Lecture Notes in Computer Science 4328

Commenced Publication in 1973
Founding and Former Series Editors:
Gerhard Goos, Juris Hartmanis, and Jan van Leeuwen

Dave Penkler   Manfred Reitenspiess
Francis Tam (Eds.)

Service Availability

Third International Service Availability Symposium, ISAS 2006
Helsinki, Finland, May 15-16, 2006
Revised Selected Papers

 Springer

Volume Editors

Dave Penkler
Hewlett-Packard
5, avenue Raymond Chanas - Eybens, 38053 Grenoble Cedex 9, France
E-mail: dave.penkler@hp.com

Manfred Reitenspiess
Fujitsu Siemens Computers GmbH
Domagkstr. 28, 80807 München, Germany
E-mail: Manfred.Reitenspiess@fujitsu-siemens.com

Francis Tam
Nokia Research Center
P.O. Box 407, 00045 Nokia Group, Finland
E-mail: francis.tam@nokia.com

Library of Congress Control Number: 2006938409

CR Subject Classification (1998): C.2, H.4, H.3, I.2.11, D.2, H.5, K.4.4, K.6

LNCS Sublibrary: SL 3 – Information Systems and Application, incl. Internet/Web
and HCI

ISSN   0302-9743
ISBN-10   3-540-68724-6 Springer Berlin Heidelberg New York
ISBN-13   978-3-540-68724-5 Springer Berlin Heidelberg New York

Springer is a part of Springer Science+Business Media

springer.com

© Springer-Verlag Berlin Heidelberg 2006

Typesetting: Camera-ready by author, data conversion by Scientific Publishing Services, Chennai, India
Printed on acid-free paper   SPIN: 11955498   06/3142   5 4 3 2 1 0

General and Program Chairs' Message

The 3rd International Service Availability Symposium (ISAS 2006) continued with the tradition of its predecessors by bringing together researchers and practitioners from both academia and industry to address the problems of service availability. The unique characteristic of a strong academic and industrial partnership was vividly reflected in this year's event, from the Organizing Committee to the contributions and the participants. Recognizing the value of broadening the scope of ISAS 2006, we included new topic areas that cover service-oriented architectures, dependability of information and communications technology services, and Java.

We received a total of 38 submissions, each of which was thoroughly reviewed by at least three members of the Program Committee. Due to the limited time allocated for the symposium, many worthwhile manuscripts unfortunately did not make it into the final program. Our sincere thanks go to the Program Committee for conducting a vigorous review process in a rather tight time schedule. The detailed review and their generous comments have shaped the contributions into an excellent program.

Under a Nokia Research Center scientific conference sponsorship, we introduced a one day pre-symposium tutorial. We are grateful to Kishor Trivedi, Veena Mendiratta, and Miroslaw Malek for stepping forward to deliver the presentations "Assurance for Continuous Availability" and "Predictive Algorithms and Technologies for Availability Enhancement". Another new feature in this year's program was a special session on European Union Sixth Framework Programme (FP6) projects and actions in the area of dependability and security, for which we thank Manfred Reitenspiess for its organization. The presentations, which were not formally reviewed, can still be accessed under http://www.saforum.org/events.

We are indebted to the University of Helsinki and Nokia Research Center for providing the support and resources needed for hosting ISAS 2006 in Finland. The local arrangements team, Minna Uimonen and Lauri Liuhto, did a tremendous job of assisting the planning, organizing, and coordinating all the local activities. Their dedication and precise execution deserve our special thanks. We would also like to acknowledge the involvement and support given by the Service Availability Forum and GI/ITG Technical Committee on "Dependability and Fault Tolerance".

We hope that you will find many contributions that are of interest to you in this volume. And of course, we look forward to seeing you at ISAS 2007, which will be held at the University of New Hampshire, Durham, NH in May 2007. The call for papers can be downloaded under http://www.saforum.org/events.

October 2006

Francis Tam
Kimmo Raatikainen
Dave Penkler
Kishor Trivedi

Organization

ISAS 2006 was organized by the Software and Application Technologies Laboratory, Nokia Research Center and the Department of Computer Science, University of Helsinki in cooperation with GI (German Computer Society) and Service Availability Forum (http://www.saforum.org).

ISAS 2006 Steering Committee

Miroslaw Malek (Humboldt Universität, Germany)
Dave Penkler (Hewlett-Packard, France)
Manfred Reitenspiess (Fujitsu Siemens Computers, Germany)
Francis Tam (Nokia Research Center, Finland)

Program Committee

General Co-chairs: Francis Tam (Nokia Research Center, Finland)
                         Kimmo Raatikainen (University of Helsinki, Finland)
Program Co-chairs: Dave Penkler (Hewlett Packard, France)
                         Kishor S. Trivedi (Duke University, USA)
Tutorials: Francis Tam (Nokia Research Center, Finland)

Referees

A. Avritzer (Siemens, USA)
D. Bakken (University of Oslo/WSU)
S. Benlarbi (Alcatel)
A. Bobbio (University of Turin)
A. Bondavalli (University of Florence)
I. Chen (Virginia Tech)
T. Dohi (Hiroshima, Japan)
C. Fetzer (TU Dresden)
S. Garg (Avaya)
M. Garzia (Microsoft)
R. German (University of Erlangen)
H. Hermanns (University of
  Saarland)
S. Hunter (IBM)
M. Kaaniche (LAAS)
G. Le Lann (INRIA, France)
M. Lyu (CUHK, Hong Kong)

M. Malek (Humboldt University,
  Germany)
R. Mansharamani (TCS, India)
M. Marathe (Cisco)
V. Mendiratta (Lucent)
B. Murphy (Microsoft)
E. Nett (University of Magdeburg)
V. Nicola (University of Twente)
P. Portugal (University of Porto)
J. Posegga (TU Hamburg)
A. Rodriguez Vargas (Siemens)
H. Sun (Sun Microsystems)
N. Suri (Darmstadt, Germany)
H. Szczerbicka (University of
  Hannover)
A. Van Moorsel (University of
  Newcastle)

B. Vashaw (IBM, USA)   J. Xu (University of Leeds)
A. Wolski (Solid Tech.)   M. Yin (Cal State Poly University)

Sponsoring Institutions

Nokia Research Center, Helsinki, Finland

Table of Contents

International Service Availability Symposium 2006

Availability Modeling, Estimation and Analysis

Dependability Techniques and Their Applications

Performability: Measurements and Assessments

Service Availability Standards: Experience Reports and Futures

Model Based Approach for Autonomic Availability Management

Kesari Mishra and Kishor S. Trivedi

Dept. of Electrical and Computer Engineering, Duke University
Durham, NC 27708-0294, USA
{km, kst}@ee.duke.edu

Abstract. As increasingly complex computer systems have started playing a controlling role in all aspects of modern life, system availability and associated downtime of technical systems have acquired critical importance. Losses due to system downtime have risen manifold and become wide-ranging. Even though the component level availability of hardware and software has increased considerably, system wide availability still needs improvement as the heterogeneity of components and the complexity of interconnections has gone up considerably too. As systems become more interconnected and diverse, architects are less able to anticipate and design for every interaction among components, leaving such issues to be dealt with at runtime. Therefore, in this paper, we propose an approach for autonomic management of system availability, which provides real-time evaluation, monitoring and management of the availability of systems in critical applications. A hybrid approach is used where analytic models provide the behavioral abstraction of components/subsystems, their interconnections and dependencies and statistical inference is applied on the data from real time monitoring of those components and subsystems, to parameterize the system availability model. The model is solved online (that is, in real time) so that at any instant of time, both the point as well as the interval estimates of the overall system availability are obtained by propagating the point and the interval estimates of each of the input parameters, through the system model. The online monitoring and estimation of system availability can then lead to adaptive online control of system availability.

1 Introduction

Growing reliance upon computer systems in almost all the aspects of modern life has made things more manageable and controllable but at the same time has imposed stricter requirements on the dependability of these systems. System availability and associated downtime of technical systems have acquired critical importance as losses due to downtime have risen manifold. The nature of losses due to downtime vary, depending upon the field of deployment. In e-commerce applications like online brokerages, credit card authorizations, online sales etc., system downtime will directly translate into financial losses due to lost transactions in the short term to a loss of customer base in the long term.

D. Penkler, M. Reitenspiess, and F. Tam (Eds.): ISAS 2006, LNCS 4328, pp. 1–16, 2006.

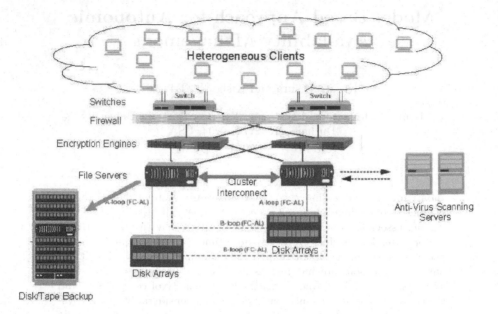

Fig. 1. A high availability data storage setup

In the infrastructure field, a downtime of the controlling systems may lead to disruption of essential services. In safety-critical and military applications, the dependability requirements are even higher as system unavailability would most often result in disastrous consequences. In such critical systems, there is a need to continuously monitor the availability of various components in the system and to take corrective/control actions in a timely manner, to maximize the system availability.

While the availability of hardware and software has significantly improved over time, the heterogeneity of systems, the complexity of interconnections and the dependencies between components has grown manifold. As a result, though the node level availability has improved, system level availability still needs improvement. Figure 1 shows a commonly deployed high availability data storage setup. In this common setup, the switches, the fire-wall (h/w or s/w), the encryption engines, file servers, disk arrays, backup system, anti-virus servers, fiber channel loops etc. are all interconnected with very complex dependencies. Most likely, all of these components will be from different manufacturers, following different best-practices guides and behaving differently, making it extremely difficult to plan for and anticipate every interaction between these components in the design phase of the setup.

The heterogeneity of system components(both hardware and software) and the complexity of their interconnections now makes the task of availability monitoring and management even more important as it will be more difficult to predict and design for all the interactions between these diverse components in the design phase and these interactions will need to be handled at runtime.

Therefore, in this paper we propose an approach for autonomic [11] management of system availability, which provides real-time evaluation, monitoring and management of the availability of systems in critical applications.

In this approach, an analytic model captures the interactions between system components and the input parameters of the model are inferred from data obtained by online (realtime) monitoring of the components of the system. The system availability model is solved online using these estimated values, thereby obtaining a realtime estimate of the system availability. The confidence interval for the overall system availability is obtained by propagating the confidence intervals of the individual parameter estimates through the system model, using a generic Monte-Carlo approach. Based on the parameter estimates and the overall system availability, control strategies such as alternate hardware and software configurations [17,10] or load balancing schemes can be decided. Optimal preventive maintenance schedules can also be computed [16,18]. This automates the whole process of availability management to ensure maximum system availability, making the system autonomic.

This paper is organized as follows: Section 2 discusses the background and related work in the field of availability evaluation, section 3 describes realtime availability estimation for a system viewed as a black box (when the whole system can be monitored from a single point). Section 4 discusses the steps in implementing autonomic availability management for a system (viewed as a grey box) with many hardware and software components, Section 5 illustrates this concept with the help of a simple prototype system and Section 6 finally concludes the paper.

2 Background and Related Work

Availability of a system can be defined as the fraction of time the system is providing service to its users. Limiting or steady state availability of a (non-redundant) system is computed as the ratio of mean time to failure (MTTF) of the system to the sum of mean time to failure and mean time to repair (MTTR). It is the steady state availability that gets translated into other metrics like uptime or downtime per year. In critical applications, there also needs to be a reasonable confidence in the estimated value of system availability. In other words, the quality or precision of the estimated values needs to be known too. Therefore, computing the interval estimates (confidence interval) of availability is also essential.

Availability evaluation has been widely researched and can be broadly classified into two basic approaches, measurement-based and model-based. In the model-based approach, availability is computed by constructing and solving an analytic or simulation model of the system. In the model-based approach, the system availability model is prepared (offline), based on the system architecture to capture the system behavior taking into account the interaction and dependencies between different components/subsystems, and their various modes of failures and repairs. Model-based approach is very convenient in the sense that it can be used to evaluate several what-if scenarios (for example, alternate system configurations), without physically implementing those cases. However, for the results to be reasonably accurate, the model should capture the system behavior as closely as possible and the failure-repair data of the system components is needed as inputs. In measurement-based approach, availability can be estimated from measured failure-repair data (data comes from a real system or its prototype) using statistical inference techniques. Even though the results would be more accurate than using the availability modeling approach, elaborate measurements need to be made and the evaluations of what-if scenarios would be possible only after implementing each of them. Direct measurements may also provide lesser insight into the dependencies between various components in the system. Furthermore it is often more convenient to make measurements at the individual component/subsystem level rather than on the system as a whole [13]. The availability management approach advocated in this paper, combines both measurement based and model based availability evaluation approaches to complement each other's deficiencies and makes use of the advantages of both the approaches.

Traditionally, availability evaluation has been an offline task using either the model based or the measurement based approach. A few projects combined availability modeling with measurements, but they did not produce the results in an online manner [4,19,7]. In other words, these previous approaches were good only for a post-mortem type analysis. In today's complex and mission-critical applications, there is a need to continuously evaluate and monitor system availability in real-time, so that suitable control actions may be triggered. The growing heterogeneity of systems and complexity of their interconnections indicate the need for an automated way of managing system availability. In other words, the system should ultimately self-manage its availability to some degree (autonomic system). Kephart et. al. [11,31] suggest that an autonomic system needs to comprise of the following key components : a continuous monitoring system, automated statistical analysis of data gathered upon monitoring, a behavioral abstraction of the system (system model) and control policies to act upon the runtime conditions. This paper describes ways to implement each of these key components and hence outlines a way for autonomic availability management of technical systems.

3   Realtime Availability Estimation for a System Viewed as a Black Box

Availability evaluation addresses the failure and recovery aspects of the system. In cases where it is possible to ascertain the operational status of the whole system by monitoring at a single point (thus considering the system as a black-box), the availability of such systems can be computed by calculating the mean time to failure (MTTF) and mean time to repair (MTTR) from direct measurements of times to failure(TTF) and times to repair(TTR) of the system. To monitor the status of a system, two approaches can be followed. Either the system under observation sends heartbeat messages to the monitoring station or the monitoring station polls the monitored system for its status. Each poll will either return the time of the last boot up or an indication of the system's failure. The heartbeat message will also contain similar information. In either case the information about the monitored system is stored as the tuple (*current time stamp, last boot time, current status*). The ith time to failure is calculated as the difference between i^{th} failure time and the $(i-1)^{st}$ boot up time, (assuming the system came up for the first time at $i = 0$). The ith repair time is calculated as the difference between i^{th} boot up time and the ith failure time. At any observation i, the time to failure(ttf) and time to repair(ttr) are calculated as

$$ttf[i] = failure\ time[i] - bootup\ time[i-1]$$
$$ttr[i] = bootup\ time[i] - failure\ time[i]$$

The sample means of mean time to failure and mean time to repair are calculated as the averages of these measured times to failure and times to repair. If at the current time of observation, the system is in an up interval, the last time to failure will be an incomplete one and the point estimate of MTTF can be obtained as

$$M\hat{T}TF = \frac{\sum_{i=1}^{n} ttf[i] + x_{n+1}}{n}$$

where, x_{n+1} is the current(unfinished) time to failure. The point estimate of MTTR can be obtained as

$$M\hat{T}TR = \frac{\sum_{i=1}^{n} ttr[i]}{n}$$

Similarly, if the system is in a down state at the current time of observation, the last time to repair will be an incomplete one and in this case, the MTTR can be estimated as

$$M\hat{T}TR = \frac{\sum_{i=1}^{n-1} ttr[i] + y_n}{n-1}$$

where, y_n is the current(unfinished) time to repair. The point estimate of MTTF can be obtained as

$$M\hat{T}TF = \frac{\sum_{i=1}^{n} ttf[i]}{n}$$

The point estimate of the steady state availability of the system is then obtained as $\hat{A} = \frac{M\hat{T}TF}{M\hat{T}TF + M\hat{T}TR}$. It can be shown that the point estimate of steady state availability depends only on the mean time to failure and mean time to repair and not on the nature of distributions of the failure times and repair times [1]. However, the nature of distributions of the failure and repair times will govern the interval estimates of availability.

Assuming the failure and repair times to be exponentially distributed, both the two sided and the upper one-sided confidence interval of the system availability can be obtained with the help of *Fischer-Snedecor F distribution*. If at the current time of observation, the system is in an up state, the $100(1 - \alpha)\%$ upper one-sided confidence interval for availability $(A_L, 1)$, can be obtained as

$$A_L = \frac{1}{1 + \frac{1/\hat{A}-1}{f_{2n,2n;1-\alpha}}}$$

where $f_{2n,2n;1-\alpha}$ is a critical value of the F distribution with $(2n, 2n)$ degrees of freedom. The $100(1 - \alpha)\%$ two-sided confidence interval (A_L, A_U) for this case, can be computed as

$$A_L = \frac{1}{1 + \frac{1/\hat{A}-1}{f_{2n,2n;1-\alpha/2}}}$$

$$A_U = \frac{1}{1 + \frac{1/\hat{A}-1}{f_{2n,2n;\alpha/2}}}$$

where $f_{2n,2n;\alpha/2}$ and $f_{2n,2n;1-\alpha/2}$ are critical values of the F distribution with $(2n, 2n)$ degrees of freedom.

If the system is in the down state at the time of the current observation, the $100(1 - \alpha)\%$ upper one-sided confidence for availability $(AL, 1)$ is computed as:

$$A_L = \frac{1}{1 + \frac{1/\hat{A}-1}{f_{2n,2n-2;1-\alpha}}}$$

The $100(1 - \alpha)\%$ two-sided confidence interval (A_L, A_U) for this case, can be computed as

$$A_L = \frac{1}{1 + \frac{1/\hat{A}-1}{f_{2n,2n-2;1-\alpha/2}}}$$

$$A_U = \frac{1}{1 + \frac{1/\hat{A}-1}{f_{2n,2n-2;\alpha/2}}}$$

where, $f_{2n,2n-2;1-\alpha}$, $f_{2n,2n-2;\alpha/2}$ and $f_{2n,2n-2;1-\alpha/2}$ are critical values of the F distribution with $(2n, 2n - 2)$ degrees of freedom [1,3].

Figure 2 shows a screenshot of the online point and interval estimates of availability of a system viewed as a black-box, with exponentially distributed time between failures and repairs. The monitored system was forced to crash and bootup at exponentially distributed times and the boot up and crash times were recorded at the monitoring station. As the number of samples increases, the confidence interval for the system availability, becomes tighter. In cases, where calculation of exact confidence intervals is time consuming (and hence, non-feasible for an online application), approximate confidence intervals are calculated using

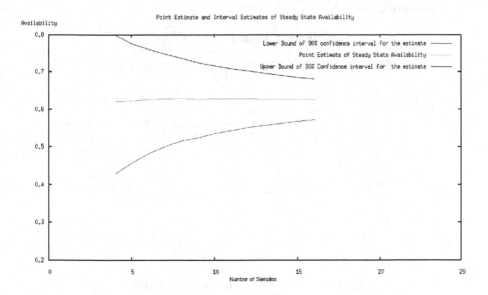

Fig. 2. Point and Interval Estimates of Steady State Availability of a Black box System

normal distribution assumptions [19]. Fricks and Ketcham [21] have proposed the method of *Cumulative Downtime Distribution*(CDD) that makes use of the sample means of the cumulative system outage time and provides both the point estimate as well as confidence intervals for the system availability without a need to make any assumption about the lifetime or time to repair distributions of the system being monitored.

4   Availability Management for a Complex System

High availability systems in critical applications have diverse and redundant hardware and software components configured together into a system with the help of complex interconnections. Availability/unavailability of these components affects the overall system availability. It might be difficult to ascertain the status of the whole system by monitoring a single point [13]. In this section, we outline the basic steps needed to implement autonomic availability management for such systems. The steps in its implementation can be summarized as:

1. Development of System Availability model (Behavioral Abstraction of the System)
   Based on the system architecture, the system availability model is constructed to capture the system behavior with respect to the interaction and dependencies between different components/subsystems, and their various modes of failures and repairs [22]. State-space, non-state space or hierarchical models are chosen based on the level of dependency in failure and

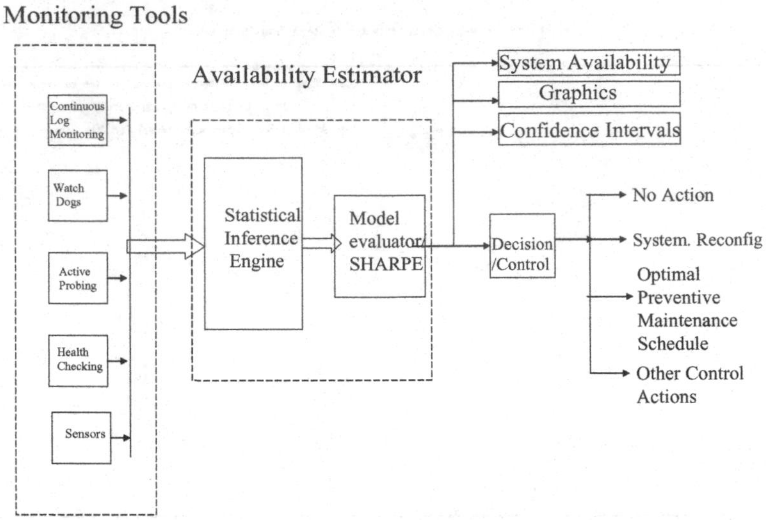

Monitoring Tools

Fig. 3. The Availability Management System

repair between different components. In the case where all the components have statistically independent failures and repairs, non-state space models (e.g. Fault Trees, Reliability Block Diagrams) can be used. The non-state space models like fault trees and reliability block diagrams cannot easily handle dependencies in failure/repair of components or shared repair facilities. Therefore, in such complex cases, state space models are required. State space models like Markov chains [1,14], stochastic reward nets [5,8], semi-Markov process [18] and Markov regenerative process [20,23] have been widely used to model the availability of complex computer systems. Hierarchical availability models can be constructed for cases where failures and repairs across subsystems are independent of each other. They are used in cases when it is more intuitive to model the parts of the system(sub-systems) individually rather than the whole system at once and then have a model on top of these sub-system models to account for the interactions between these lower level models. Hierarchical models scale better with the number of subsystems and subsystem components than does a composite model and thus help avoid largeness of the state space of models [9].

2. Development of Monitoring Tools

For every component/subsystem in the system availability model, in order to gather its failure-repair data, there needs to be a mechanism to assess its operational status, at regular intervals. The monitoring mechanism needs to be designed to facilitate the monitoring of all the subsystems and components from a central location (the monitoring station). The system needs to be configured so that all the *relevant* (of the required severity) system log messages are directed to the monitoring station. Some of the steps needed in developing a monitoring mechanism have been summarized below.

- The system event logging mechanism in the monitored systems, should be configured so that the messages of required severity, from components being monitored are directed to the monitoring station. The monitoring station needs to be configured also as the log server for the log messages from all the monitored systems. Tools need to be developed to continuously inspect these log messages for error messages from I/O devices, hard disk, memory, CPU and related components like caches and buses, daemons and user processes, fans and power supplies. These tools can be either one of the available log monitoring tools like Epylog [25] or a light-weight custom developed one, running at the monitoring station. In Unix or Linux based systems, hardware failures like memory failure (uncorrectable ECC error), hard disk errors, I/O device errors, cache parity errors, bus errors etc. can be kept track of, by keeping a watch on emergency, alert, critical, error and warning level messages from the kernel [32].
- Polling agents need to be developed to poll the system regularly to determine the status of some components (e.g. sending periodic ICMP echo messages for network status, probing the sensor monitoring tools for status of fans and power supplies [28]).
- In cluster systems, watchdog processes need to be developed to listen for heartbeat messages from applications running on the cluster elements. Available redundancy (both process and hardware) in the cluster systems, provides additional mechanisms for monitoring by peer cluster elements [24,29,30]. Heart beat messages and Watch dog processes [29,30] and hardware [24] help detect processor and application failures.
- If SNMP (Simple Network Management Protocol) based monitoring is used, then periodic queries need to be sent from the monitoring station [26].

3. Development of the Statistical Inference Engine

Once the monitoring tools have begun their task of data collection, parameters of the system availability model need to be estimated from the data by using methods of statistical inference. The tasks of the statistical inference engine are :

- The statistical inference engine should first perform goodness of fit tests (Kolmogorov-Smirnov test and probability plot) upon the failure and repair data of each monitored component or subsystem. The parameters of the closely fitting distribution need to be calculated next.
- The point estimate of limiting availability for any component or subsystem will be calculated as the ratio of mean time to failure and sum of mean time to failure and mean time to repair.
- Depending upon the distribution of time to failure and time to repair, exact or approximate confidence intervals are calculated for the limiting availability of each component as discussed in the case of availability estimation for the non-redundant system.

4. Evaluation of the System Availability Model

   The point estimates of the parameter values are used to solve the system availability model using the software package SHARPE [2] to obtain the point estimate of the overall system availability. The confidence interval for overall system availability is calculated as discussed in section 5.

5. Deciding the Control Action

   Some of the possible control actions that may be suggested online, based on the estimated parameter values are :

   – At any set of parameter values, for system availability below a threshold, the availability of the system in different possible configurations can be calculated by evaluating the system availability models for those configurations at the current set of parameter values. The system configuration with maximum availability at that set of parameter values, could be suggested as an alternative.

   – Optimal preventive maintenance schedule (repair/replacement schedule for ageing components, scrubbing interval for memory or memory-type elements, rejuvenation schedule to avoid software ageing) can be obtained in terms of the parameters of the maintenance model [18,20]. In this case, since the parameter values are being constantly updated, there is a need to recalculate these schedules at each set of parameter values.

   – Diagnostics are performed to increase system availability by detecting latent faults(for example, failure of a standby component). The availability of the system as a function of period between diagnostics has been obtained in [1]. For a required availability and at the current set of parameter values, the schedule for diagnostics to detect failures in standby components can be adjusted.

The flow diagram in figure 4 summarizes the above described steps.

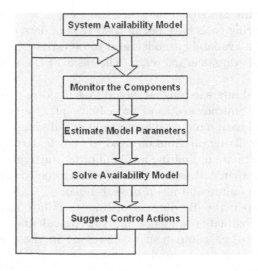

Fig. 4. Flow Diagram of the Autonomic Availability Management Approach

5   Illustration with a Specific System Model

In this section, the availability management approach is illustrated with an example. A simple online transaction processing system with two back end nodes for transaction processing and one front end machine forwarding the incoming requests to the backend nodes based on some load balancing scheme, is set up in our laboratory. The backend machines have apache servers running on them and the frontend machine has the load generator httperf [33] running on it, which sends requests to each of the backend machines. All the machines have the Redhat Linux 9 as their operating system. The setup is shown in figure 5. The steps in the availability management of the above described setup is discussed next.

- Development of system model
  Based on the conditions for the system to be available, the system availability model is constructed as a two level hierarchy. The lower level model being a two-state Markov chain for each of the components and the upper level is a fault tree shown in figure 6. The events considered are failures of network, hard disk drive, memory, cpu and the application, on each of the systems. The system is up as long as the front end machine and at least one of the two backend machines are working. Each of the machines is considered up when their network, memory, hard disk and the application software are all up.
- Development of monitoring tools
  The monitoring system is designed as
  - The Linux system event logging mechanism known as *syslog* provides flexibility in selectively directing log messages from a source (known as

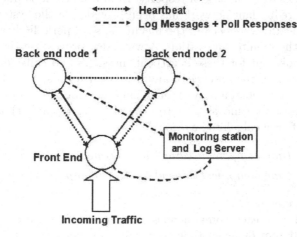

Fig. 5. The Experimental Setup

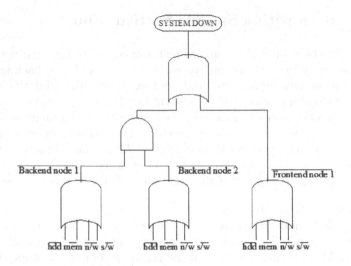

Fig. 6. Fault Tree for the setup

facility) and of a given *severity* to any remote location (the log server). The monitoring station is configured as the log server for all the machines. On each of the monitored system, the messages from facility *kernel* and of severity *error*, *critical* and *emergency* are forwarded to the monitoring station.

- A log-parser at the monitoring station continuously inspects the incoming log messages for error messages from all the three machines' memory (ECC errors), hard disk and CPU related errors.
- The network status is obtained by probing the machines at regular intervals. To ensure that lack of response from a machine is due to network failure, a redundant network has been provided in the system.
- The applications on each of the machines, send periodic heartbeat messages to the monitoring station. A watchdog process on the monitoring station looks out for these heartbeat messages and considers the application down on the absence of any heartbeat for a specific duration.
- For each component, at any observation i (assuming the component came up for the first time at $i = 0$), the time to repair(ttr) and time to failure(ttf) are calculated as

$$ttr[i] = \textit{time component came up}[i] - \textit{time component went down}[i]$$
$$ttf[i] = \textit{time comp. went down}[i] - \textit{time comp. came up}[i - 1]$$

– Statistical Inference

The availability of each component is calculated as the ratio of mean time to failure and sum of mean time to repair and mean time to failure. The availability of each component serves as input to the fault tree and the point estimate of overall system availability is calculated by evaluating the

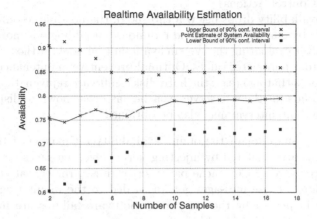

Fig. 7. Realtime Availability Estimation of the experimental setup

fault tree using SHARPE. The time to failure and time to repair data are fitted to some known distributions (e.g. Weibull, lognormal, exponential) and the parameters for the best fitting distribution are calculated. Using exact or approximate methods, the confidence intervals for these parameters are calculated. The estimators of each of the input parameters in the system model themselves being random variables, have their own distribution and hence their point estimates have some associated uncertainty which is accounted for, in the confidence intervals. The uncertainty expressed in confidence intervals of the parameter needs to be propagated through the system model to obtain the confidence interval of the overall system availability. We follow a generic Monte Carlo approach for uncertainty [15]. The system availability model can be seen as a function of input parameters. If $\Lambda = \{\lambda_i, i = 1, 2, \ldots, k\}$ be the set of input parameters, the overall availability can be viewed as a function g such that $A = g(\lambda_1, \lambda_2, \ldots, \lambda_k) = g(\Lambda)$. Suppose the joint probability density function of all the input parameters is $f(\Lambda)$ then A can be calculated through a simple simulation:

- Draw Samples $\Lambda^{(j)}$ from $f(\Lambda)$, where $j = 1, 2, \ldots, J$, J being the total number of samples
- Compute $A^{(j)} = g(\Lambda^{(j)})$
- Summarize $A^{(j)}$

In the case when $\lambda_i s$ are mutually independent and so the joint probability density function $f(\Lambda)$ can be written as the product of marginal density functions, samples can be drawn independently. Drawing enough number of samples from the distributions of the input parameters, the confidence interval for the overall system availability is computed from values obtained by evaluating the system availability model at each of these sample values.

– Suggesting Control Actions
  When the availability drops below a threshold, the possible reconfigurations
  may be done by making the frontend redundant or adding one more backend
  machines, after evaluating the system availability model for those configurations at current parameter values. Optimal preventive maintenance schedule
  for components that age (e.g., the hard disk), software rejuvenation schedule
  for the backends (as the web server Apache has been shown to display aging
  [12]) or scrubbing interval may also be obtained.

Figure 7 shows a snapshot of the online availability estimation of this setup.
Hardware failures are emulated by injecting kernel level messages for hardware
failures like uncorrected ECC, cache parity error, bus error etc. at each of the
monitored stations. These messages get forwarded to the monitoring station ,
where they are inspected by the log parser. Software failures are injected by
killing of the processes. Absence of heartbeat messages is detected by the watchdog process on the monitoring station as a failure. The times between failure
and repair injections are exponentially distributed. As the number of samples increases from observation to observation, the confidence interval becomes tighter.

6   Conclusion

In this paper, an autonomic availability management approach for complex systems in critical applications is presented. The approach consists of monitoring
these systems to continuously estimate their availability and its confidence intervals by exercising their availability model. Based on their availability and other
inferred lifetime characteristics, appropriate control actions to increase the system availability may be suggested, in real time. The approach combines both
the measurement based and model based approaches of availability estimation
and at the same time provides continuous realtime monitoring and control of
the system availability. This automates the whole process of availability management to ensure maximum system availability, making the system autonomic.

References

1. Trivedi, K.S. (2001),*Probability and Statistics with Reliability, Queuing and Computer Science Applications*, John Wiley & Sons, New York.
2. Sahner R.A., Trivedi K.S. and Puliafito A. (1996),*Performance and Reliability
   Analysis of Computer Systems: An Example-Based Approach Using the SHARPE
   Software Package*, Kluwer Academic Publishers.
3. Leemis, L.M. (1995),*Reliability. Probabilistic Models and Statistical Methods*, Pren-
   tice Hall, New Jersey.
4. Tang, D. and Iyer, R.K. (1993), Dependability Measurement and Modeling of a
   Multicomputer System, *IEEE Transactions on Computers*, **42** (1), 62–75.
5. Malhotra, M. and Trivedi, K.S.(1995), Dependability Modeling Using Petri Net
   Based Models, *IEEE Transactions on Reliability*, **44** (3), 428–440.

6. Cristian, F., Dancey, B. and Dehn J. (1996), Fault Tolerance in Air Traffic Control Systems, *ACM Transactions on Computer Systems*, **14**, 265–286.
7. Morgan, P., Gaffney, P., Melody, J., Condon, M., Hayden, M. (1990), System Availability Monitoring, *IEEE Transactions on Reliability*, **39** (4), 480–485.
8. Ibe, O., Howe, R., and Trivedi, K.S. (1989), Approximate availability analysis of VAXCluster systems, *IEEE Transactions on Reliability*, **R-38** (1), 146–152.
9. Blake, J.T. and Trivedi, K.S. (1989), Reliability analysis of interconnection networks using hierarchical composition, *IEEE Transactions on Reliability*, **32**, 111–120.
10. Albin, S.L.. and Chao, S. (1992), Preventive Replacement in Systems with Dependent Components, *IEEE Transactions on Reliability*, **41** (2), 230–238.
11. Kephart., J.O. and Chess, D.M. (Jan. 2003), The Vision of Autonomic Computing, *Computer magazine*, 41–50.
12. Li, L., Vaidyanathan, K. and Trivedi, K.S. (2002), An Approach for Estimation of Software Aging in a Web Server, *Proc. of Intl. Symposium on Empirical Software Engineering (ISESE-2002)*.
13. Garzia, M.R. (2003), Assessing the Reliability of Windows Servers, *Proc. of Dependable Systems and Networks, (DSN-2002)*.
14. Hunter, S.W. and Smith, W.E. (1999), Availability modeling and analysis of a two node cluster, *Proc. of 5th Int. Conf. On Information Systems, Analysis and Synthesis*.
15. Yin, L., Smith, M.A.J. and Trivedi, K.S. (2001), Uncertainty Analysis in Reliability Modeling, *Proc. of the Annual Reliability and Maintainability Symposium, (RAMS-2001)*.
16. Dohi, T., G.-Popstojanova,K., Trivedi, K.S. (2000), Statistical Non-Parametric Algorithms to estimate the Optimal Software Rejuvenation Schedule, *Proc. of Pacific Rim Intl. Symposium on Dependable Computing, (PRDC)*.
17. Garg, S., Huang, Y., Kintala, C.M.R., Trivedi, K.S. and Yajnik S. (1999), Performance and Reliability Evaluation of Passive replication Schemes in Application Level fault Tolerance, *Proc. of 29th Annual Intl. Symposium on Fault Tolerant Computing (FTCS)*.
18. Chen, D.Y. and Trivedi, K.S. (2001), Analysis of Periodic Preventive Maintenance with General System Failure Distribution, *Pacific Rim Intl Symposium on Dependable Computing (PRDC)*.
19. Long, D., Muir, a., and Golding, R. (1995), A Longitudinal Survey of Internet Host Reliability, *Proc. of the 14th Symposium on Reliable Distributed Systems*.
20. Garg, S., Puliafito, A., Telek, M. and Trivedi, K. (1995), Analysis of Software Rejuvenation using Markov Regenerative Stochastic Petri Net, *Proc. of Intl. Symposium on Software Reliability Engineering (ISSRE)*.
21. Fricks, R.M. and Ketcham, M. (2004), Steady State Availability Estimation Using Field Failure Data, *Proc. Annual Reliability and Maintainability Symposium (RAMS-2004)*.
22. Sathaye, A., Ramani, S., Trivedi, K.S. (2000), Availability Models in Practice, *Proc. of Intl. Workshop on Fault-Tolerant Control and Computing (FTCC-1)*.
23. Logothetis, D. and Trivedi, K. (1995), Time-dependent behavior of redundant systems with deterministic repair, *Proc. of 2nd International Workshop on the Numerical Solution of Markov Chains*.
24. G. Hughes-Fenchel (1997), A Flexible Clustered Approach to High Availability, *27th Int. Symp. on Fault-Tolerant Computing (FTCS-27)*.
25. Epylog Log Analyzer, *http://linux.duke.edu/projects/epylog*.

26. Sun SNMP Management Agent Guide for Sun Fire B1600, *http://docs.sun.com/ source/817-1010-10/SNMP_intro.html*.
27. Simple Network Management Protocol, *http://www.cisco.com/univercd/cc/td/ doc/cisintwk/ito_doc/snmp.htm*.
28. Hardware Monitoring by lm_sensors, *http://secure.netroedge.com/~lm78/info.html*.
29. Windows 2000 Cluster Service Architecture, *www.microsoft.com/serviceproviders/ whitepapers/win2k*.
30. SwiFT for Windows NT, *http://www.bell-labs.com/project/swift*.
31. IBM Research—Autonomic Computing, *http://www.research.ibm.com/autonomic/ index.html*.
32. Linux Syslog Man Page, *http://www.die.net/doc/linux/man/man2/syslog.2.html*.
33. Mosberger, D. and Jin, T., httperf—A Tool for Measuring Web Server Performance, *http://www.hpl.hp.com/personal/David_Mosberger/httperf.html*.

Analysis of a Service Degradation Model with Preventive Rejuvenation

Hiroyuki Eto and Tadashi Dohi

Department of Information Engineering, Hiroshima University
Higashi-Hiroshima 739–8527, Japan
dohi@rel.hiroshima-u.ac.jp

Abstract. The preventive maintenance is very useful to improve effectively the service availability for software systems with service degradation. In this paper, we present a stochastic model to describe an operational software, which consists of one operating system and multiple applications and provides a service in continuous time. Two kinds of maintenance strategies are taken: reconfiguration of applications as a corrective maintenance and preventive rejuvenation of an operating system. We derive the optimal preventive rejuvenation schedule maximizing the steady-state service availability in the framework of semi-Markov decision process and study analytically the optimality structure on it. We give a simple numerical example to determine the condition-based optimal rejuvenation schedule via the decision table.

Keywords: service degradation, service availability, software aging, software rejuvenation, semi-Markov decision process.

1 Introduction

The value of service provided through computer systems is more increasing day by day rather than that of service equipments themselves. Hence, the notions of *service reliability* and *service availability* are becoming popular in our highly information-oriented society. As Michael Tortorella mentions in his good survey papers [19], [20], service reliability engineering enables service providers to design and operate an infrastructure in order to deliver services that meet the stated reliability and availability requirements. Also, he defines the standard service reliability engineering procedure consists of four steps: (i) setting service reliability requirements, (ii) sources of service reliability requirements, (iii) design for service reliability, (iv) service reliability monitoring. In fact, since service reliability theory provides both analytical model-based and measurement-based frameworks to quantify the service failure mode, its concept can be involved completely in the usual dependable computing. More specifically, the software fault-tolerant computing is mainly classified into design diversity technique and environment diversity technique. The former is an engineering approach to realize the redundant design of equipments (hardware and software systems) for tolerating failures, the latter achieves the temporal redundancy by changing

D. Penkler, M. Reitenspiess, and F. Tam (Eds.): ISAS 2006, LNCS 4328, pp. 17–29, 2006.

the operation environment occasionally. Especially, if one focuses on the service provided by software, the environment diversity technique leads to an effective improvement to prevent a severe service failure. The typical examples are check-pointing to back up the service data, reconfiguration of application software and software rejuvenation.

As another examples on service reliability, Clossbrenner [12] introduces the notions of reliability and availability for switched telecommunication services. Calabria *et al.* [2] report a case study on the service dependability for real rail-way transit systems. Cristian [7] introduces a distributed system service called *availability management service* which is responsible for ensuring that the critical services of a distributed system remain continuously available to users despite arbitrary numbers of concurrent node removals and node restarts caused by fail-ures, maintenance and growth. Mainkar [14] deals with transaction-processing systems based on user-perceived performance by introducing the so-called *per-formability*. Chu *et al.* [6] consider a radio access telecommunications network and define what is known as *service accessibility* for a wireless access service. Reisinger [17] discusses experimentally how the quality of service control by middleware can be established in a client-server system. Chan and Tortorella [4] consider a simple stochastic model for sizing the spare inventory to meet an end-to-end service availability objective. Dislis [9] describes some of the challenges in providing continuous service and the impact of upgrade related outages for mobile telephone networks. Recently, Reinecke *et al.* [16] treat the restart policy to speed up the completion of service as a representative application-level service dependability technique. Choi and Kim [5] introduce the concept of *performable availability* as the probability that the systems are in one of some available states such that meet the minimum service requirement for cluster software systems. These papers [5], [16] focus on the typical software rejuvenation techniques [1], [3] for internet applications subject to system failures or unpredictable delays and cluster systems, respectively. Actually, for long periods of service time, op-erating system resources such as swap space and free memory available may be progressively depleted due to defects in software such as memory leaks and incomplete cleanup of resources after use. Software rejuvenation is a preventive and proactive maintenance policy that is particularly useful for counteracting the phenomenon of *software aging*, which is due to the phenomenon of resource exhaustion.

When software application executes continuously for long periods of time, some of the faults cause software to age due to the error conditions that ac-crue with time and/or load. Software aging will also affect the performance of the application service and eventually cause it to fail. In fact, it is observed in widely-used communication software like Internet Explorer, Netscape and xrn as well as commercial operating systems and middleware. Huang *et al.* [13] con-sider a stochastic model to trigger the software rejuvenation as a preventive and proactive solution, which involves stopping the running software occasionally, cleaning its internal state and restarting it. Cleaning the internal state of a soft-ware might involve garbage collection, flushing operating system kernel tables, reinitializing internal data structures, and hardware reboot. Since the seminal contribution by Huang *et al.* [13], many stochastic models have been developed to trigger the software rejuvenation effectively to improve both system and service availabilities. Pfening *et al.* [15] model a performance degradation process by the gradual decrease of the processing rate in a non-stationary Markovian queueing system, and formulate a determination problem of the optimal software rejuvenation schedule by a Markov decision process. Garg *et al.* [11] consider a transaction-based software system, which involves arrival and queueing of jobs, and analyze both effects of aging; hard failures that result in an unavailability and soft failures that result in performance degradation. Eto and Dohi [10] consider a simple condition-based rejuvenation policy via a semi-Markov decision process and prove that the control-limit type of software rejuvenation is always the cost-optimal policy which minimizes the steady-state expected operating cost rate. Vaidyanathan and Trivedi [21] develop a comprehensive stochastic model for software rejuvenation from both points of view; analytical approach and measurement-based approach.

In this paper we present a stochastic model to describe an operational software, which consists of one operating system and multiple applications, and provides a service in continuous time. As Yurcik and Doss [22] point out, the software fault-tolerant with preventive rejuvenation and corrective reconfiguration is a commonly used reactive technique in our daily service circumstance, where software reconfiguration can use redundant resources for real-time recovery while dynamically considering a large number of factors, such as operating system services, processor load, memory variables, *etc.* As a simple but realistic example, consider the situation where two kinds of maintenance strategies are taken: reconfiguration of applications as a corrective maintenance and preventive rejuvenation of an operating system like garbage collection. More precisely, when the software performance deteriorates, the reconfiguration of some applications on the system will be made reactively by listing executing processes and the time delay as a set up cost will be incurred. In addition to the software reconfiguration, the software rejuvenation will be performed before the system failure occurs. In this situation, if the software rejuvenation seldom takes place, the much more set up cost for software reconfiguration and the down cost due to a system failure will be needed, otherwise, *i.e.*, the frequent trigger of software rejuvenation leads to much more preventive maintenance cost. By taking account of these tradeoff relationships, we derive the optimal preventive rejuvenation schedule maximizing the steady-state service availability (equivalently, minimizing the steady-state service unavailability) in the framework of semi-Markov decision process and study analytically the optimality structure on it.

The rest part of this paper proceeds as follows: In Section 2, we consider an operational software system with multistage degradations, and suppose that the state of software system deteriorates stochastically and is described by a right-skip free continuous-time Markov chain (CTMC) with an absorbing state [10]. In Section 3, we formulate the semi-Markov decision process with set up delay time and derive the value iteration algorithm to calculate the optimal software

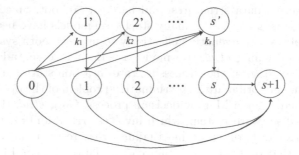

Fig. 1. Semi-Markov transition diagram of a service degradation model

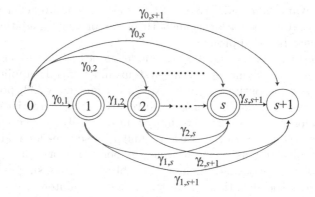

Fig. 2. Aggregated Markovian transition diagram

rejuvenation policy maximizing the steady-state service availability. Section 4 concerns the optimality structure of the software rejuvenation policy. Especially, we show analytically that the control-limit type of software rejuvenation policy is optimal. In Section 5, we give a simple numerical example to determine the condition-based optimal rejuvenation schedule via the decision table. Finally, the paper is concluded with remarks in Section 6.

2   Service Degradation Model

Consider a software system which consists of one operating system and multiple applications. The system can provide a service in continuous time and, at the same time, may deteriorate with time. Suppose that State 0 and State $s+1$ are the normal (highly robust) state and the service down state, respectively. The service starts with State 0 at time 0 and makes a transition to s degradation levels $k = 1', 2', \cdots, s'$ stochastically at any random time. At each change of state, the corrective maintenance, *i.e.*, the reconfiguration of some applications on the system, will be made reactively by listing executing processes. Then, the service state becomes from k $(= 1', 2', \cdots, s')$ to j $(= 1, \cdots, s)$ after the corrective maintenance, where the constant set up time, k_j, depending on the state j $(= 0, 1, \cdots, s)$ will be required. However, since the service can not become as good as new only by the reconfiguration of applications, the state just after the corrective maintenance makes a transition from j $(= 1, \cdots, s - 1)$ to k $(= 2', \cdots, s')$.

Suppose that the service level of software at time t is described by a semi-Markov process (SMP) with $2(s + 1)$ states and constant sojourn time k_j $(j = 1, \cdots, s)$. Figure 1 illustrates the semi-Markov transition diagram of a service degradation model. Since this SMP can be simplified to a right-skip free CTMC by aggregation of states k $(= 1', 2', \cdots, s')$ and j $(= 1, \cdots, s)$, it can be reduced to the simpler form depicted in Fig. 2. More specifically, let $\{N(t), t \geq 0\}$ be a right-skip free CTMC with space state $I = \{0, 1, 2, \cdots, s, s + 1\}$, where the transition rate from i to j $(i, j = 0, \cdots, s+1, i < j)$ is given by $\gamma_{i,j}$ (> 0) and $\sum_{j=i+1}^{s+1} \gamma_{i,j} = \Gamma_i$ for all i $(= 0, 1, \cdots, s)$ in Fig. 2. When the service failure occurs, the service is down and the state makes a transition from an arbitrary state j $(= 0, 1, \cdots, s)$ to State $s+1$. Then, both the recovery operation and the rejuvenation of operating system immediately start, where the time to complete the recovery operation is an independent and identically distributed (i.i.d.) random variable having the cumulative distribution function (c.d.f.) $H_{s+1}(x)$ and mean $1/\omega_{s+1}$ (> 0).

On the other hand, one makes a decision whether to trigger the preventive rejuvenation of operating system like garbege collection at the time instant when the state of software service changes from i $(= 0, 1, \cdots, s - 1)$ to j $(= i + 1, i + 2, \cdots, s)$. If one decides to continue operation (Action 2), the state is monitored until the next change of state, otherwise, the rejuvenation (Action 1) is preventively triggered, where the time to complete the rejuvenation is also an i.i.d. random variable with the c.d.f. $H_i(x)$ and mean $1/\omega_i$ (> 0), depending on the state i $(= 0, 1, \cdots, s)$. When the service failure occurs, i.e. the service state becomes $j = s + 1$, the recovery operation (Action 3) is taken. Let $q_{i,j}(\delta)$ denote the probability that the service state changes from i to j under Action δ $(= 1, 2, 3)$. Then it is seen that

(i) Case 1:

$$q_{i,0}(1) = \int_0^\infty dH_i(t) = 1, \quad i = 0, 1, \cdots, s. \tag{1}$$

where the mean rejuvenation time (overhead) is given by

$$h_i = \int_0^\infty t \, dH_i(t). \tag{2}$$

(ii) Case 2:

$$q_{i,j}(2) = \gamma_{i,j}/\Gamma_i, \quad i, j = 0, 1, \cdots, s + 1, i < j. \tag{3}$$

(iii) Case 3:

$$q_{i,0}(3) = \int_0^\infty dH_{s+1}(t) = 1, \tag{4}$$

where the mean recovery time (overhead) is given by

$$h_{s+1} = \int_0^\infty t dH_{s+1}(t).$$ (5)

After completing preventive rejuvenation and recovery operations, the service state becomes as good as new, *i.e.* $j = 0$ in Eqs. (1) and (4), and the same cycle repeats again and again over an infinite time horizon. We define the time interval from the initial point to the completion of rejuvenation or recovery operation whichever occurs first, as one cycle.

3   Semi-markov Decision Process

Observing the service state of software, we sequentially determine the optimal timing to trigger the software rejuvenation so as to minimize the steady-state service unavailability. Define the following functions:

$\mu(i)$: action taken at state i, *i.e.*,

$$\mu(i) = \begin{cases} 1 : 0 \le i \le s \\ 2 : 0 \le i \le s \\ 3 : i = s+1. \end{cases}$$ (6)

$G(i, \mu(i))$: expected service down time between successive two decision points when action $\mu(i)$ is taken at state i,

$$G(i, \mu(i)) = \begin{cases} h_i : & \mu(i) = 1 \\ k_i : & \mu(i) = 2 \\ h_{s+1} : \mu(i) = 3. \end{cases}$$ (7)

$\pi_i(\mu(i))$: total expected time between successive two decision points when action $\mu(i)$ is taken at state i,

$$\pi_i(\mu(i)) = \begin{cases} h_i : & \mu(i) = 1 \\ 1/\Gamma_i : \mu(i) = 2 \\ h_{s+1} : \mu(i) = 3. \end{cases}$$ (8)

$U(i)$: action space at state i,
$v(i)$: value function at state $i \in I$,
UA: service unavailability in the steady state, where **UA*** denotes the minimum one.

From the preliminary above, the Bellman equation based on the principle of optimality [18] is given by

$$v(i) = \min_{\mu \in U(i)} \left[G(i, \mu) - \mathbf{UA} \cdot \pi_i(\mu) + \sum_{j=0}^{s+1} q_{i,j}(\mu) \cdot v(j) \right].$$ (9)

It is well known that the software rejuvenation policy satisfying Eq. (9) is the best policy among all the Markovian policies [18]. To solve the above functional equation numerically, we can easily develop the well-known value iteration algorithm for the semi-Markov decision process. Define:

$w(i, \mu(i))$: value function when action $\mu(i)$ is taken at state i,
$A(n) := \min_{i \in I}\{V^n(i) - V^{n-1}(i)\}$,
$B(n) := \max_{i \in I}\{V^n(i) - V^{n-1}(i)\}$,
ϵ : tolerance level,
τ : design parameter satisfying $0 \le \tau/h_r$ for all i, $\tau\Gamma_i$ and $\tau/h_f \le 1$ (see [18]),

where $V^n(i)$ denotes the value function at n-th iteration. Then, the value iteration algorithm is given in the following:

Value Iteration Algorithm:

Step 1:

$$n := 0, \quad v^0(i) := 0. \tag{10}$$

Step 2:

$$w^{n+1}(i, 2) := \frac{k_i}{(1/\Gamma_i)} + \sum_{j=0}^{s+1} \tau\gamma_{ij}v^n(j) + \Big(1 - \sum_{j=0}^{s+1} \tau\gamma_{ij}\Big)v^n(i), \tag{11}$$

$$w^{n+1}(i, 1) := \frac{h_i}{h_i} + \Big(\frac{\tau}{h_i}\Big)v^n(0) + \Big(1 - \frac{\tau}{h_i}\Big)v^n(i), \tag{12}$$

$$v^{n+1}(i) := \min\{w^{n+1}(i, 1), w^{n+1}(i, 2)\}, \tag{13}$$

$$v^{n+1}(s+1) := \frac{h_{s+1}}{h_{s+1}} + \Big(\frac{\tau}{h_{s+1}}\Big)v^n(0) + \Big(1 - \frac{\tau}{h_{s+1}}\Big)v^n(s+1). \tag{14}$$

Step 3: If $0 \le B(n) - A(n) \le \epsilon A(n)$, then stop the procedure, otherwise, $n := n + 1$ and go to **Step 1**.

In general, it would be possible to derive the optimal software rejuvenation schedule by applying the above value iteration algorithm, if there exists a unique optimal solution. However, it is worth noting that an analytical approach to characterize the optimal rejuvenation policy, without solving the Bellman equation directly, is possible by making some parametric (but reasonable) assumptions (see [10]). In the following section, we investigate some mathematical properties for the optimal software rejuvenation policy and prove its optimality.

4   Optimality of Control-Limit Policy

In a fashion similar to the previous result by the same authors [10], we prove the optimality of the control-limit type of policy. We make the following assumptions:

(A-1) Γ_i is monotonically increasing in i ($= 0, 1, \cdots, s+1$).

(A-2) For an arbitrary increasing function f_j, $\sum_{j=i+1}^{s+1} \gamma_{i,j} f_j / \Gamma_i$ is monotonically increasing in i ($= 0, 1, \cdots, j-1$).

(A-3) For an arbitrary x, $\overline{H}_{s+1}(x) > \overline{H}_i(x)$, where in general $\overline{H}(\cdot) = 1 - H(\cdot)$.

(A-4) k_i is monotonically increasing in i ($= 0, 1, \cdots, s$).

(A-5) $k_i - h_i$ in monotonically increasing in i ($= 0, 1, \cdots, s$).

The assumption (A-1) implies that the mean sojourn time in each state decreases, as the system deteriorates. The assumption (A-2) seems to be somewhat technical, but is intuitively reasonable. For instance, let f_j be any cost parameter depending on state j. In this case, the expected down time incurred when the system state makes a transition, $\sum_{j=i+1}^{s+1} f_j(\gamma_{i,j} / \Gamma_i)$, tends to increase as the degraded level i progresses. In the assumption (A-3), one expects in the sense of probability that the recovery time from system failure is strictly greater than the rejuvenation overhead. The assumption (A-4) means that the set up time increases, but according to (A-5) the motivation to trigger the software rejuvenation becomes stronger gradually, as the software system deteriorates more and more.

We give the main results of this paper.

Lemma 4.1. The function $v(i)$ is increasing in i.

Proof. It is evident from (A-3) to show that

$$w(s, 1) = h_i + v(0) - zh_i, \tag{15}$$

$$v(s+1) = h_{s+1} + v(0) - zh_{s+1}. \tag{16}$$

Hence we have $v(s) \leq v(s+1)$ immediately. Supposing that $v(i+1) \leq v(i+2) \leq \cdots \leq v(s) \leq v(s+1)$ for an arbitrary i, from (A-2), it can be seen that

$$\sum_j \frac{\gamma_{i,j}}{\Gamma_i} v(j) \leq \sum_j \frac{\gamma_{i+1,j}}{\Gamma_{i+1}} v(j). \tag{17}$$

In Case 1 with $\mu(i+1) = 1$, we have

$$v(i+1) - v(i) \geq (h_{i+1} - h_i) - z(h_{i+1} - h_i) = 0. \tag{18}$$

This implies that $v(i+1) \geq v(i)$. In Case 2 with $\mu(i+1) = 2$, we obtain

$$v(i+1) - v(i) \geq k_{i+1} + \sum_j \frac{\gamma_{i+1,j}}{\Gamma_{i+1}} v(j) - z/\Gamma_{i+1} - k_i - \sum_j \frac{\gamma_{i,j}}{\Gamma_i} v(j) + z/\Gamma_i$$

$$= (k_{i+1} - k_i) + \left(\sum_j \frac{\gamma_{i+1,j}}{\Gamma_{i+1}} v(j) - \sum_j \frac{\gamma_{i,j}}{\Gamma_i} v(j) \right)$$

$$+ (z/\Gamma_i - z/\Gamma_{i+1})$$

$$\geq 0, \tag{19}$$

which is due to (A-1), (A-2) and (A-4). Thus, it can be shown that $v(i) \leq v(i+1)$. From the inductive argument, it can be proved that $v(i) \leq v(i+1)$ for an arbitrary i.

Theorem 4.2. There exists the optimal control limit $N^* + 1$ satisfying

$$D(i) = \begin{cases} 1 : \text{otherwise} \\ 2 : i \le N^*. \end{cases} \tag{20}$$

Proof.

$$w(i, 2) - w(i, 1) = k_i + \sum_j \frac{\gamma_{i,j}}{\Gamma_i} v(j) - z/\Gamma_i - h_i - v(0) + z h_i. \tag{21}$$

From (A-1), (A-2), (A-5) and Lemma 4.1, it is seen that Eq. (21) is a monotonically increasing function of i. Hence, the proof is completed.

From Theorem 4.2, the problem can be reduced to obtain the optimal control-limit $N^* + 1$ so as to minimize the steady-state service unavailability.

Next, we formulate the steady-state service unavailability as a function of N, i.e. $\mathbf{UA} = \mathbf{UA}(N)$. Define

$$R_{i,j} = \begin{cases} 1 & i = j, \\ \displaystyle\sum_{k=i+1}^{j} \gamma_{i,k} R_{k,j}/\Gamma_i & \text{otherwise,} \end{cases} \tag{22}$$

$$t_i = \begin{cases} \displaystyle\sum_{j=i+1}^{N} R_{i,j}/\Gamma_j & i \le N, \\ 0 & i > N, \end{cases} \tag{23}$$

where $R_{i,j}$ is the transition probability from the state i to the state j, and t_i denotes the mean time to trigger the software rejuvenation. Define the first passage time:

$$T^* = \inf\{t \ge 0 : N(t) \ge N^* + 1\}, \tag{24}$$

so that the random variable T^* is the first time when $N(t)$ is greater than the level $N^* + 1$. Using the above notation, we can get the following result without the proof.

Theorem 4.3. The optimal software rejuvenation time is given by the first passage time T^*, where the optimal threshold level N^* is the solution of $\min_{0 \le N < \infty} \mathbf{UA}(N)$ and

$$\mathbf{UA}(N) = \frac{\displaystyle\sum_{j=1}^{N} R_{0,j} \left\{ k_j + \sum_{k=N+1}^{s} \frac{\gamma_{j,k} h_k}{\Gamma_j} + \frac{\gamma_{j,s+1} h_{s+1}}{\Gamma_j} \right\}}{S_0 + \displaystyle\sum_{j=1}^{N} \sum_{k=N+1}^{s} \frac{R_{0,j}}{\Gamma_j} \left\{ \gamma_{j,k} h_k + \gamma_{j,s+1} h_{s+1} \right\}}. \tag{25}$$

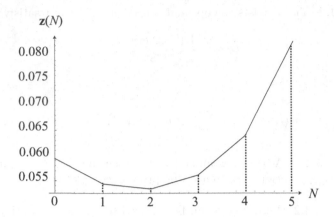

Fig. 3. Behavior of the steady-state service unavailability with respect to N

In Eq. (25), the function $\mathbf{UA}(N)$ is formulated as the expected down time for one cycle divided by the mean time length of one cycle. The minimization problem of $\mathbf{UA}(N)$ with respect to N ($= 0, 1, 2, \cdots$) is trivial. Define the difference of $\mathbf{UA}(N)$ by $\phi(N) = \mathbf{UA}(N+1) - \mathbf{UA}(N)$. If $\phi(N+1) - \phi(N) > 0$, then the function $\mathbf{UA}(N)$ is strictly convex in N. Further, if $\phi(N^* - 1) > 0$ and $\phi(N^*) \leq 0$, then there exist (at least one, at most two) optimal threshold level N^* which minimizes $\mathbf{UA}(N)$, i.e., $\mathbf{UA}^* = \mathbf{UA}(N^*)$. In fact, the convex property of the function $\mathbf{UA}(N)$ can be easily checked numerically.

Figure 3 depicts the behavior of the steady-state service unavailability with respect to N, where the model parameters used here are given by $\gamma_{0,1} = \gamma_{0,2} = \gamma_{1,4} = \gamma_{2,6} = 0.05$, $\gamma_{0,3} = \gamma_{1,5} = 0.04$, $\gamma_{0,4} = \gamma_{1,6} = 0.03$, $\gamma_{0,5} = 0.02$, $\gamma_{0,6} = 0.01$, $\gamma_{1,2} = \gamma_{1,3} = \gamma_{2,5} = 0.06$, $\gamma_{2,3} = \gamma_{2,4} = 0.07$, $\gamma_{3,4} = \gamma_{3,5} = 0.09$, $\gamma_{3,6} = 0.08$, $\gamma_{4,5} = \gamma_{4,6} = 0.15$, $\gamma_{5,6} = 0.35$, $\omega_1 = \omega_2 = \omega_3 = \omega_4 = \omega_5 = 4$ (hr^{-1}), $\omega_6 = 2$ (hr^{-1}), $k_0 = 0.05$ (hr), $k_1 = 0.10$ (hr), $k_2 = 0.15$ (hr), $k_3 = 0.20$ (hr), $k_4 = 0.25$ (hr), $k_5 = 0.3$ (hr). It can be shown that there is an optimal threshold level $N^* = 2$ in this example.

5   A Numerical Example

Here we give an illustrative example to determine the optimal rejuvenation schedule. Huang et al. [13] suppose that the number of system states is only 3: normal operation, deterioration (failure probable state) and system down (failure). In this section we consider a generalized Markovian deterioration process with 6 degradation levels (totally, 8 states). Figure 4 illustrates the Markovian transition diagram with absorption representing the deterioration process of the software service, where each transition rate is assigned on each arc.

Suppose that the rejuvenation time and the recovery time from service failure are given by $\omega_1 = \omega_2 = \omega_3 = \omega_4 = \omega_5 = \omega_6 = 4.0$ (hr^{-1}), and $\omega_7 = 2.0$ (hr^{-1}),

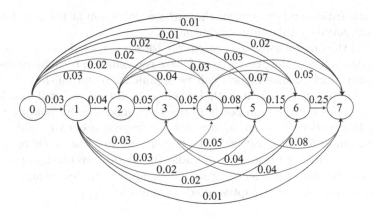

Fig. 4. An illustrative example with 6 degradation levels

Table 1. Decision Table

i	0	1	2	3	4	5	6	7
$D(i)$	2	2	2	2	1	1	1	3

respectively. Also, it is assumed that $k_0 = 0.05$ (hr), $k_1 = 0.10$ (hr), $k_2 = 0.15$ (hr), $k_3 = 0.20$ (hr), $k_4 = 0.25$ (hr), $k_5 = 0.30$ (hr), $k_6 = 0.35$ (hr). In Table 1, we obtain the so-called *decision table* to characterize the optimal software rejuvenation policy. From this result, it is optimal to trigger the software rejuvenation at the first time when the system state reaches to $i^* = N^* + 1 = 4$. Then the associated minimum service unavailability in the steady state is given by $\mathbf{UA}^* = \mathbf{UA}(N^*) = \mathbf{UA}(3) = 0.374026$.

6   Conclusions

In this paper, we have considered a service degradation model with preventive rejuvenation for an operational software system with set up delay. We have formulated the underlying optimization problem by a semi-Markov decision process and proved the optimality of control-limit type of software rejuvenation policy. A numerical example has been presented to illustrate the dynamic rejuvenation policy and its associated steady-state service unavailability. Here we have derived the decision table to characterize the optimal rejuvenation strategy through a numerical example. Service availability is of key importance for the general maintenance operations in computer systems as well as the communications network management (see *e.g.* [8]). The result can be applied to the preventive maintenance problem with garbage collection for an operating software, if the degradation level can be quantified by the total amount of memory leak. Based on the optimality of control-limit policy, the service provider monitors the level of resource exhaustion and can trigger the garbage collection at the best timing in terms of the service availability maximization.

In general the critical software systems are ideally required to be 'zero-service failure' systems. Then, the preventive software rejuvenation techniques and their dependability/performance models will be significant to establish and quantify higher availability requirement with low cost. In future, we will consider an adaptive software rejuvenation policy in the same modeling framework with set up delay. In practice, it is not so easy for service engineers to build software rejuvenation models and to estimate the transition rates from their operational experience. To challenge the above issue, adaptive algorithms like non-parametric statistics and reinforcement learning should be applied to design an autonomic rejuvenation protocol with adaptive prediction ability.

Acknowledgments

The present research was partially supported by a Grant-in-Aid for Scientific Research from the Ministry of Education, Sports, Science and Culture of Japan under Grant Nos. 15651076 and 16310116.

References

1. Adams, E. (1984), Optimizing preventive service of the software products, *IBM Journal of Research & Development*, **28** (1), 2–14.
2. Calabria, R., Ragione, L. D., Pulcini, G. and Rapone, M. (1993), Service dependability of transit systems: a case study, *Proceedings of Annual Reliability and Maintainability Symposium*, 366–371, IEEE Reliability Society.
3. Castelli, V., Harper, R. E., Heidelberger, P., Hunter, S. W., Trivedi, K. S., Vaidyanathan, K. V. and Zeggert, W. P. (2001), Proactive management of software aging, *IBM Journal of Research & Development*, **45** (2), 311–332.
4. Chan, C. K. and Tortorella, M. (2001), Spares-inventory sizing for end-to-end service availability, *Proceedings of Annual Reliability and Maintainability Symposium*, 98–102, IEEE Reliability Society.
5. Choi, C. and Kim, S. (2005), A dependability management mechanism for ubiquitous computing systems, *Embedded and Ubiquitous Computing – EUC 2005 Workshops* (eds. by T. Enokido *et al.*), LNCS **3823**, 1293–1302, Springer-Verlag.
6. Chu, L. K., Chu, S. S. and Sculli, D. (1998), Service availability of a radio access telecommunications network, *Quality & Reliability Engineering International*, **14** (5), 365–370.
7. Cristian, F. (1993), Automatic service availability management, *Proceedings of International Symposium on Autonomous Decentralized Systems (ISADS-93)*, 360–366, IEEE Computer Society Press.
8. Dahlin, M., Chandra, B. B. V., Lei, G., Nayate, A. (2003), End-to-end WAN service availability, *IEEE/ACM Transactions on Networking*, **11** (2), 300–313.
9. Dislis, C. (2002), Improving service availability via low-outage upgrades, *Proceedings of 26th Annual International Computer Software and Applications Conference (COMPSAC-2002)*, 989–993, IEEE Computer Society Press.

10. Eto, H. and Dohi, T. (2005), Optimality of control-limit type of software rejuvenation policy, *Proceedings of IEEE 11th International Conference on Parallel and Distributed Systems (ICPADS-2005)*, **II**, 483–487, IEEE Computer Society Press.

11. Garg, S., Pfening, S., Puliafito, A., Telek, M. and Trivedi, K. S. (1998), Analysis of preventive maintenance in transactions based software systems, *IEEE Transactions on Computers*, **47** (1), 96–107.

12. Glossbrenner, K. C. (1993), Availability and reliability of switched services, *IEEE Communications Magazine*, **31** (6), 28–32.

13. Huang, Y., Kintala, C., Koletti, N. and Fulton, N. D. (1995), Software rejuvenation: analysis, module and applications, *Proceedings of 25th International Symposium on Fault Tolerant Computing (FTCS-1995)*, 381–390, IEEE Computer Society Press.

14. Mainkar, V. (1997), Availability analysis of transaction-processing systems based on user-perceived performance, *Proceedings of 16th IEEE Symposium on Reliable Distributed Systems (SRDS-1997)*, 10–17, IEEE Computer Society Press.

15. Pfening, S., Garg, S., Puliafito, A., Telek, M. and Trivedi, K. S. (1996), Optimal rejuvenation for toleranting soft failure, *Performance Evaluation*, **27/28** (4), 491–506.

16. Reinecke, P., Van Moorsel, A. and Wolter, K. (2004), A measurement study of the interplay between application level restart and transport protocol, *Service Availability: First International Service Availability Symposium (ISAS-2004)* (eds. by M. Malek *et al.*), LNCS **3335**, 86–100, Springer-Verlag.

17. Reisinger, H. (2004), Quality of service control by middleware, *Service Availability: First International Service Availability Symposium (ISAS-2004)* (eds. by M. Malek *et al.*), LNCS **3335**, 61–72, Springer-Verlag.

18. Tijms, H. C. (1994), *Stochastic Models: An Algorithmic Approach*, John Wiley & Sons.

19. Tortorella, M. (2005), Service reliability theory and engineering, I: foundations, *Quality Technology & Quantitative Management*, **2** (1), 1–16.

20. Tortorella, M. (2005), Service reliability theory and engineering, II: models and examples, *Quality Technology & Quantitative Management*, **2** (1), 17–37.

21. Vaidyanathan, K. and Trivedi, K. S. (2005), A comprehensive model for software rejuvenation, *IEEE Transactions on Dependable and Secure Computing*, **2** (2), 124–137.

22. Yurcik, W. and Doss, D. (2001), Achieving fault-tolerant software with rejuvenation and reconfiguration, *IEEE Software*, **18** (4), 48–52.

Estimating SLAs Availability/Reliability in Multi-services IP Networks

Saida Benlarbi

Manager, System Reliability Engineering
Alcatel – IP Division
600 March Road, Kanata - Ottawa, Ontario, Canada K2K 2E6
Voice: (613)-784-6433
Saida.Benlarbi@alcatel.com

Abstract. Multi-Services IP Networks are being required to deliver unprecedented high volumes of diverse traffic that span two ends of the reliability requirements spectrum. On one end of the spectrum real-time services such as voice and real time TV require high sensitivity to delays and jitter. On the other end of the spectrum best effort services such as data content delivery services requires zero traffic losses and traffic integrity. This paper focuses on investigating the challenges of measuring the end to end service availability given the different layers of resilience in the hierarchical network architecture. It proposes a layered approach to modeling and measurement of multi-services IP networks from which composite availability/reliability estimation models combining convoluted levels of fault resilience can be derived. The resulting models can be readily used to show a Service Level Agreement reliability measure is met from both the service provider and the end user standpoints.

Keywords: Reliability, Availability, Service Level Agreement, Multi-service IP network, Markov Modeling.

1 Introduction

IP is becoming the next generation communication services delivery mean that makes service providers and Telecom operators face a number of networking design and reliability challenges. Multi-services IP networks are currently touted as being up to these challenges. However, they need to meet a set of design and reliability requirements in order to be carrier-grade performance and reliability hence secure low costs and increased profits for vendors, network operators and services providers [8],[1],[3],[10]. In particular, a multi-services IP network has to deliver high volumes of diverse traffic that span two ends of the reliability requirements spectrum. On one end of the spectrum real-time services such as voice or real time TV require high sensitivity to delays and jitter. On the other end of the spectrum best effort services such as data content delivery require zero traffic losses and high traffic integrity.

As service providers and network operators deploy these services they face the challenges of designing the IP network that is capable of supporting a number of

D. Penkler, M. Reitenspiess, and F. Tam (Eds.): ISAS 2006, LNCS 4328, pp. 30–42, 2006.

application service classes with predictable and/or guaranteed levels of service. In order to deliver predictable service levels that are bound to meet required Service Level Agreements (SLA)s every service class has to be defined in terms of availability/reliability/serviceability targets measured in terms of the network architecture design and traffic management parameters such as topology and network configuration dimensioning, latency, jitter, packet loss, and bandwidth.

Over decades of development, the Telecom industry came to agree on well established and standardized communication systems reliability estimation methods and techniques that allow quantifying their behavior and measuring it against service level agreement targets [7]. However, these estimation practices present a number of limits and challenges that need to be overcome in order to be able to leverage their use for multi-services IP networks SLAs estimation. For example, most of the currently industry used methods and techniques are based on connection oriented traffic moving that focuses on L1 (node hardware and Automatic Protection Systems) and L2 (link and connection protection) of the IP network whereas the availability/reliability models of multi-services IP network need to take into account the complexity and the intricacy of the various levels of the networking functions and their binding with the infrastructure behavior. Moreover, the service IP path failure/repair behavior has to be considered under network load performance conditions in order to demonstrate that an SLA is met under for given engineered bandwidth. One of the major issues in this respect is to be able to demonstrate that an end-to-end service path meets its SLA reliability targets under a given network dimensioning and services configuration. For example, how to show that an end-to-end service path meets 99.999% availability often coined from the well proven PSTN[1] reliability under average and worst case load? How to show that an IP path carrying voice traffic meets the tight voice requirement of 150ms max delay from mouth to ear dictated by the max window of a perceivable degradation in voice quality? How to show that an end-to-end IP path incurs zero packet loss for a real-time TV service?

Liu & Trivedi [1] propose a general framework for survivability estimation where one can distinguish various angles of network reliability focus for each of which a suitable reliability model can be constructed. However, it still does not answer the need for a binding view between the service behavior and the network behavior that has to be defined in order for service providers, network operators and vendors have a common service quantification mean. To answer this need we are currently investigating various design and measurement approaches that pave the way for building viable modeling and measurement techniques that answer specific SLAs quantification.

In this paper, we propose a layered approach to modeling and measurement of multi-services IP networks from which composite availability/reliability estimation models combining convoluted levels of fault resilience can be derived. The resulting models can be readily used to show an SLA is met from both the service provider and the end user standpoints.

Section 2 provides a mapping between the service view, the network functions view and the network infrastructure view. In section 3 we identify the four layers of network resilience and discuss the limitations of measuring multi-service IP network

---

[1] If not defined in this paper, the acronyms used are well established Telecom terms. The reader is advised to consult the Telecom literature for an exhaustive glossary.

availability/reliability and performance separately. In section 4 we show the need for using an integrated modeling approach that is more reflective of the network resilience layers contribution to the service availability/reliability. We then propose a layered approach that allows assessing the service availability/reliability in a multi-service IP network that help in demonstrating SLAs are met under given network load conditions and behavior.

2   Overview of Service Resilience in Multi-services IP Networks

As new communication technologies are developed new services can be created and the need to demonstrate they meet customer requirements becomes crucial in differentiating these technologies. Fig. 1 shows a simple mapping between data communication based services, the networking infrastructure that provides it and the networking functionality or service protocol that delivers it [1].

Multi-services data networks are designed in a hierarchical architecture where various resilience options are deployable. At the Physical Layer (L 1) of the network a number of transport options with different resilience characteristics are possible. A first option is the well established Telecom carrier transport systems TDM ring based on SONET and SDH. The second one which comes from the packet world is the packet rings where a range of options is available: token ring, FDDI, etc. Since Gigabit Ethernet packet switching at line rate is becoming the multi-services IP networks preferred traffic delivery method, Resilient Packet Ring (RPR IEEE 802.17) presents itself as the MAN/WAN transport option that leverages packet rings based on the TDM ring resilience concepts. Both categories offer physical protection since when a link is cut or a port is down traffic keeps on flowing through a redundant path. On a failure, the target switchover delays are typically of less than 50ms in order to meet the stringent requirements of time sensitive services.

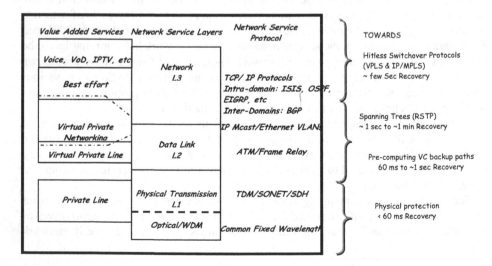

Fig. 1. Mapping Services, Networking Functionality and Network Infrastructure

At the Link Layer (L 2) of the network, technology choices are less diverse. ATM provides resilience by pre-computing backup paths that are activated within a given delay typically in the order of less than one second for switched Virtual Circuits (VC)s depending on the number of connections to reroute. Ethernet provides resilience through the re-computation of its spanning tree in the event of a failure (IEEE 802.1d). Because this mechanism may take a delay in the order of the minutes it fails to meet stringent real-time service recovery requirements. Recently it has been extended with the Rapid Spanning Tree Protocol (RSTP, IEEE 802.1w) with target convergence times of the order of the second.

At the Network Layer (L 3) of the network, the most common protocol option is IP. IP uses ICMP to detect and recover from L3 type of failures. The IP resilience is provided by the L2/L3 control protocol functions which maintain forwarding information, manage failure detections, perform topology discovery and routing table updates in the event of a network topology or load conditions changes. However, IP networking function must also rely on the Transmission layer (L4) to ensure a reliable delivery of the packet. Depending on where a given networking system is located in the network and on local preferences, different protocols are used: within the same domain, intra-domain protocol such as ISIS, OSPF, EIGRP, or RIP is used; between different domains, an inter-domain protocol is used with BGP being the most dominant. The L4 resilience is based on TCP functionality for connection based packet routing and UDP for connectionless packet routing. Hence, in case of a failure or poor network performance behavior the routing and network configuration information have to be re-computed.

One main problem with L3 resilience is that it is coupled with a working routing protocol run at L4. If the latter fails, the routing system can no longer be active in reconfiguring the network topology and re-establishing new routes. Depending on the protocol used the recovery times in this case are in the order of 10s of minutes unless a duplication of devices and networking functions is put in place which of course comes with a high cost. The separation of the routing plane from the forwarding plane allows for a better resilience especially when a failure event impacts only the routing plane. In this case it is possible to try to restart the routing engine without impacting the service. The failure may then be recoverable with target recovery time in the order of 10 seconds. In this respect, many quick restart extensions have been added by the IETF to the common routing protocols. However, at GigE line rate switching, a failure translates in high impacts even in case of 10's of seconds of interruption as thousands of traffic flows and user/subscribers get cut from the service. Hence the network re-convergence may pose a number of performance tuning challenges. A much higher availability solution is to architect a fully redundant routing plane in a hot standby mode where regardless of the protocols running, the L3 and L4 protocol activities incur a hitless switchover in the event of a failure or poor network load behavior. This means the active and standby routing planes must maintain synchronized L3/L4 states and traffic management information so the traffic is handed over within 10's of milliseconds. Currently, VPLS and IP/MPLS network architecture designs are targeting L3/L4 recovery times in the order of few seconds.

3   Estimating Multi-services IP Networks Service Availability/Reliability

The main difficulty in modeling and estimating multi-services IP networks is to aggregate the measures from all the levels of networking functions and work with a viable model that reflects the network behavior from the service provider and the service user standpoints. The second difficulty is that for functions of L1 and L2 types, availability/reliability parameters can be easily distinguished from performance ones hence estimated separately. On the other hand, functions of L3 and L4 types exhibit most of the time a degraded performance state before they fail completely. This makes it difficult to distinguish between failures modes resulting in a complete loss of service (e.g. unreachable destination or link loss) and failures modes resulting in a partial loss or temporary corruption of the service (e.g. overflow of buffer capacity to forward traffic). Hence, demonstrating multi-services IP networks reliability and robustness requires a careful balancing act of probing and measurement of the various network layers resilience that are impacted by both scalability limits and failure events that affect the various networking layers.

As a first step of the estimation approach a careful definition and identification of the service affecting failure modes that can be generated by any of the L1 to L4 of the networking functions has to be laid out.

Figure 2 depicts the growing complexity and interactions that stem from failure modes dependencies which can originate at the different networking functions layers of the multi-service IP network. Failure modes attributable to particular hardware infrastructure, software system or network element running a particular network protocol have to be identified and assessed in terms of their effects on the network service layers which in turn have to be mapped to specific type of provider/end-user service failure effects.

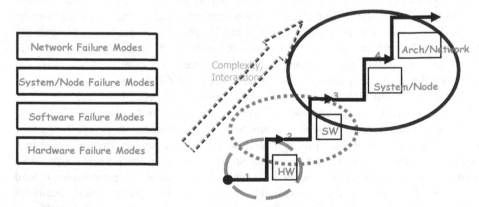

Fig. 2. Networking Function Failure Modes Complexity and Interactions Levels

3.1 Models for L1 and L2 Types of Resilience

Two major modeling approaches are used to evaluate networking systems availability: discrete-event simulation or analytical modeling [5]. A discrete-event simulation model mimics dynamically detailed system behavior to evaluate specific measures such rerouting delays or resources utilization. An analytical model uses a set of mathematical equations to describe the system behavior. The measures are obtained from solving these equations, for e.g. the system availability, reliability and Mean Time Between Failure (MTBF). The analytical models can be divided in turn into two major classes: non-state space and state space models. Three main assumptions underlie the non-state space modeling techniques: the system is either up or down (no degraded state is captured), the failures are statistically independent and the repairs actions are independent. Two main modeling techniques are used in this category: Reliability Block Diagram (RBD) and Fault Trees. The RBD technique mimics the logical behavior of failures whereas the fault tree mimics the logical paths down to one failure. Fault trees are mostly used to isolate catastrophic faults or to perform root cause analysis.

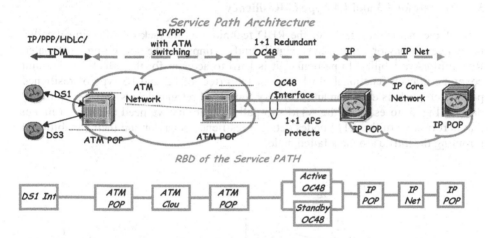

Fig. 3. Example of a Multi-Services IP Path RBD

RBD is the most used method in the Telecom industry to estimate the Reliability/Availability of the L1 and L2 type of resilience in a networking system [7]. It is simple to develop and grasp and it does reflect typical L1/L2 reliability behavior as network functions at these level are either up or down. It is also a straightforward mean to isolate the network single points of failure. An RBD captures a network function or a deployed service as a set of inter-working blocks (e.g. a SONET ring) connected in series and/or in parallel to reflect their operational dependencies. In a series connection all the components are needed for the block to work properly i.e. any of them goes down the function/service goes down. In a parallel connection at least one of the components is needed to work for the block to work. Given the failure rate λi of a block i and the Mean Time to Repair (MTTR) μ, the steady state availability of the block is given by:

$$A_i = \frac{MTBF_i}{MTBF_i + MTTR} = \frac{\lambda_i}{\lambda_i + \mu}$$

Fig. 3 shows an example of a service path RBD.

The path is composed of a DS3 source point then traverses and ATM network then gets out to an IP network ending on an IP point of presence (PoP) through a protected OC48 link. The availability of the IP path can be simply estimated as:

$$A_{path} = \prod_i A_i = A_{DS3} A_{PoP}^2 A_{ATM\_Net} A_{OC48} A_{IP\_PoP}^2 A_{IP\_net}$$

And the availability of the OC48 link is estimated by:

$$A_{OC48} = 1 - (1 - A_{SimplexOC48})^2$$

3.2   Models for L3 and L4 Type of Resiliency

One of the major drawbacks of the RBD technique is its lack of reflecting detailed resilience behavior that can significantly impact the resulting estimated Reliability/Availability. In particular, it is hard to account for the effects of the fault coverage of each functional block and for the effect of L2 and L3 type of resilience parameters such as detection and recovery times and reroute delays. For e.g. in the IP path of Fig. 3, to estimate the ATM sub-path availability we need to create a model that is reflective of the ATM nodes detailed resilience behavior and their capability of rerouting the traffic around a failed node.

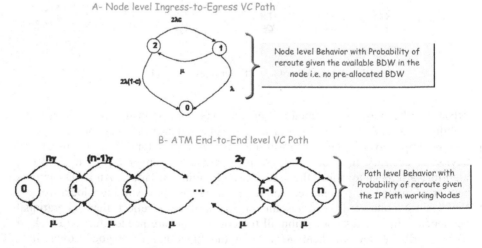

Fig. 4. Markov chain Modeling of an ATM VC Path Reliability Behavior

State space modeling allows tackling complex reliability behavior such as failure/repair dependencies and shared repair facilities. Among these techniques Markov chains has been established as a proven and reasonably easy to use approach in the Telecom industry [7]. Let's consider the ATM VC sub path of our Fig. 3 service path example. Fig. 4 shows the Markov chain models that we have used to estimate the end-to-end VC path availability in order to demonstrate it does meet 99.999% availability under a target node bandwidth available for reroute.

In order to better reflect the L2 resiliency and how it gets impacted by the available node bandwidth to reroute traffic around failed nodes, we constructed a composite Markov chain that mimics the ATM VC path states based on the ATM node behavior. In Fig. 4-B, let γ be the ATM node failure rate and μ the MTTR. The ATM VC path is up if at least one of the n ATM nodes is operational. After a node failure, the VC gets rerouted if the node traffic load allows it. For k=0, 1, ..., n-1, state k represents the VC path is up and the failed node has enough bandwidth to reroute, but k out of n nodes are down because either the node is down or it has no available bandwidth to reroute the traffic. State n represent the VC path is down i.e. all the ATM nodes in the path are down or none of them can reroute the traffic. The path availability is estimated as A_{path} = 1- U_{path} and the U_{path} its unavailability is defined as a function of n, the number of nodes in the path. U_{path} can be computed using the steady state probability πi of each state i as:

$$U_{path} = \pi_n = \frac{\rho^n n!}{\sum_{k=0}^{n} \rho^k \frac{n!}{(n-k)!}}$$

$$A_{path} = 1 - \pi_n = \sum_{k=0}^{n-1} \rho^k \frac{n!}{(n-k)!};$$

$$\pi_{n-1} = \frac{\rho^{n-1}(n-1)!}{\sum_{k=0}^{n} \rho^k \frac{n!}{(n-k)!}}; \qquad where \ \rho = \frac{\gamma_{node}}{\mu}$$

$$\lambda_{path} = \gamma_{node} * \frac{\pi_{n-1}}{1 - \pi_n} \Rightarrow \lambda_{path} = \gamma_{node} * \frac{\rho^{n-1}(n-1)!}{\sum_{k=0}^{n-1} \rho^k \frac{(n-1)!}{(n-k)!}}$$

The node failure rate γ is estimated using the Markov chain depicted in Fig. 4-A. It takes into account the probability of reroute given the available bandwidth in the node and the node infrastructure behavior. State2 represents the node is up and a failure is either covered with a probability c of reroute success, or not covered with (1-c) probability of not rerouting because of lack of bandwidth. A fault is covered if it is detected and recovered from without taking down the service. State1 represents the node is up but in simplex mode with no alternative routes. State0 represents the node down (all routes failed or no capacity available). The node mean time between failures (MTBF) can be estimated by:

$$MTBF = \frac{\lambda(1+2c)+\mu}{2\lambda(\lambda+\mu(1-c))}$$

We have run the model on a network composed of an average of 5 to 6 nodes end-to-end VC path and with an MTTR of < 3 hours and demonstrated that 99.999% VC path availability is reached only if the probability of reroute success is at least 50% given the way the bandwidth has been engineered. Fig. 5 show the resulting availability as function of the probability of re-route given the number of the nodes on the path.

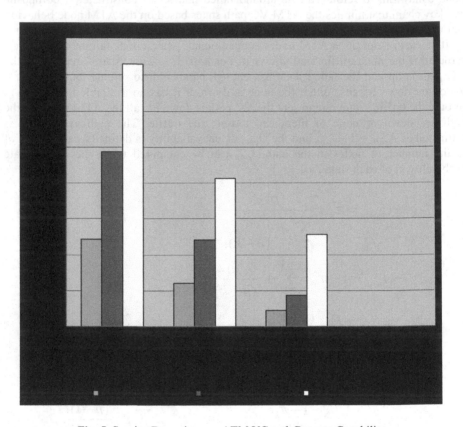

Fig. 5. Service Downtime vs. ATM VC path Reroute Capability

A similar approach to ours has been used in [5] to estimate the service availability for the purpose of a network architecture tradeoff analysis.

4   Towards a Hierarchical Approach for Service Availability Modeling and Measurement

At 10GE line rate packet switching, IP networks service availability is tightly dependent on both the infrastructure it is deployed on, the way it is deployed and the way the bandwidth is engineered. Separate reliability and performance models do not answer the need to reflect the interdependencies between the L2, L3 and L4 failure modes. For example, in the ATM VC path model of Fig. 4, we have assumed the reroute delay times were quite negligible in terms of service downtime impacts. This is a realistic assumption for an ATM path where recovery times are of the order of the sub second. However, if we wanted to account for the impact of the reroute delays on the path availability as it is the case for a L3/L4 type of resilience behavior, we need to construct a Markov chain that details the path behavioral states when it is in recovery because of reroute delays due to reroute protocols states recovery and re-convergence times.

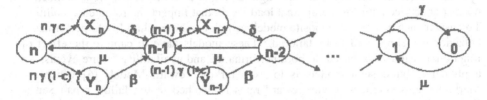

Fig. 6. Markov chain Model of a Service IP Path Reliability Behavior with Reroute Delays

Fig. 6 shows an example of such a Markov chain we have created to estimate the service IP path availability from end-to-end in a multi-services IP network given the reroute delays. The network is designed as a typical resilient VPLS architecture targeted for triple play solution with RSTP rings deployed at the metro access and with IP/MPLS routing at the metro core.

Let γ be the failure rate of the IP node, and μ its MTTR. A node failure is covered with a probability c and not covered with probability 1-c. After a node covered fault the path is up in a degraded mode until a release of the active routing engine activities to the standby one is complete and the traffic is running through the new active routing engine. However, after an uncovered fault, the path is down until the failed node is taken out from the path and the network reconfigured itself with a new routing table regenerated and broadcast. The routing engine switchover time and the network reconfiguration time are assumed to be exponentially distributed with means $1/\delta$ and $1/\beta$ respectively. The routing engine switchover time is in the order of the second. However, the path reconfiguration time may be in the order of the minutes. These two parameters are assumed to be small compared to the node MTBF and MTTR hence no failures and repairs are assumed to happen during these actions. The path is up if at least one of its n nodes is operational. The state i, $1 \leq i \leq n$, represents node i is operational and n-i nodes are down waiting for repair. The states Xn-i and Yn-i ($0 \leq i \leq n-2$) reflect the path recovery state and the path reconfiguration state respectively. The path availability A(n) is computed as a function of the number of nodes n given by its unavailability computed from the steady state probability πi of each state i as:

$$UA(n) = 1 - \sum_{i=1}^{n} \pi_i$$

We have run our model to show that the end-to-end IP path meet 99.999% voice service availability for various target network dimensioning and an average and max reroute delays. We are currently running the model with various failures/recovery scenarios to characterize the service availability behavior given different network dimensioning targets and variable reroute delays.

However, with pure reliability models it still would not be possible to show the impact of various performances levels at various functional/operational states. On the other hand modeling the performance separately from the reliability misses to reflect failure/repair behavior and makes it difficult to demonstrate an SLA is met under a given engineered bandwidth. A key practical question in network dimensioning for optimal service availability that meet tight SLAs is to estimate the right number of nodes per service path for the optimal load levels that impact the reroute capabilities. To answer such question composite models which combine reliability to performance behavior modeling need to be tailored. These models have to capture the effect of functional degradation based on both performance and availability failure events. An approach to build such models is to use Markov Reward Models [6] which are Markov chains augmented with reward rates r_i attached to the failure/repair states. Different reward schemes can be devised to account for the impact of performance features on the availability. For example for the IP path dimensioning, we are investigating the use of the Markov chain in Fig. 6 augmented with a reward system where ri =1 for the down states and ri=f(p_i,q_i) where p_i is the probability to drop traffic in case of service impacting packet loss and q_i is the service recovery time given i operational nodes in the path and f an appropriately chosen function that reflects the relationship between congestion and recovery time. The recovery time can be defined in turn as a function of the network delay and its jitter.

The state space technique may still suffer from a number of practical limiting factors. As the modeled block complexity grows, the state space model complexity may grow exponentially. For e.g., in the case of the ATM path model we have used a simplified time discrete Markov chain that does not distinguish between hardware and software failures i.e. we assumed the same recovery times for both. It also assumes a common repair facility for the all the nodes (same MTTR for all the nodes). In order to mimic such complex behavior very large Markov chain are needed. This makes the numerical solution of these models a daunting task. Currently, a number of techniques are explored in order to help in limiting the complexity of the numerical resolution of such chains. These techniques include structured analysis of Markov Chains such as the approximation techniques based on fixed point computations, bounding techniques, and hybrid techniques combining simulation and transient numerical analysis.

Our current view is to reduce the Markov Chain network resilience modeling complexity by taking advantage of the communication network specifics based on known information abot its functional and topological behaviors. Since the levels of traffic and the levels of reliability required at each layer of the network architecture are different even though the same service runs across all the layers, a hierarchal modeling approach can be used to aggregate the various layers of resilience behavior in the network with the level of details required for each layer. As we illustrated it in the previous section, the first layer of the modeling consists of defining an RBD that describes the basic functional blocks of the service. Then in turn each functional block can be estimated by using either a pure availability/reliability model if it is an L1 or L2 type of functional block or a composite model that reflects both the availability and performance if it is a L3 or L4 type of functional block. Hence the choice of the modeling technique suitable for a networking resilience level is now dictated by the need to account for the impact of the resilience parameters on the service availability, the level of details of the node/network/service behavior to be represented and the ease of construction and use of the set of models.

In summary the steps of the approach is as follows:

    a) partition the service path into sub paths, each sub path operating according to a set of respective network functions;

    b) estimate a reliability measure for each sub path according to the network functions parameters and constraints that impacts it;

    c) estimate the service reliability measure over the end to end path as the aggregate of the sub paths reliability measures.

Based on this hierarchical modeling approach, one can show tight reliability/availability SLA targets are met under a given network designed infrastructure with a given engineered bandwidth to provide a set of value added services each one predictable through a set of network functions scalability and robustness attributes.

For example, to engineer the required bandwidth in a resilient network architecture, reliability combined with performance modeling will help in two main aspects. First, it will help identifying and eliminating single points of failure by design. Second, it will help in constructing the optimal and cost effective resilience behavior by design and implementation choices where the network service will gracefully continue operating in the face of a wide variety of traffic anomalies, fault conditions, or operational changes to the network.

5 Summary and Future Directions

In this paper we showed that a multi-services IP network has different layers of resilience. They are basically tied up to the networking infrastructure deployed and the way the latter is engineered to handle the offered services. We have then discussed the issue of estimating the contribution of the 4 different layers of the network resilience to the reliability of the network architecture and the services it offers. We have discussed in particular the challenges posed by measuring the service availability/reliability given the effects of failure modes rooted in both the network infrastructure and the performance behavior of the network. We have then proposed a service availability modeling approach based on a layered structure using increasingly powerful and detailed analytical models that aggregate availability/reliability measures which can be estimated from each resilience layer with the suitable modeling technique. The multi-layered approach combines state-space and non-state space analysis techniques to aggregate availability/reliability measures that can be estimated and proven to meet tight SLA's.

There are a number of investigation leads that we are currently pursuing. Among these, our next step is to run various experiments with our approach to validate and calibrate its viable use for SLAs estimation in terms of end-to-end IP path service availability/reliability. For example, it would be useful to understand the scalability and limits of the method with the network dimensioning or the mix and makeup of services deployed changes. Second, in validating and calibrating our modeling approach we would like to compare it to the currently used Markov Chain structured analysis approaches.

References

1. P. Buchholz and G. Ciardo , "Tutorial on Structured analysis of Markov chains"; 1st International Conference on the Quantitative Evaluation of Systems (QEST) 2004; September 2004, University of Twente, Enschede, The Netherlands
2. R. Bynum, "Generic Data Communications Services Models" ; IEEE 10GigE p802.3ae and EFM 802.3ah Task Forces; June 2001
3. IETF group work on IP over Resilient Packet Rings (iporpr), http://www1.ietf.org/html.charters/iporpr-charter.html
4. Y. Liu and K.S. Trivedi. A General Framework for Network Survivability Quantification. 12th GI/ITG Conference on Measuring, Modeling and Evaluation of Computer and Communication Systems (MMB) and 3rd Polish-German Telegraphic Symposium (PGTS), Dresden, Germany, September 2004
5. Y. Liu, V. B. Mendiratta, and K. S. Trivedi. Survivability Analysis of Telephone Access Network. 15th IEEE International Symposium on Software Reliability Engineering (ISSRE'04), November, Saint-Malo, Bretagne, France
6. J. Muppala, R. Fricks, and K. S. Trivedi. Techniques for System Dependability Evaluation. Computational Probability, W. Grassman (ed.), pp. 445-480, Kluwer Academic Publishers, The Netherlands, 2000
7. Telcordia GR-512-CORE, issue 2, 1998; GR-929-CORE issue 8, 2002
8. M. Tortorella, Reliability Challenges of Converged Networks and Packet-Based Services. Industrial Engineering Working Paper, February 5th, 2003
9. K.S. Trivedi, "Probability and Statistics with Reliability, Queuing and Computer Science Applications; John Wiley &Sons Publisher, Second Edition, 2002
10. http://www.vpls.org/

Making Services Fault Tolerant

Pat. P.W. Chan[1], Michael R. Lyu[1], and Miroslaw Malek[2]

[1] Department of Computer Science and Engineering
The Chinese University of Hong Kong
Hong Kong, China
{pwchan, lyu}@cse.cuhk.edu.hk
[2] Department of Computer Science and Engineering
Humboldt University Berlin, Germany
malek@informatik.hu-berlin.de

Abstract. With ever growing use of Internet, Web services become increasingly popular and their growth rate surpasses even the most optimistic predictions. Services are self-descriptive, self-contained, platform-independent and openly-available components that interact over the network. They are written strictly according to open specifications and/or standards and provide important and often critical functions for many business-to-business systems. Failures causing either service downtime or producing invalid results in such systems may range from a mere inconvenience to significant monetary penalties or even loss of human lives. In applications where sensing and control of machines and other devices take place via services, making the services highly dependable is one of main critical goals. Currently, there is no experimental investigation to evaluate the reliability and availability of Web services systems. In this paper, we identify parameters impacting the Web services dependability, describe the methods of dependability enhancement by redundancy in space and redundancy in time and perform a series of experiments to evaluate the availability of Web services. To increase the availability of the Web service, we use several replication schemes and compare them with a single service. The Web services are coordinated by a replication manager. The replication algorithm and the detailed system configuration are described in this paper.

Keywords: Web service, availability, redundancy, reliability.

1 Introduction

As the use of Web services is growing, there is an increasing demand for dependability. Service-oriented Architectures (SOA) are based on a simple model of roles. Every service may assume one or more roles such as being a service provider, a broker or a user (requestor).

The use of services, especially Web services, became a common practice. In Web services, standard communication protocols and simple broker-request architectures are needed to facilitate an exchange (trade) of services, and this

D. Penkler, M. Reitenspiess, and F. Tam (Eds.): ISAS 2006, LNCS 4328, pp. 43–61, 2006.

model simplifies interoperability. In the coming years, services are expected to dominate software industry. As services begin to permeate all aspects of human society, the problems of service dependability, security and timeliness are becoming critical, and appropriate solutions need to be made available.

Several fault tolerance approaches have been proposed for Web services in the literature [1,2,3,4,5,6,7,8], but the field still requires theoretical foundations, appropriate models, effective design paradigms, practical implementations, and in-depth experimentations for building highly-dependable Web services.

In this paper, related work on dependable services is presented in Section 2, in which the problem statement about reliable Web services is presented. In Section 3, a methodology for reliable Web services is described, in which we propose experimental settings and offer a roadmap to dependable Web services. Experimental results and reliability modeling are presented in Sections 4 and 5. Finally, conclusions are made in Section 6.

2   Related Work

It is a well-known fact that fault tolerance can be achieved via spatial or temporal redundancy, including replication of hardware (with additional components), software (with special programs), and time (with the diversified of operations) [9,10,11].

Spatial redundancy can be dynamic or static. Both use replication but in static redundancy, all replicas are active at the same time and voting takes place to obtain a correct result. The number of replicas is usually odd and the approach is known as n-modular redundancy (NMR). For example, under a single-fault assumption, if services are triplicated and one of them fails, the remaining two will still guarantee the correct result. The associated spatial redundancy cost is high (i.e., three copies plus a voter). The time overhead of managing redundant modules such as voting and synchronization is also considerably large for static redundancy. Dynamic redundancy, on the other hand, engages one active replica at one time while others are kept in an active or in a standby state. If one replica fails, another replica can be employed immediately with little impact on response time. In the second case, if the active replica fails, a previously inactive replica must be initialized and take over the operations. Although this approach may be more flexible and less expensive than static redundancy, its cost may still be high due to the possibility of hastily eliminating modules with transient faults. It may also increase the recovery time because of its dependence on time-consuming error-handling stages such as fault diagnosis, system reconfiguration, and resumption of execution. Redundancy can be achieved by replicating hardware modules to provide backup capacity when a failure occurs, or redundancy can be obtained using software solutions to replicate key elements of a business process.

In any redundant systems, common-mode failures (CMFs) result from failures that affect more than one module at the same time, generally due to a common cause. These include design mistakes and operational failures that may be caused externally or internally. Design diversity has been proposed in the past to protect redundant systems against common-mode failures [12,13] and has been used in both firmware and software systems [14,15,16]. The basic idea is that, with different design and implementations, common failure modes can be reduced. In the event that they exist and are manifested, they will probably cause different failure effects. One of the design diversity techniques is N-version programming, and another one is Recovery Blocks. The key element of N-version programming or Recovery Blocks approaches is diversity. By attempting to make the development processes diverse it is anticipated that the independently designed versions will also contain diverse faults. It is assumed that such diverse faults, when carefully managed, will minimize the likelihood of coincident failures.

Based on the discussed techniques, a number of reliable Web services techniques appeared in the recent literature. A Web Services Reliable Messaging Protocol is proposed in [1], which employs flooding and acknowledgement to ensure that messages are delivered reliably among distributed applications, in the presence of software component, system, or network failures.

WS-FTM (Web Service-Fault Tolerance Mechanism) is an implementation of the classic N-version model with Web services [2] which can easily be applied to systems with a minimal change. The Web services are implemented in different versions and the voting mechanism is in the client program.

FT-SOAP [3], on the other hand, is aimed at improving the reliability of the SOAP when using Web services. The system includes different function replication management, fault management, logging/recovery mechanism and client fault tolerance transparency. FT-SOAP is based on the work of FT-CORBA [4], in which a fault-tolerant SOAP-based middleware platform is proposed. There are two major targets in FT-SOAP: 1) to define a fault-tolerant SOAP service standard recommendation, and 2) to implement an FT-SOAP service prototype.

FT-Grid [5] is another design, which is a development of design-diverse fault tolerance in Grid. It is not specified for Web services but the techniques are applicable to Web services. The FT-Grid allows a user to manually search through any number of public or private UDDI repositories, select a number of functionally-equivalent services, choose the parameters to supply to each service, and invoke those services. The application can then perform voting on the results returned by the services, with the aim of filtering out any anomalous results.

Although a number of approaches have been proposed to increase the Web service reliability, there is a need for systematic modeling and experiments to understand the tradeoffs and verify reliability of the proposed methods.

3   Problem Statement

There are many fault-tolerant techniques that can be applied to Web services including replication and diversity. Replication is one of the efficient ways for creating reliable systems by time or space redundancy. Redundancy has long been used as a means of increasing the availability of distributed systems, with key components being re-executed (replication in time) or replicated (replication in space) to protect against hardware malfunctions or transient system faults. Another efficient technique is design diversity. By independently designing software systems or services with different programming teams, diversity provides an ultimate resort in defending against permanent software design faults.

In this paper, we focus on the systematic analysis of the replication techniques when applied to Web services. We analyze the performance and the availability of the Web services using spatial and temporal redundancy and study the tradeoffs between them. A generic Web service system with spatial as well as temporal replication is proposed and experimented with.

4   Methodologies for Reliable Web Services

4.1   Failure Response Stages of Web Services

Web services go through different operation modes, so when failures occur and the failure response of Web services can be classified into different stages [17]. When a failure occurs, the Web service should confine the failure by applying fault detection techniques to find out the failure causes and the failed components should be repaired or recovered. Then, reconfiguration, restart and reintegration should follow. The flow of the failure response of a Web service is shown in Figure 1 and the details of each stage are described as follows:

Fault confinement. This stage limits the fault impact by attempting to contain the spread of fault effects in one area of the Web service, thus preventing contamination of other areas. Fault-confinement can be achieved through the

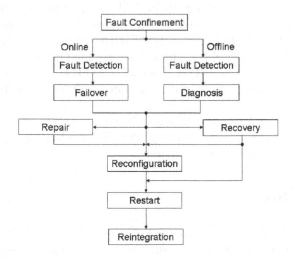

Fig. 1. Flow of the failure response of Web services

use of fault detection within the Web services, consistency checks, and multiple requests/confirmations.

Fault detection. This stage recognizes that something unexpected has occurred in a Web service. Fault latency is the period of time between the occurrence of a fault and its detection. Techniques fall here into two classes: off-line and on-line. With off-line techniques, such as diagnostic programs, the service is not able to perform useful work while under test. On-line techniques, such as duplication, provide a real-time detection capability that is performed concurrently with useful work.

Diagnosis. This stage is necessary if the fault detection technique does not provide information about the fault location. Typically, fault diagnosis encompasses both fault detection and fault location.

Reconfiguration. This stage occurs when a fault is detected and located. The Web service can be composed of different components. When providing the service, there may be a fault in individual components. The system may reconfigure its components either to replace the failed component or to isolate it from the rest of the system.

Recovery. This stage utilizes techniques to eliminate the effects of faults. Three basic recovery approaches are available: fault masking, retry and rollback. Fault-masking techniques hide the effects of failures by allowing redundant information to outweigh the incorrect information. Web services can be replicated or implemented with different versions (NVP). Retry undertakes a second attempt at an operation and is based on the premise that many faults are transient in nature. Web services provide services through a network, and retry would be a practical approach as requests/replies may be affected by the state of the network. Rollback makes use of the fact that the Web service operation is backed up (checkpointed) at some point in its processing prior to fault detection and operation recommences from that point. Fault latency is important here because the rollback must go back far enough to avoid the effects of undetected errors that occurred before the detected error.

Restart. This stage occurs after the recovery of undamaged information.

 - Hot restart: resumption of all operations from the point of fault detection and is possible only if no damage has occurred.
 - Warm restart: only some of the processes can be resumed without loss.
 - Cold restart: complete reload of the system with no processes surviving. The Web services can be restarted by rebooting the server.

Repair. At this stage, a failed component is replaced. Repair can be off-line or on-line. Web services can be component-based and consist of other Web services. In off-line repair, either the Web service will continue if the failed component/sub-Web service is not necessary for operation or the Web services must be brought down to perform the repair. In on-line repair, the component/sub-Web service may be replaced immediately with a backup spare or operation may continue without the component. With on-line repair, the Web service operation is not interrupted.

Reintegration. At this stage the repaired module must be reintegrated into the Web service. For on-line repair, reintegration must be performed without interrupting the Web service operation.

4.2 Proposed Technique

In the previous section, we describe a general approach in system fault tolerance which can be applicable to Web services. In the following section, we propose a replication Web service system for reliable Web services. In our system, the dynamic approach is considered and its architecture is shown in Figure 2.

Scheme details. In the proposed system, one Web server works as the active server and others are used for backup purpose to tolerate a single server failure. The Web service is replicated on different machines, but only one Web service provides the requested service at a time, which is called the primary Web service. The Web service is replicated identically on different machines; therefore, when the primary Web service fails, the other Web services can immediately provide the required service. The replication mechanism shortens the recovery time and increases the availability of the system.

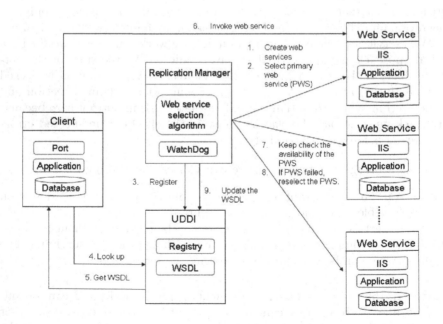

Fig. 2. Proposed architecture for dependable Web services

The main component of this system is the replication manager, which acts as a coordinator of the Web services. The replication manager is responsible for:

1. Creating a Web service.
2. Choosing (with anycasting algorithm) the best (fastest, most robust, etc.) Web service [18] to provide the service which is called the primary Web service.
3. Registering the Web Service Definition Language (WSDL) with the Universal Description, Discovery, and Integration (UDDI).
4. Continuously checking the availability of the primary Web service by using a watchdog.
5. Selecting another Web service provider if the primary service fails, so as to ensure fault tolerance.

When the primary Web service fails, the replication manager selects the most suitable Web service again to continue providing the service. The replication manager maps the new address of the new primary Web service to the WSDL, thus the clients can still access the Web service with the same URL. This failover process is transparent to the users. The detailed procedure is shown in Figure 2.

The workflow of the replication manager is shown in Figure 3. The replication manager is running on a server, which keeps checking the availability of the Web services by the polling method. It sends messages to the Web services periodically. If it does not get the reply from the primary Web service, it will select another Web service to replace the primary one and map the new address to the WSDL. The system is considered failed if all the Web services have failed. If a Web service replies with the logging, the replication manager will record the information of the Web service.

4.3 Roadmap for Experimental Research

We take a pragmatic approach by starting with a single service without any replication. The only approach to fault tolerance in this case is the use of redundancy in time. If a service is considered as an atomic action or a transaction where the input is clearly defined, no interaction is allowed during its execution and the termination has two outcomes: correct or incorrect. In this case, the only way to make such service fault tolerant is to retry or reboot it. This approach allows tolerance of temporary faults, but it will not be sufficient for tolerating permanent faults within a server or a service. One issue is how much delay can a user tolerate, and another issue is the optimization of the retry or the reboot time; in other words, deciding when a current request should be timed out. By handling services as atomic transactions, exception handling does not help in dealing directly with inherent problems of a service. Consequently, continuous service is only possible by performing re-execution using a retry or reboot at the termination points or after a timeout period.

If redundancy in time is not appropriate to meet dependability requirements or time overhead is unacceptable, the next step is redundancy in space. Redundancy in space for services means replication where multiple copies of a given

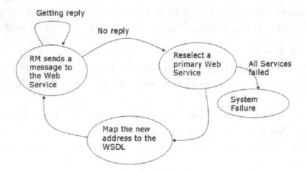

Fig. 3. Workflow of the Replication Manager

service may be executed sequentially or in parallel. If the copies of the same services are executed on different servers, different modes of operation are possible:

1. Sequentially, meaning that we await a response from a primary service and in case of timeout or a service delivering incorrect results, we invoke a backup service (multiple backup copies are possible). It is often called failover.
2. In parallel, meaning that multiple services are executed simultaneously and if the primary service fails, the next one takes over [1]. It is also called a failover. Another variant is that the service whose response arrives first is taken.
3. There is also a possibility of majority voting using n-modular redundancy, where results are compared and the final outcome is based on at least $\lfloor n/2 + 1 \rfloor$ services agreeing on the result.
4. If diversified versions of different services are compared, the approach can be seen as either a Recovery Blocks (RB) system where backup services are engaged sequentially until the results are accepted (by an Acceptance Test), or an N-version programming (NVP) system where voting takes place and majority results are taken as the final outcome. In case of failure, the failed service can be masked and the processing can continue.

NVP and RB have undergone various challenges and vivid discussions. Critics would state that the development of multiple versions is too expensive and dependability improvement is questionable in comparison to a single version, provided the development effort equals the development cost of the multiple versions. We argue that in the age of service-oriented computing, diversified Web services permeate and the objections to NVP or RB can be mitigated. Based on market needs, service providers competitively and independently develop their services and make them available to the market. With abundance of services for specific functional requirements, it is apparent that fault tolerance by design

---

[1] In such case service parameter compatibility must be checked or aligned. Services are assumed to have equivalent functionality.

diversity will be a natural choice. NVP should be applied to services not only for dependability but also for higher performance purpose.

Finally, a hybrid method may be used where both space and time redundancy are applied, and depending on system parameters, a retry might be more effective before switching to the backup service. This type of approach will require a further investigation.

We also need to formulate several additional quality-of-service parameters to service customers. We propose a number of fault injection experiments showing both dependability and performance with and without diversified Web services. The outlined roadmap to fault-tolerant services leads to ultra reliable services where hybrid techniques of spatial and time redundancy can be employed for optimizing cost-effectiveness tradeoffs. In the next section, we describe the various approaches and some experiments in more detail.

4.4 Experiments

A series of experiments are designed and performed for evaluating the reliability of the Web service, including single service without replication, single service with retry or reboot, and a service with spatial replication. We will also perform retry or failover when the Web service is down. A summary of five (1-5) experiments is stated in Table 1.

Table 1. Summary of the experiments

		None	Retry/Reboot	Failover	Both(hybrid)
1	Single service, no retry	1	–	–	–
2	Single service with retry	–	2	–	–
3	Single service with reboot	–	3	–	–
4	Spatial replication	–	–	4	–
5	Spatial replication	–	–	–	5

Our experimental system is implemented with Visual Studio .Net and runs with .Net framework. The Web service is replicated on different machines and the primary Web service is chosen by the replication manager.

In the experiments, faults are injected in the system and the fault injection techniques are similar, for example, to the ones referred in [6,22]. A number of faults may occur in the Web service environment [20,21], including network problem, resource problem, entry point failure, and component failure. These faults are injected in the experimental system to evaluate the reliability of our proposed scheme. Our experimental environment is defined by a set of parameters. Table 2 shows the parameters of the Web service in our experiments.

Experimental results. We compare five approaches for providing the Web services. The details of the experiments are described as follows:

Table 2. Parameters of the experiments

	Parameters	Current setting/metric
1	Request frequency	1 req/min
2	Polling frequency	10 per min
3	Number of replicas	5
4	Client timeout period for retry	10 s
5	Failure rate λ	number of failures/hour
6	Load (profile of the program)	percentage or load function
7	Reboot time	10 min
8	Failover time	1 s

1. **Single service without retry and reboot.** The Web service is provided by a single server without any replication. No redundancy technique is applied to this Web service.
2. **Single service with retry.** The Web service provides the service and the client retries another Web service when there is no response from the original Web service after timeout.
3. **Single service with reboot (restart).** The Web service provides the service and the Web service server will reboot when there is no response from the Web service. Clients will not retry after timeout when there is no response from the service.
4. **Spatial replication with failover.** We use a generic spatial replication: The Web service is replicated on different machines and the request is transferred to another machine when the primary Web service fails (failover). The replication manager coordinates among the replicas and carries out a failover in case of a failure. Clients will only submit the request once and will not retry.
5. **Spatial replication with failover and retry.** This is a hybrid approach. Similar to the Experiment 4 where the Web service is replicated on different machines and the request is transferred to another one (failover) when the primary Web service fails. But the client will retry if there is no response from the Web service after timeout.

The Web services were executed for 720 hours generating a total of 720x60 req/hr = 43200 requests from the client. A single failure is counted when the system cannot reply to the client. For the approach with retry, a single failure is counted when a client retries five times and still cannot get the result. A summary of the results is shown in Table 3 and the Figures 4 to 7 depict the number of failures as the time increases.

The reliability of Web services is tested under different scenarios, including normal operation, resource problem by increasing the load of the server, entry point failure by rebooting the server periodically, and a number of faults by fault injection techniques.

In the fault injection, WS-FIT fault injection is applied. The WS-FIT fault injection method is a modified of Network Level Fault Injection. WS-FIT differs from

Table 3. Experimental results

Experiments over 720 hour period (43200 reqs)	Normal	Resource Problem	Entry Point Failure	Network Level Fault Injection
Exp1	4928	6130	6492	5324
Exp2	2210	2327	2658	2289
Exp3	2561	3160	3323	5211
Exp4	1324	1711	1658	5258
Exp5	1089	1148	1325	2210

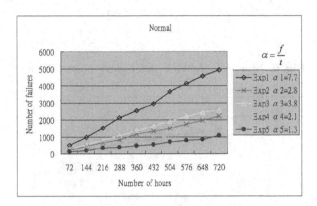

Fig. 4. Number of failures when the server operates normally

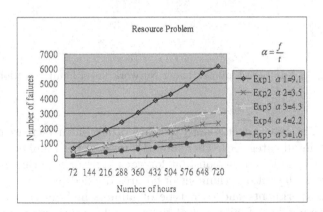

Fig. 5. Number of failures under resource problem

standard Network Level Fault Injection techniques in that the fault injector decodes the SOAP message and injects faults into individual remote procedure call (RPC) parameters, rather than randomly corrupting a message, for instance by bit-flipping. This enables API-level parameter value modification to be performed in a non-invasive way as well as the standard Network Level Fault Injection.

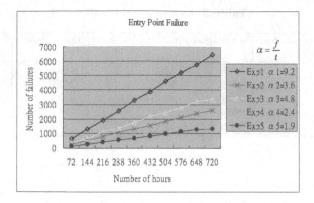

Fig. 6. Number of failures under entry point failure

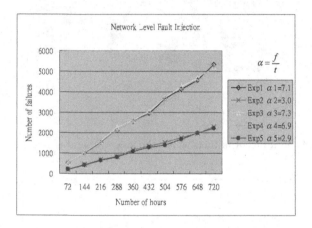

Fig. 7. Number of failures under Network Level Fault Injection

Discussion. The experiments barely indicate rather linear increase of the number of failures in all categories. Therefore, the ratio of the number of failures to the amount of time is almost constant for each type of experiments and each type of failures. The ratio α (number of failures divided by time t) is given for each type of experiments and each type of failures in Figures 4 to 7. So the communicative number of failures f at time t can be approximate by $f = \alpha \times t$.

When there is no redundancy techniques applied on the Web service system (Exp 1), it is clearly shown that the failure rate of the system is the highest. Consequently, we try to improve the reliability of the Web service in two different ways, including spatial redundancy with replication and temporal redundancy with retry or reboot.

Resource Problem and Entry Point Failure. Under different situations, our approach improves the availability of the system differently. When the system is under resource problem and entry point failure, the experiment shows that the temporal redundancy helps to improve the availability of the system.

For the Web service with retry (Exp 2), the percentage of failures of the system (number of failed requests/total number of requests) is reduced from 11.97% to 4.93%. This shows that the temporal redundancy with retry can significantly improve the availability of the Web service. When there is a failure occurrence in the Web service, on the average, the clients need to retry twice to get the response from the Web service.

Another temporal redundancy is Web service with reboot (Exp 3). From the experimental result, it is found that the failure rate of the system is also reduced: from 11.97% to 6.44%. The improvement is good, but not as substantial as the temporal redundancy with retry. It is due to the fact that when the Web service cannot be provided, the server will take time to reboot.

Spatial redundancy is applied in the system in Exp 4, which is the approach we have proposed. The availability of the system is improved even more significantly: the failure rate of the system is reduced from 11.97% to 3.56%. The Web service performs failover when the Web service cannot respond. The replication manager keeps checking the availability of the Web services. If the primary service fails, the replication manager selects another Web service to provide the service. The replication manager sends a message to the Web server to check the availability every 5 ms. It shortens the potential downtime of the Web service, thus the failure rate is reduced. In the experiment, on the average, the replication manager detects that there are around 600 failures in the Web services and performs the failovers accordingly.

To further improve the reliability of the Web service, both spatial and temporal redundancy is applied in the system in the Experiment 5. The failure rate is reduced from 11.97% to 2.59%. In the experiment, the Web service is replicated on five different machines and the clients will retry if they cannot get response correctly from the service. It is demonstrated that this setting results in the lowest failure rate. This shows that spatial and temporal redundancy (a hybrid approach) achieve the highest gain in reliability improvement of the Web service.

Network Level Fault Injection. When the system is under network level fault injection, the temporal redundancy reduces the failure rate of the system from 12.32% to 5.12%. When there are fault injected into the SOAP message, the system cannot process the request correctly, which will cause error in the system. However, with temporal redundancy, the clients can resubmit the result to the system when there is a fault injected into the previous message; thus, the failure rate of the system is reduced. However, the spatial redundancy approach cannot improve the availability of the system. It is because even the message has injected faults and it will not trigger a failover of the system.

Failure Rate. The failure rate of a system is defined as:

$$\lambda = \lim_{\Delta \longrightarrow 0} \frac{F(t + \Delta t) - F(t)}{\Delta t} \tag{1}$$

Fig. 8. Reliability of the system over time

The failure rate of our system, using a specific scenario, has improved from 0.114 to 0.025. The reliability of the system can be calculated with

$$R(t) = e^{-\lambda(t)t} \tag{2}$$

and Figure 8 shows the reliability of the discussed system.

Availability of the system is defined as:

$$A = \frac{MTTF}{MTTF + MTTR} \tag{3}$$

And in our case

$$MTTF = \frac{1}{\lambda(t)}$$
$$= \frac{1}{0.025} = 40$$
$$MTTR = 3s$$

$$A = \frac{40}{40 + 3} = 0.93$$

which is quite of an improvement from $A = 0.75$ but still not up to standards of today's expectations.

5 Reliability Modeling

We develop the reliability model of the proposed Web service paradigm using Markov chains [23]. The model is shown in Figure 9. The reliability model is analyzed and verified through applying the reliability evaluation tool SHARPE [25].

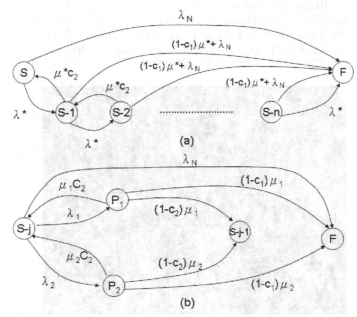

Fig. 9. Markov chain based reliability model for the proposed system

In Figure 9(a), the state s represents the normal execution state of the system with n Web service replicas. In the event of an error, the primary Web service fails, and the system will either go into the other states (i.e., $s-j$ which represents the system with $n-j$ working replicas remaining, if the replication manager responds on time), or it will go to the failure state F with conditional probability $(1-c_1)$. λ^* denotes the error rate at which recovery cannot complete in this state and c_1 represents the probability that the replication manager responds on time to switch to another Web service.

When the failed Web service is repaired, the system will go back to the previous state, $s-j+1$. μ^* denotes the rate at which successful recovery is performed in this state, and c_2 represents the probability that the failed Web service server reboots successfully. If the Web service fails, it switches to another Web service. When all Web services fail, the system enters the failure state F. λ_n represents the network failure rate.

In Figure 9, $(s-1)$ to $(s-n)$ represent the working states of the n Web service replicas and the reliability model of each Web service is shown in Figure 9(b).

Table 4. Model parameters

ID	Description	Value
λ_N	Network failure rate	0.01
λ^*	Web service failure rate	0.025
λ_1	Resource problem rate	0.142
λ_2	Entry point failure rate	0.150
μ^*	Web service repair rate	0.286
μ_1	Resource problem repair rate	0.979
μ_2	Entry point failure repair rate	0.979
C_1	Probability that the RM responds on time	0.9
C_2	Probability that the server reboots successfully	0.9

Fig. 10. Reliability with different failure rate and repair rate is 0.286

There are two types of failures simulated in our experiments: P_1 denotes recourses problem (server busy) and P_2 denotes entry point failures (server reboot). If a failure occurs in the Web service, either the Web service can be repaired with μ_1 (to enter P_1) or μ_2 (to enter P_2) repair rates with conditional probability c_1, or the error cannot be recovered, and the system enters the next state $(s - j - 1)$ with one less Web service replica available. If the replication manager cannot respond on time, it will go to the failure state. From the figure, two formulas can be obtained:

$$\lambda^* = \lambda_1 \times (1 - C_1)\mu_1 + \lambda_2 \times (1 - C_2)\mu_2 \tag{4}$$

$$\mu^* = \lambda_1 \times \mu_1 + \lambda_2 \times \mu_2 \tag{5}$$

From the experiments, we obtain the error rates and the repair rates of the system, and the values are shown in Table 4.

According to the parameters obtained from the experiments, the reliability of the system over time is calculated with the tool SHARPE. In Figure 10, the

Fig. 11. Reliability with different failure rate and repair rate is 0.572

repair rate μ^* is 0.286 failure/s (from the experiment), the reliability is plotted under different failure rate λ^*. Note that the failure rate obtained from the experiments is 0.025 failure/s. This failure rate is measured under an accelerated testing environment. By considering the test compression factor [26], the failure rate of the system in a real situation will be much less. A similar reliability curve is plotted in Figure 11 with repair rate μ^* equal to 0.572 failure/s.

6 Conclusions

In the paper, we surveyed and addressed applicability of replication and design diversity techniques for reliable services and proposed a hybrid approach to improving the availability of Web services. Our approach reduces the number of failures in comparison to normal singular method by a factor of about 5. Furthermore, we carried out a series of experiments to evaluate the availability and reliability of the proposed Web service system. From the experiments, we conclude that both temporal and spatial redundancy are important to the availability improvement of the Web service. In the future, we plan to test the proposed schemes with a wide variety of systems, environments and fault injection scenarios and analyze the impact of various parameters on reliability and availability. Moreover, we will evaluate effectiveness of the schemes with design diversity techniques in handling permanent design faults in Web services.

Acknowledgement

We would like to thank Prof. Kishor Trivedi for providing SHARPE for our reliability analysis. The work described in this paper was fully supported by two grants: One from the Research Grants Council of the Hong Kong Special

Administrative Region, China (Project No. CUHK4205/04E), and another from the Shun Hing Institute of Advanced Engineering (SHIAE) of The Chinese University of Hong Kong.

References

1. R. Bilorusets, A. Bosworth et al, "Web Services Reliable Messaging Protocol WS-ReliableMessaging," EA, Microsoft, IBM and TIBCO Software, http://msdn.microsoft.com/library/enus/dnglobspec/html/ws-reliablemessaging.asp, Mar. 2004.
2. N. Looker and M. Munro, "WS-FTM: A Fault Tolerance Mechanism for Web Services," University of Durham, Technical Report, 19 Mar. 2005.
3. D. Liang, C. Fang, and C. Chen, "FT-SOAP: A Fault-tolerant Web Service, " Institute of Information Science, Academia Sinica, Technical Report 2003.
4. D. Liang, C. Fang and S. Yuan, "A Fault-Tolerant Object Service on CORBA," Journal of Systems and Software, Vol. 48, pp. 197-211, 1999.
5. P. Townend, P. Groth, N. Looker, and J. Xu, "Ft-grid: A fault-tolerance system for e-science," Proc. of the UK OST e-Science Fourth All Hands Meeting (AHM05), Sept. 2005.
6. M. Merideth, A. Iyengar, T. Mikalsen, S. Tai, I. Rouvellou, and P. Narasimhan, "Thema: Byzantine-Fault-Tolerant Middleware for Web-Service Application," Proc. of IEEE Symposium on Reliable Distributed Systems, Orlando, FL, Oct. 2005.
7. A. Erradi and P. Maheshwari, "A broker-based approach for improving Web services reliability", Proc. of IEEE International Conference on Web Services, vol. 1, pp. 355-362, 11-15 Jul. 2005.
8. W . Tsai, Z. Cao, Y. Chen, Y and R. Paul, "Web services-based collaborative and cooperative computing," Proc. of Autonomous Decentralized Systems, pp. 552-556, 4-8 Apr. 2005.
9. D. Leu, F. Bastani and E. Leiss, "The effect of statically and dynamically replicated components on system reliability," IEEE Transactions on Reliability, vol.39, Issue 2, pp.209-216, Jun. 1990.
10. B. Kim, "Reliability analysis of real-time controllers with dual-modular temporal redundancy," Proc. of the Sixth International Conference on Real-Time Computing Systems and Applications (RTCSA) 1999, pp.364-371, 13-15 Dec. 1999.
11. K. Shen and M. Xie, "On the increase of system reliability by parallel redundancy," IEEE Transactions on Reliability, vol.39, Issue 5, pp.607-611, Dec. 1990.
12. A. Avizienis, and L. Chen, "On the implementation of N-version programming for software fault-tolerance during program execution," Proc. of First International Computer Software and Applications Conference, pp.149-155, 1977.
13. A. Avizienis, and J. Kelly, "Fault Tolerance by Design Diversity: Concepts and Experiments," IEEE Transactions on Computer, pp. 67-80, Aug. 1984.
14. M.R. Lyu and A. Avizienis, "Assuring Design Diversity in N-Version Software: A Design Paradigm for N-Version Programming," in Fault-Tolerant Software Systems: Techniques and Applications, H. Pham (ed.), IEEE Computer Society Press Technology Series, pp. 45-54, Oct. 1992.
15. J. Lala, and R. Harper, "Architectural principles for safety-critical real-time applications," Proc. of the IEEE, vol. 82, no.1, pp.25-40, Jan. 1994.

16. R. Riter, "Modeling and Testing a Critical Fault-Tolerant Multi-Process System," Proc. the 25th International Symposium on Fault-Tolerant Computing, pp.516-521, 1995.
17. M. Lyu and V. Mendiratta, "Software Fault Tolerance in a Clustered Architecture: Techniques and Reliability Modeling," Proc. of 1999 IEEE Aerospace Conference, Snowmass, Colorado, vol.5, pp.141-150, 6-13 Mar. 1999.
18. M. Sayal, Y. Breitbart, P. Scheuermann, and R. Vingralek, "Selection algorithms for replicated web servers," Proc. of Workshop on Internet Server Performance 98, Madison, WI, Jun. 1998.
19. N. Looker, M. Munro, and J. Xu, "Simulating Errors in Web Services," International Journal of Simulation: Systems, Science and Technology, vol.5, pp.29-38, 2004.
20. Y. Yan, Y. Liang and X. Du, "Controlling remote instruments using Web services for online experiment systems," Proc. of IEEE International Conference on Web Services (ICWS) 2005, 11-15 Jul. 2005.
21. Y. Yan, Y. Liang and X. Du, "Distributed and collaborative environment for online experiment system using Web services," Proc. the Ninth International Conference on Computer Supported Cooperative Work in Design 2005, vol.1, pp.265-270, 24-26 May 2005.
22. N. Looker and J. Xu, "Assessing the Dependability of SOAP-RPC-Based Web Services by Fault Injection," Proc. of the 9th IEEE International Workshop on Object-oriented Real-time Dependable Systems, pp.163-170, 2003.
23. K. Goseva-Popstojanova and K. Trivedi, "Failure correlation in software reliability models," IEEE Transactions on Reliability, vol.49, Issue 1, pp.37-48, Mar. 2000.
24. H. Guen, R. Marie and T. Thelin, "Reliability estimation for statistical usage testing using Markov chains," Proc. of the 15th International Symposium on Software Reliability Engineering (ISSRE) 2004, pp.54-65, 2-5 Nov. 2004.
25. R. Sahner, K. Trivedi, and A. Puliafito, "Performance and Reliability Analysis of Computer Systems. An Example-BasedApproach Using the SHARPE Software Package," Kluwer, Boston, MA (1996).
26. M. Lyu, "Handbook of Software Reliability Engineering," IEEE Computer Society Press and McGraw-Hill Book Company.

Performability Analysis of Storage Systems in Practice: Methodology and Tools

Hairong Sun, Tina Tyan, Steven Johnson, Richard Elling,
Nisha Talagala, and Robert B. Wood

Storage Group, Sun Microsystems, USA
{hairong.sun, tina.tyan, steven.johnson, richard.elling,
nisha.talagala, robert.b.wood}@sun.com

Abstract. This paper presents a methodology and tools used for performability analysis of storage systems in Sun Microsystems. A Markov modeling tool is used to evaluate the probabilities of normal and fault states in the storage system, based on field reliability data collected from customer sites. Fault injection tests are conducted to measure the performance of the storage system in various degraded states with a performance benchmark developed within Sun Microsystems. A graphic metric is introduced for performability assessment and comparison. An example is used throughout the paper to illustrate the methodology and process.

Keywords: Performability, storage, Markov model.

1 Introduction

Performability was first defined in the 1970's [1] by J.F. Meyer, et al to address performance in a degradable system in the presence of operational faults. It integrates performance, reliability, and availability to evaluate a system's ability to deliver a specified service. Most storage systems today are inherently degradable, from RAID (Redundant Array of Independent Disks) arrays designed to withstand a failed disk, to larger scale high availability systems utilizing redundant components such as controllers, power supplies, and cards to ensure that the system continues to provide service in the presence of faults. However, the storage industry still relies primarily on using separate performance and dependability/availability measures to evaluate systems. Traditional performance analysis, which tends to measure the best case performance of fully-functional systems, and binary availability analysis, which views the system as being either up or down, are not sufficient to evaluate how the system performs when in a degraded state, or how it recovers from degraded modes with fault recovery and tolerance design.

This paper uses a general purpose methodology for performability evaluation of storage systems within Sun Microsystems. It uses a combination of Markov modeling and fault injection testing to measure the probability and performance impact of various faulty states, which is subsequently used to generate metrics useful in comparing and evaluating storage systems against performability requirements. Although the examples in this paper focus on block-level storage systems, this

D. Penkler, M. Reitenspiess, and F. Tam (Eds.): ISAS 2006, LNCS 4328, pp. 62–75, 2006.

methodology has been applied to evaluate various products from Sun Microsystems, including NAS, clusters, and blade servers.

The organization of the paper is as follows. Section 2 describes related work in this area, including a quick overview of performance and availability analysis. Section 3 presents the methodology in detail, including examples showing this methodology in practice on a few of Sun's storage products. Section 3.1 focuses on availability modeling and assessment, while Section 3.2 delves into fault injection and performance measurements. Section 3.3 describes the P-Graph, a metric we have developed to combine the analytical results on fault probabilities and test results on fault impacts, and how it is used to evaluate the performability of the system. Conclusions are given in Section 4.

2 Related Works

Since its introduction 20 years ago, performability has been studied extensively, but is still primarily a niche coinage used by researchers in academia. The mainstream computer and storage industry still relies on using performance and binary dependability/availability separately to evaluate a system. Performance benchmarks such as TPC-C, TPC-W, TPC-H [2], and SPC (Storage Performance Council) [3] have been defined to compare the performance of systems from different vendors. These usually give the performance for the best-case scenario, when there are no faults in the system. The traditional availability in terms of number of 9's is generally derived from calculating the probability that the system is completely down, and subtracting this probability from one. Our quantitative analysis shows that the probability of most RAID systems being available, where availability is defined as fully functional without any faults or degradation in the system, is around 2-9's, whereas the probability of the same systems being available, where availability is defined as being able to deliver any data service, is around 4-9's. Thus, there is a significant chance that at any given time, some kind of fault will exist in the system, and that the system will only be able to provide services at a degraded level. The separate measures of performance and availability are usually optimistic, and are not sufficient to analyze a system that can continue to provide service in the presence of faults.

Most previous efforts on performability measures have either tried to find a moment-based single-valued metric or a complicated probability density function (or cumulative distribution function) to capture the statistics of performance over the system state space. The former is oversimplified, and a great deal of information will be lost after the single-valued metrics are calculated, while the latter is too complicated to be applied practically to engineering. Beaudry [13] used the notation of computation availability to calculate a weighted sum of the effective performance at and the probability of the various states of the system. Huslende [14] considered performance reliability by assuming a minimum performance threshold and defined a threshold-based performability measure. Wu [15] defined the transient probability of the system operating at a specific level, and used it as a performability measure. Smith et al [5] used complementary distribution of time-averaged accumulated performance measure (bandwidth in their case) to assess performability. An overview of these measures and other similar metrics can be found in [5].

Performability analysis should take both the probability and the impact of the faults into account. Markov modeling and stochastic Petri net modeling have been widely used to analyze the performability of degradable systems [4][5][6]. Previous studies used composite or hierarchical approaches to build Markov models for performance and availability, and then calculated performability as a function of the performance and availability metrics. However, this pure analytical modeling approach may not be applicable to storage systems, where a plethora of processes that impact performance (e.g., seek time, locality of I/O requests, read-ahead algorithm, cache destage algorithm) are not Markovian, and are difficult to model analytically.

Recent work by X. He, et al [7] introduced a benchmark tool, Storage Performance Evaluation Kernel Module (SPEK), for evaluating the performance of block-level storage systems in the presence of faults, as well as under normal operation. This work treats all faults as equal, examining the performance of faulty states without considering the probability of occurrence of each state. A full understanding of a system's performability needs to consider both the performance of faulty states and the amount of time the system is expected to spend in the degraded state. This work therefore provides only one piece of the performability puzzle, i.e., performance. In addition, there does not seem to be much advantageous to going to kernel mode in generating the workload in Unix. DTrace [8] is an elegant and useful solution to get similar instrumentation, and does not require being in kernel mode.

Krian Nagajara, et al [9] proposed a two-phase methodology for quantifying the performability of cluster-based Internet services. In the first phase, a fault-injection infrastructure is used to measure the impact of faults on the server's performance. In the second phase, an analytical model is used to combine an expected fault load with the measurements from the first phase to assess the server's performability. While this paper does address both aspects of performability, i.e., performance and availability, its emphasis was on developing single-valued metrics such as average throughput, average availability, and a performability metric, which lose a lot of information about the performance and availability of the system under different states. It also lacked a formal solution on how to estimate the probabilities of the faulty states.

3 Performability Assessment Methodology

There are two dimensions to performability assessment, i.e., performance and availability. Availability modeling is used to calculate the probability of the various faulty and normal states, giving a more thorough understanding of the expected behavior of the system. In particular, the probabilities can be used to calculate the expected amount of time the system is in each state, allowing the various faulty states to be weighted according to expected impact. States that are expected to occur for a longer proportion of time should be given more consideration than those that rarely occur. Performance testing during fault injection tests measures the effective performance of the system during degraded states. States that have a higher performance impact should also be given more weight than those causing minimal degradation. This section describes a methodology for combining availability and performance evaluation to generate a set of performability metrics that can be used in assessing and comparing the performability of systems.

3.1 Availability Modeling and Assessment

Before a model of the system can be built, the various system states must be identified. Failure Modes and Effects Analysis (FMEA), part of the Six Sigma process [16], is an engineering technique used to define, identify, and mitigate known and/or potential failures, problems, errors, and so on from the system, design, process, and/or service. Part of this process includes the generation of system state diagrams, which can be used in identifying the states of interest to be modeled and tested. The set of states examined in evaluating the performability of a system should be comprehensive, covering those states that are most likely to occur or to have a high performance impact, but tractable, so as to keep the size of the model and the number of test cases within reason.

For availability analysis, each component in a system may have different reliability and fault impact characteristics. We use Markov models, i.e. constant failure and repair rates of each component, to determine the staying time in each state for each component. For example, a disk drive has an expected failure rate. A repair model, which is based on typical service agreements for Sun customers, is used, from which we can predict the downtime per year of a disk drive. We describe this time as mean annual staying time for the broken disk state. Disks can be made redundant using RAID techniques, which can also be modelled to determine the staying time for each of the states of a RAID system: nominal, one disk down, hot spare synchronization, copy back, etc.

The NSCC (Network Storage Command Center) is the data repository for Sun storage telemetry data collected remotely from the Storage Automated Diagnostic Environment (StorADE). These data can be used to track the reliability of network storage products from Sun Microsystems, and are used to estimate the Mean Time Between Failure (MTBF) of the various components within these products. Using these data, we build a Markov model utilizing RAScad, a Markov model solver developed in Sun Microsystems, to calculate the probabilities of the various types of failures and system states. Alternatively, stochastic Petri net modelling can also be used.

3.1.1 Architecture of a Storage Product
Throughout this paper, we will be presenting examples of this methodology in practice using Sun array products. Figure 1 illustrates the architecture and HA (High Availability) configuration for a typical Sun storage product. Two controller tray units are looped to create a configuration with hot-swap redundant controllers and redundant data and management paths, allowing for cache mirroring, controller failover, and path failover capability. Each drive tray can be configured with a number of hot-spare drives that are used by the RAID controller to replace the failed drive when a drive within the controller unit has failed. The two controllers are configured as master/alternate master. If the alternate master controller fails, no administrative changes are needed. If the master controller fails, then the alternate master must take over the role of the master controller. Each array tray includes two redundant power and cooling units (PCUs). Each tray also includes two unit interconnect cards (UICs), each of which connects to one of the two Fiber Channel ports on each disk drive, and to one of the back-end ports on the RAID controller board. The dual UICs function together in a master/alternate master relationship.

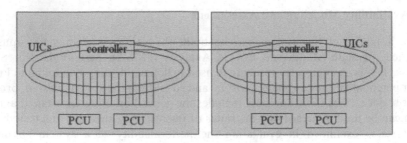

Fig. 1. 2x2 HA Configuration of Sun Storage

3.1.2 Reliability Data

As described above, the NSCC is the repository for Sun storage telemetry, and can be used to track the reliability of products and components. Table 1 gives the Mean Time Between Failure (MTBF) estimates for various components.

Table 1. MTBF Estimates

MTBF for UIC	1,000,000 hours
MTBF for FC drive	800,000 hours
MTBF for controller	200,000 hours
MTBF for midplane	2,000,000 hours
MTBF for PCU	200,000 hours
Reconstruction time for one 73GB FC drive	2 hours
MTTR	24.5 hours

3.1.3 Availability Modeling

Figure 2 shows the Markov model for the storage system in Figure 1, configured with four RAID 5 parity groups (each with 7 disk drives), with one hot spare drive shared with the four parity groups.

The λ_xxx parameters are the failure rates, and μ_yyy are the repair rates, which are the reciprocals of the corresponding MTBF/MTTR listed in Table 1.

At state (m,n,k), there are m total functional disk drives in the system, with n disk drives under reconstruction and k hot spare disk drives. Therefore, state (28, 0, 1) is the initial state where there are 28 functional drives, one of which is a hot spare. The remaining disk failure cases reflect different circumstances under which different combinations of failed, reconstructing, and spare drives exist, see Table 2 for details. States 1 PCU_Dn, 1 UIC_Dn and 1 Ctlr_Dn are the states in which there is one PCU, UIC, or Controller failure in the system. There are transitions from state (28,0,1) to 1 PCU_Dn, 1 UIC_Dn, 1 Ctlr_Dn if one of the redundant PCU, UIC or controller fails. The system fails if the midplane, the second PCU, UIC or controller fails. The system goes to (27,0,0) upon the failure of the spare disk drive. Failure of any disk

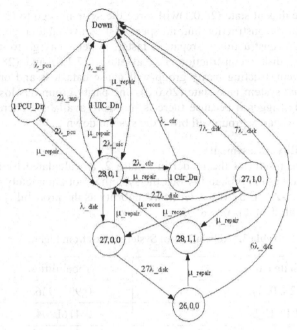

Fig. 2. Markov Model for 2x2 HA Configuration of the Storage System

Table 2. States and Transition rates in Figure 2

State	Explanation	Transition rate	Explanation
28,0,1	No failures	μ_repair	Repair rate (=1/MTTR)
1 UIC_Dn	1 UIC is down	λ_uic	UIC failure rate
Down	System is down	λ_mp	Midplane failure rate
1 Ctlr_Dn	1 Controller is down	λ_cntl	Controller failure rate
1PCU_Dn	1 PCU is down	λ_pcu	PCU failure rate
27,1,0	1 disk is under reconstruction	λ_recon	Disk reconstruction rate
28,1,1	1 disk is under reconstruction, 1 spare disk available	λ_disk	Disk failure rate
27,0,0	No spare disk		
26,0,0	One parity group loses 1 disk, no spare available, no disk reconstruction		

except the spare disk at state (28,0,1)will force the system to go to (27,1,0) state, i.e., one disk is under reconstruction and no spare disk is available anymore. Depending on whether the reconstruction or repair is faster, system may go to state (27,0,0) or (28,1,1). During disk reconstruction, i.e., at state (27,1,0) and (28,1,1), any disk failure in the reconstructing parity group will cause data loss and bring the system down. When the system is at state (26,0,0), one parity group has lost a disk but no reconstruction is triggered because there is no spare available. Therefore any more disk failure in this parity group will bring the system down.

3.1.4 Availability Assessment

Table 3 lists the results of the model in Figure 2, as calculated by RAScad. If we define availability as the probability that the system is not completely down, then it is 0.9999758 (i.e., 1-2.42E-5). If we define availability as the probability that the system is fully functional, then it is 0.9985936.

Table 3. Probabilities of System States from Figure 2

State name	Probabilities
(28, 0, 1)	0.9985936
1 PCU_Dn	2.416E-04
1 Ctrl_Dn	2.416E-04
1 UIC_Dn	4.83E-05
(27, 1, 0)	6.23E-05
(28, 1, 1)	5.20E-06
(27, 0, 0)	7.83E-04
(26, 0, 0)	6.390E-07
Down	2.420E-05

By summing the probabilities of all the states except the first and last in Table 3, we get 0.0013822, the probability that the system will be in a degraded state. Multiplying this number by 8760 hours in a year, we get the number of hours the system will spend in degraded mode per year, 12.11 hours.

3.2 Performance Measurement

Each system state has an associated performance impact which can be measured in the lab through a combination of fault injection testing and performance measurement. The performability of a system is very workload-dependent. Ideally, the system should be tested under workloads that are similar to the expected actual workload it will handle when deployed. However, this may not always be possible or practical.

3.2.1 Vdbench and Workload

Vdbench [12] is a command line Java-based synthetic I/O driver developed by Sun Microsystems that is portable across multiple platforms. It can generate a wide variety of controlled disk I/O workloads allowing control over workload parameters such as I/O rate, file sizes, transfer sizes, thread count, volume count, volume skew, read/write ratios, read and write cache hit percentages, random or sequential workloads or any combination of the two. Vdbench is multi-platform and has been tested on Solaris Sparc and x86, Windows NT and higher, HP/UX, AIX, and Linux. Vdbench is the basis for the SPC benchmark 1, an industry-standard performance benchmark for storage systems created by the Storage Performance Council (SPC) [11]. The SPC benchmark could potentially be used as a standard to characterize the performance of the system in its various faulty states; however, this will require further investigation before being put into practice. An alternative method of assessing the system is to establish the bounds of expected system performance through a combination of extreme corner-case workloads.

Our set of workloads consists of four corner case workloads and two "typical" workloads, which were derived from a collection of real-world traces of workloads from customer sites.

-100% Read Hit (RH) (maximum read performance)
-100% Write Hit (WH) (maximum write performance)
-100% Read Miss (RM) (minimum read performance)
-100% Write Miss (WM) (minimum write performance)
-"Typical Read" (TypR): 70% Reads, 35% Read Hits, 85% Write Hits
-"Typical Write" (TypW): 40% Reads, 35% Read Hits, 85% Write Hits

Read and Write Hits can be created by generating I/O requests to a 4MB "hit area". These workloads can be generated by vdbench, and are random IOs. The transfer size is 8kB.

3.2.2 Fault Injection Testing

Fault injection is used to induce each of the system states in the Markov model, and performance is measured under each of the workloads described in the previous section. For overall system modeling and assessment, the steady state performance of each state can be measured. Each fault can also be examined in more detail to understand the transient performance as the system responds to and recovers from the fault. It is important to note that one of the states of the Markov model should be the initial state with no failures, and that the performance in this baseline state must also be measured. This baseline performance can be used to calculate degradation percentage or relative performance in the degraded states, and is crucial to understand the impact of the various faults.

In order to understand the degraded mode performance of a system in the presence of failures, it is useful to understand how the system behaves when these failures occur. For example, caches on arrays commonly go into write through mode when there is a problem with the power supply, in case the system is about to fail. Some of these behaviors reflect design or configuration decisions that may have been made without performance issues in consideration. Correlating the performance effect of each failure may help in increasing understanding of how the system is functioning, as well as the tradeoff between availability and performance inherent in these decisions.

3.2.3 Steady State Performance Assessment

Steady state performance assessment measures the average steady state performance of the system after it has stabilized from the injection of a fault. This is the average degraded performance of the system before it is repaired when in the given faulty state. For each test, the failure is induced, the system is given some time to stabilize, and then a workload is run to measure the performance. After the workload is completed, the failure is repaired, and the storage brought back to normal state before the next failure is induced. Normal state can be verified by checking system status as well as running short verification workloads to check that performance has returned to baseline. Each failure should be examined independently. If multiple failures are to be considered, these should be classified as separate system states and treated as such, with probabilities of occurrence calculated and performance measured. Understanding the steady state degraded performance of the individual states of the system can help developers to improve system design, allowing them to better understand the performance impact of design decisions, and make tradeoffs between performance and other desired characteristics.

In the example of the storage system in Figure 1 with the 2x2 configuration, the following failure conditions were examined:

1)Broken drive (drive physically pulled out of tray)
2)Drive Reconstruction (physically replace pulled out drive)
3)UIC disabled (using command on array)
4)Power supply off (switch off one of the two power supplies)
5)Controller disabled (using command on array)

Early on, a few workloads were run with the controller physically removed, as well as the UIC physically removed, and compared against the results of using the disable command to ensure that the disable command had the same effect as a physically induced failure. Once verified, the disable command was used in all subsequent tests for those failure conditions. Table 4 gives the results of IOPS of measured during fault injection testing.

Table 4. Steady State Performance (IOPS)

RH	24269.24	23986.88	24160.1	14489.6	12767.88	16009.99
WH	2797.78	1386.71	982.1	2635.86	1711.62	1435.38
RM	1189.96	1184.91	1184.14	1041.79	869.49	1105.86
WM	762.07	382	382.48	689.16	680.03	363.16
TypR	1945.65	970.25	772	1658.47	1233.34	902.22
TypW	2246.33	1059.58	559.26	1738.54	1481.86	1011.46

A close examination of Table 4 provides useful information that helps us understand how the system performs under different workloads and fault situations. For example:

The failure of a power supply will disable the write cache and force the system into writethrough mode, which deteriorates write performance dramatically.

Read miss performance does not drop much when one UIC or controller fails, implying that the bottleneck is reading from the disk, rather than the surviving UIC or controller.

This kind of deeper understanding can help developers improve system design, for example by increasing the processing power of the controllers so that the surviving controller can service all I/O requests when one controller fails, or in making the tradeoff between fast reconstruction and resource consumption.

3.2.4 Transient Performance Assessment

A more detailed study of the transient performance of each fault, including fault detection, recovery, and repair, is very useful to further reveal any design flaws that may exist. In this case, the workload is started and performance measurement begun while the system is still in the faultless baseline state. The fault is then induced, and the system allowed to respond to it and stabilize. After the system has been given enough time to reach its degraded steady state, the fault is then repaired and the system allowed to stabilize once again. The performance throughout all these stages is captured and graphed, giving a clear depiction of the performance impact and amount of time spent by the system in recovering from a fault. In our testing, we have identified four distinct stages in a system's response to failure injection and recovery. The system initially goes into a period of shock after the fault is injected, which often results in a sharp drop in performance for a short period of time. It then goes through a period of recovery, which may still have poor performance, before stabilizing to a degraded steady state that may or may not have better performance than the recovery state. It stays in this degraded steady state until the fault is repaired. After the fault is repaired, the system once again reacts with changes in the performance before stabilizing back to normal performance. This gives us specific targets for improvement when engineering for performability. It also gives a better sense of the kinds of requirements and guarantees that can be imposed on a system,

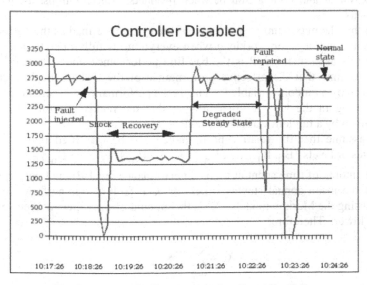

Fig. 3. Transient Performance during Controller Failure

and how the system may interact with application timeouts in the event of a fault. The annual staying time calculated in the availability assessment does not give a sense of how long individual outages may take, which is important information to have when taking into account the requirements of the applications running on the system.

Figure 3 depicts the performance in IOPS under the typical write workload during controller failure and recovery for a new product from Sun Microsystems. The different stages of failure response and recovery are marked on the graph. The failure of one controller causes an initial 10 second outage due to the resynchronization and multi-path functions in the controllers. This is followed by an approximately 2 minute period of recovery during which the system can only achieve about half of the baseline performance. Once the failover is complete, the system is back to full performance, implying that the remaining controller can handle the full workload, unlike the previous product as shown in Table 4. After the fault is repaired, the system performance once again dips and fluctuates, possibly due to multi-pathing functions as the new controller is brought online. The initial outages right after the fault is injected and after it is repaired are potential problems for the overriding application, and targets for improvement, along with the degraded performance during the recovery period. Improvements could include improving the performance or shortening the duration of these stages of response.

3.3 P-Graph

Given that performability is the combination of performance and availability, and not just the two taken separately, a performability metric is needed that integrates the results of the availability and performance assessments described above and can be used to evaluate and compare the performability of systems. The P-Graph is a graphical representation of performability data that provides a more coherent view into the nature of system performability than traditional single-valued metrics, and allows assessment and comparison between products, configurations, architectures, and workloads.

Assume that the maximum performance of the system, defined as the performance of the system under a given workload when everything is fully operational, is given by MP. In this assessment, MP is the baseline performance under the workload in question. Assume that the effective performance of the system (in throughput or IOPs) is given by a random variable P. This is the performance measured during fault injection testing in the lab. Further assume that the relative performance of the system is given by a random variable B and $P = B*MP$.

Further assume that the relative performance can be classified into a set of n distinct states or levels $\{B_0, B_1, \ldots, B_{n-1}\}$ where $B_0 < B_1 < \ldots < B_{n-1}$.

T_i is the amount of time spent at a given performance level B_i, and corresponds to the sum of the mean annual staying times for each fault at this performance level, calculated using the Markov models. X_i is the amount of time spent at a performance level B_i or lower. Therefore,

$$X_i = \sum_{k=0}^{i} T * p_k$$

(1)

$$T_i = T * p_i \tag{2}$$

$$X_i = \sum_{k=0}^{i} T_k \tag{3}$$

The P-Graph is given by:

$$Pgraph(x) = \begin{cases} B_0 & 0 \leqslant x < X_0 \\ B_1 & X_0 \leqslant x < X_1 \\ . & . \\ . & . \\ . & . \\ B_{n-1} & X_{n-2} \leqslant x < X_{n-1} \end{cases} \tag{4}$$

The resulting graph is a step function. Alternatively, the P-Graph can be graphed using effective performance Pi rather than relative performance, or using degradation, calculated as 1-Bi. An example of the P-Graph for the product using effective performance is given in Figure 4.

In the P-Graph, any point (x, y) on the curve represents that the system spends x amount of time in the time interval [0,T] with performance less than or equal to y, where y goes from 0 to the maximum performance of the system, corresponding to the state without faults. This time period of interest T can be a year (projected from modeling or testing), the duration of an experiment, or the amount of time the system has been running in the field. In the case of the performability assessment methodology described in this paper, T is one year, and the P-Graph shows the mean cumulative annual time in minutes for each performance level.

This graph provides a clear visualization of the performability of the system. The graph of a perfect system with no degradation would be a horizontal line at MP, y=MP. The better the performability of the system is, the higher or further to the left the curve will be. There are several ways to improve the performability of a system: increase its overall baseline performance (MP), which will push the overall graph up; increase the performance of any particular faulty state, pushing that segment of the graph up; and decreasing the amount of time spent in degraded mode, pushing the graph to the left. This latter can be accomplished by increasing the reliability of a product, reducing the recovery and repair time, or implementing high-availability strategies such as redundancy. Many of the strategies used to improve performance or availability have an effect on the other dimension of performability. For instance, increasing the reconstruction rate of disks can improve the availability, but will generally result in a severe performance impact. Conversely, improving the performance during reconstruction may require lowering the reconstruction rate, thus adversely affecting availability. The P-Graph graphically depicts the tradeoff between severity of degradation and duration of degradation, or performance vs availability, inherent in these design or configuration decisions.

In addition to providing a graphical depiction of the performability of a system, the P-Graph allows the comparison of a system's performability against a performability requirement. For instance, a requirement could be set stating that the system shall not fall below 1000 IOPS for longer than 300 minutes per year, and depicted on the graph as a point (300, 1000) against which the P-Graph can be compared. If the curve falls below and to the right of the point, then it fails to meet the requirement.

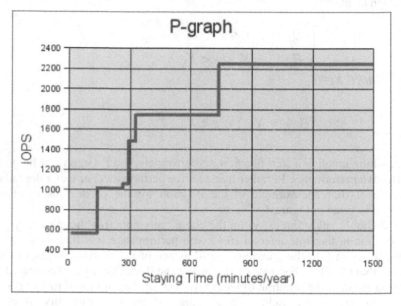

Fig. 4. P-Graph under Typical Write Workload

4 Conclusions

This paper presented a complete methodology for performability evaluation, from stochastic modeling, reliability analysis and modeling tool to fault injection testing, performance benchmarking, and performability metrics. Markov modeling utilizing the RAScad Markov model solver was used to calculate the probabilities of failure and normal states based on field MTBF data and system state diagrams from FMEA. The performance impacts of these states were measured utilizing the vdbench storage benchmark during fault injection tests. Combining the analytical results on fault probabilities, and test results on fault impacts, we developed a new metric called the P-Graph to evaluate and compare storage systems from performability point of view. This methodology has been applied extensively to analyze the performability of Sun storage products, and some of the results were presented in this paper. Although the examples and analysis in this paper focused on traditional block-level storage systems, this methodology has been applied to evaluate various products from Sun Microsystems, including cluster systems and blade servers.

References

1. J.F.Meyer, On Evaluating the Performability of Degradable Computing Systems,   Proc. 8th International Symposium on Fault-Tolerant Computing, pp.44-49, 1978
2. Transaction Processing Performance Council, http://www.tpc.org/
3. Storage Performance Council, http://www.storageperformance.org/home
4. Performability Modeling Tools and Techniques, edited by B. Haverkort, R. Marie and G. Rubino, and K. S. Trivedi, John Wiley & Sons, Chichester, England, 2001
5. R. M. Smith, K. S. Trivedi, and A. Ramesh, Performability Analysis: Measures, An Algorithm and a Case Study, IEEE Transactions on Computers, Vol. C-37, No. 4, pp. 406-417, Apr. 1988.
6. J. Muppala and K. Trivedi, Composite Performance and Availability Analysis Using a Hierarchy of Stochastic Reward Nets, Proc. Fifth Int l Conf. Modeling Techniques and Tools for Computer Performance Evaluation, Feb. 1991
7. Xubin He, Ming Zhang, and Qing (Ken) Yang, SPEK: A Storage Performance Evaluation Kernel Module for Block-Level Storage Systems under Faulty Conditions, IEEE Trans. On Dependable and Secure Computing, Vol.2, No.2, pp. 138-149, April 2005
8. Big Admin System Administration Portal : Dtrace, http://www.sun.com/bigadmin/content/dtrace/
9. Kiran Nagaraja, Xiaoyan Li, Ricardo Bianchini, Richard P. Martin, Thu D. Nguyen, Using Fault Injection and Modeling to Evaluate the Performability of Cluster-Based Services, In Proceedings of the 4th USENIX Symposium on Internet Technologies and Systems (USITS), Seattle, WA, March 2003.
10. D. Tang and K. S. Trivedi, ?Hierarchical Computation of Interval Availability and Related Metrics, DSN'2004, June 2004, pp. 693-698.
11. Storage Performance Council, www.storageperformance.org.
12. Henk Vandenbergh, vdbench,
13. M.Beaudry, Performance Related Reliability for Computer Systems, IEEE Trans. Computers, Vol. 27, pp.540-547, June 1984
14. R. Huslende, A Combined Evaluation of Performance and Reliability for Degraded Systems, ACM/SIGMETRICS, pp.157-164, 1981
15. L.T Wu, Operational Modes for the Evaluation of Degradable Computing Systems, ACM/SIGMETRICS, pp.179-185, 1982
16. Edward Abramowich, Six SIGMA for Growth: Driving Business Growth Using Six SIGMA, Wiley, John & Sons

Using Web Service Transformations to Implement Cooperative Fault Tolerance

Toshiyuki Moritsu[1], Matti A. Hiltunen[2], Richard D. Schlichting[2],
Junichi Toyouchi[1], and Yasuharu Namba[1]

[1] Systems Development Laboratory, Hitachi Ltd.
292, Yoshida-cho, Totsuka, Yokohama, Kanagawa, 244-0817 Japan
[2] Shannon Laboratory, AT&T Labs–Research
180 Park Avenue, Florham Park, NJ 07932, USA

Abstract. Developing techniques to increase the availability of web services in the event of failure has become increasingly important given their key role in providing access to online information, financial, and retail resources. This paper describes an approach to improving availability by using failover between similar but not identical services, and the use of cooperative fault tolerance between the providers of these services. With this approach, a similar service can be used as a backup, with the protocol and service differences between the two services masked by the use of transformation web services that are generated semi-automatically. The basic idea of cooperative fault-tolerance using similar services is presented based on an example involving two stock broker services. The software architecture and the process for generating the transformation web services using a code generation tool are also described, along with experimental results from the stock broker example. These results suggest that the transformation overhead is modest compared with the typical cost of communication.

1 Introduction

Web services have become the central unifying abstraction that enable client programs to access computer-based information, financial, and retail resources across networks using standardized interfaces and access methods. Because of this, the issue of dealing with service unavailability caused by events such as machine failures is increasingly important. Indeed, numerous research efforts and commercial offerings in the areas of web server clustering (e.g., BEA WebLogic[1] and IBM WebSphere[2]), disaster recovery (e.g., VERITAS Volume Replicator[3]) and even CDNs (e.g. Akamai Technologies) can be viewed as addressing different aspects of the service availability issue. Fundamental to all of this approaches, however, is the notion that there is a single underlying service, with replication of the service or data used to handle potential unavailability.

---

[1] WebLogic is a registered trademark of BEA Systems Inc.
[2] WebSphere is a registered trademark of IBM Corporation.
[3] VERITAS Volume Replicator is a registered trademark of Symantec Corporation.

D. Penkler, M. Reitenspiess, and F. Tam (Eds.): ISAS 2006, LNCS 4328, pp. 76–91, 2006.
© Springer-Verlag Berlin Heidelberg 2006

In this paper, we describe an approach to handling unavailability in which failover is done between similar, but not identical, services potentially owned and operated by separate companies. These similar services are not identical replicas, but rather simply provide close to the same functionality. There are many services that fit this description. For example, hotel reservation systems all have similar transaction flows for similar functions such as specifying the date or room type, checking availability, or registering payment information even though the exact details of the interfaces may differ. This is not surprising since the underlying business flows that drive each transaction are essentially identical despite these differences. Unfortunately, it is precisely these differences that make it difficult to use similar services interchangeably.

Our approach is based on the business principle of *cooperative fault tolerance* and implemented by semi-automatic service transformations. With cooperative fault tolerance, providers of similar services agree on a common service backup strategy based on their separate services. This could involve, for example, medium or small service providers that do not have enough resources to construct their own backup center using one another's services as failover sites. Or a collection of providers with similar services could contract with a network service provider to construct a shared disaster recovery site, with the transformation mechanism absorbing the difference between each service and the shared backup system. The fundamental idea behind cooperative fault tolerance is to realize enhanced availability at a very high level, essentially doing replication at a *business* level rather than at the service or lower levels.

The core enabling technology of the approach is the semi-automatic transformation of similar services. Our solution is based on two guiding principles. The first is that the performance of the transformation mechanism is of key importance. As a result, our approach uses static techniques to generate the appropriate transformation modules rather than relying on runtime composition. The second is that a semi-automated approach provides the best balance between the effort required for a manual approach and the complexity of a fully automated approach. This approach requires developers to specify the transformation flow manually, but in a way that is guided based on the interface description of the original services. Based on these directions, a code generator then generates a *transformation web service* that enables a service to use a similar service as its backup. These services are generated from WSDL definitions [1] of the similar services, transformation flow definitions provided by the developer, and extensible transformation logic libraries.

Other existing research focuses on problems that are related to the issues being addressed in this paper. For example, a number of efforts are attempting to improve the reliability of web services, including work on message reliability [2], and mechanisms for managing replication and recovery strategies [3,4]. The work on automatic service composition from existing web services (e.g., [5,6,7,8]) is related to our transformation mechanisms. In these efforts, compatible services are identified by using interface descriptions such as WSDL, or ontology descriptions such as DAML-S [9] and OWL [10], and then dynamically gathered to compose a new web service. Such an approach could be used, in principle, to construct a new web service that replaces the failed original web service. However, such general approaches do not address specific fault-tolerance issues such as state sharing between the original and new web service, or state restoration after recovery of the original service. Furthermore, while very flexible, such dynamic composition approaches impose a runtime penalty that may be unacceptably large to use as a basis for failover. Finally, it may in fact be impossible to compose an appropriate transformation path unless the description of every difference between services has been standardized. While this may be feasible for basic transformations like currency unit conversion or type conversion, it is less straightforward if applications use, for example, their own code systems (e.g., product or error codes) or data formats.

In contrast with the above, our work focuses on providing interoperability between similar services and doing so in a way that customizes the transformation code to the pair of services, rather than providing a completely flexible and dynamic mechanism that can connect to any service. This is more suitable for cooperative fault-tolerance where the backup provider is known in advance, some service state may need to be shared between the service and its backup, and where performance is perhaps more of an issue. In cases such as these, the key is to provide an efficient transformation mechanism that works between specific similar services.

The remainder of this paper is organized as follows. In Sect. 2, we describe the goals of this work and give an overview of the software architecture for our solution. Section 3 then illustrates the approach with a sample application. The code generator used to generate the transformation web service that masks differences between the similar services is described in Sect. 4. Section 5 gives experimental results demonstrating the performance of the transformation web service. Finally, in Sect. 6, we summarize our work.

2   Cooperative Fault Tolerance

Establishing provisions for continued availability of web services in the event of failures using traditional fault-tolerance or disaster recovery mechanisms can be expensive and burdensome, especially for small and medium size providers. By using cooperative fault-tolerance techniques that exploit similar services, however, various strategies can be adopted. Examples of several such strategies are shown in Fig. 1. In Case 1, one provider makes arrangements with another provider with a similar service to act as its backup; such an arrangement may in fact be symmetric, with each serving as backup for the other in a mutual assistance relationship. In Case 2, providers that are engaged in the same field of business and have similar services might establish a common shared disaster recovery site to reduce backup cost. Another possible scenario shown in Case 3 is a company that upgrades its service but maintains its older similar service as a backup. Case 4 illustrates a final scenario, in which two merging companies might use separately developed services as mutual backups. The sample application described in detail in section 3 is an example of a Case 1 strategy.

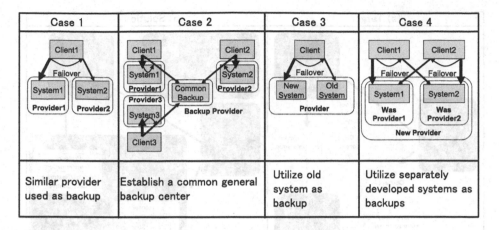

Fig. 1. Cooperative Fault Tolerance Usage Cases

There are at least three challenges to implementing failover between similar services: *replicated state maintenance, protocol compatibility,* and *service compatibility.* As an example, consider Fig. 2(a). Here, we assume that Provider A and Provider B have similar services, and that A (primary) plans to use B's service as its backup. The first challenge relates to how to maintain A's state at the backup B in anticipation of a possible failure. The choice of possible strategies, shown in Fig. 3, depends largely on the semantics of the services involved. The primary difficulty comes when, for contractual or other reasons, data may not be shared as frequently or as completely in this cross-enterprise scenario than would be the case when identical services are replicated using a tightly-coupled strategy.

Several strategies that are especially appropriate in these cases are shaded in the figure and highlighted below:

- State updates using batch transfer. In cases where a delay of the state update is acceptable (e.g., video streaming service, map direction service), a periodic batch transfer strategy can be adopted to reduce the data exchange frequency between A and B.
- Partitioning service resources. In cases where the resource managed by the service can be divided (e.g., hotel or ticket reservations), a strategy can be adopted in which B only accepts requests after a failure for resources that were previous assigned to it [11].
- Queuing requests. Some service state might be too confidential to be shared with the backup service B and as a result, the backup B is not able to fully serve all requests. In such cases, it may be sufficient, depending on the service semantics, to queue requests from clients at B and then resolve them after A recovers.

The second challenge is dealing with protocol incompatibilities between the primary A and the backup B. This impacts A's clients on failover, since they

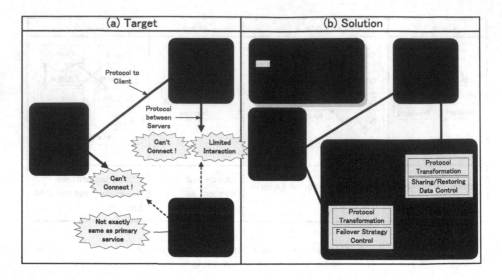

Fig. 2. System Structure

are unlikely to be able to connect to B directly. In addition, it also affects the communication between A and B needed to implement data transfer for the state maintenance described above, as well as for recovery.

The last challenge is that, since our approach is based on services that are similar but not identical, the backup service B likely does not provide clients exactly the same service as the primary A. The details of the interfaces may be different, for example. The particular state maintenance strategy used can also have a significant influence on service differences. In particular, it may not even be possible for B to implement the same service if data sharing is limited or B lacks authorization to proceed with certain types of requests.

Our solution to these challenges is based on the use of transformation web services that are generated semi-automatically using a code generation tool. The *client transformation web service* (see Fig. 2(b)) transforms the client's request, which uses A's protocol, into the protocol for B. It also controls the failover strategies according to the contents of the request. Similarly, the *server transformation web service* transforms the interactions needed between A and B for data sharing; for state maintenance, these would typically be requests from A to B transferring state, while for recovery, the data flow would be the reverse. It also provides the control mechanisms needed in these cases based on the failover strategy chosen.

3   Example: Similar Stock Broker Services

To illustrate our approach, we present an extended example based on a securities brokering application (Fig. 4). There are four principals in this scenario. Broker A and broker B provide similar brokering services, and we assume that they

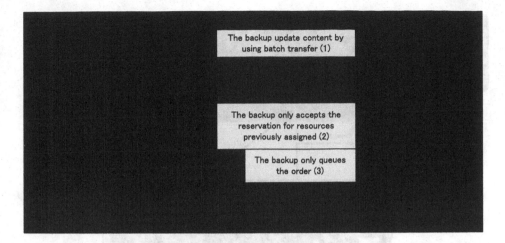

Fig. 3. Possible State Maintenance Strategies

have negotiated a cooperative fault-tolerance agreement in which B acts as A's backup in the event of failure. Each broker handlers orders to buy and sell over-the-counter stocks, as well as similar transactions for their own collections of mutual funds. The stock exchange market settles trades for stocks, while the mutual fund orders are handled locally at each broker. The client is a customer of broker A. The numbers and the letters used below match those in Fig. 4.

In the normal case, the primary service (broker A) receives a stock order from the client (1) and forwards it to the stock exchange market (2). If the transaction is settled in the market (3), the primary receives the result and stores it in its database. Mutual fund orders are handled locally at broker A. In the event that the primary fails, the client stub detects the failure and switches the connection to the backup service (a). In our prototype, the failure detection and switching mechanisms needed to provide failure transparency for the client are placed in the the client stub,[4] but other approaches such as having a server-side detection and switching mechanism are also possible. The backup receives the order from the client via the client transformation web service, which masks the protocol and service differences (b). For stock transactions, the backup accepts the order and handles it as if it was the primary (c, d and e). After the primary recovers, the backup sends the results of transactions that have been performed during the failure to the primary via the server transformation web service (f), which again masks the service differences. In the case of mutual funds, we assume that these are private items that can be managed only by the primary and that the providers do not share enough information to allow the backup to process the order in the event of failure. So when the backup receives a buy or sell order for a mutual fund (f), it only queues it (g) and asks the primary in lieu of the client to execute the order after recovery (h and i).

---

[4] The stub could easily be generated by our generator, but this has not yet been implemented.

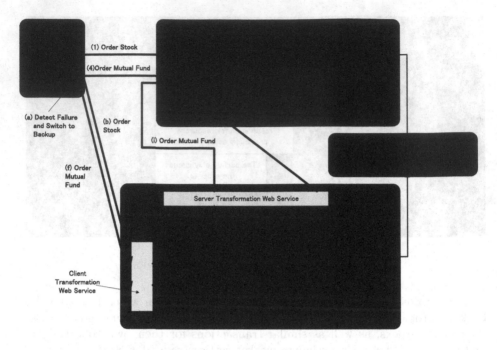

Fig. 4. Sample Application

For the purposes of this example, we assume the following differences between the primary and backup services; the relevant messages are shown in Fig. 5:

- Message Format. We assume that the primary and backup use different message formats. In this example, the primary uses XML-based message passing in which all parameter values are included in an XML document. On the other hand, the backup uses parameter-based message passing in which the values are sent as parameters of the remote procedure call.
- Different Code Systems. We assume that the primary and backup use different code systems for some parameters, and that the types of some parameters are different. In this example, the primary service uses character security codes and operation indicators (SELL/BUY), while the backup service uses numeric codes.
- Missing Parameters. We assume that there are some missing parameters that only the backup requires that are not included in the primary's message. In this example, only the backup requires the currency unit.
- Extra Parameters. We assume that there are some extra parameters that only the primary service requires. In this example, only the primary requires the order time.
- Request Granularity. We assume that there is a different granularity associated with the requests encapsulated in a remote procedure call. In this example, the primary accepts multiple orders per procedure call, while the backup accepts only one order.

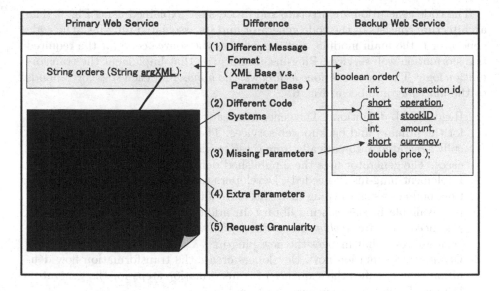

Primary Web Service	Difference	Backup Web Service
String orders (String argXML);	(1) Different Message Format (XML Base v.s. Parameter Base) (2) Different Code Systems (3) Missing Parameters (4) Extra Parameters (5) Request Granularity	boolean order(int transaction_id, short operation, int stockID, int amount, short currency, double price);

Fig. 5. Service Differences

In the next section, we describe how transformation web services that mask the above differences are generated.

4   Code Generation

In this section, we describe the code generation tool and how it works to generate the transformation web services in a semi-automated way. We do this by outlining its architecture and control flow, and then giving an example of the code generated by the tool.

4.1   Architecture and Control Flow

The code generator is based on the following design principles:

- *Transformation web services.* Web services are used as the basis for the transformation modules, meaning that they can be accessed in the same way as the original web service.
- *Original interface definitions.* The original WSDL definitions of the primary and backup web services are used to generate transformation modules that bridge the differences between these interfaces.
- *Transformation flow definition.* Code generation is performed based on guidance from the user in the form of the required sequence of transformation logic; this sequence is specified using a development environment.
- *Plug-in architecture.* The transformation logic implementation can be customized using plug-ins, which makes the architecture extensible and able to handle scenarios beyond those possible with a fixed architecture.

The code generation architecture and process are explained using Fig. 6. The architecture consists of the code generator and its associated plug-ins. The code generator is the main module, and it generates the source code for the required transformation web services. Plug-ins are libraries that implement the transformation logic. The process is done as follows; the number for each step corresponds to the matching number in Fig. 6.

1. Read WSDL definitions. The generator reads the original WSDL definitions for the primary and backup web services. These WSDL definitions are typically generated automatically from these services and also published in many cases. The generator uses these published definitions.
2. Implement plug-ins (if needed). Developers can implement new transformation modules using the plug-in architecture if the desired transformations are not available in the existing library. In addition to the plug-in itself, they also need to write a *plug-in definition file*, which enables the generator to generate code that invokes the new plug-in.
3. Define transformation flow. Developers create the transformation flow definition that specifies the sequence of transformation steps for the generator. Details of this step are given in section 4.2.
4. Generate source code. The generator generates source code for the transformation web services using the WSDL definitions, the plug-in definitions, and the transformation flow definition.
5. Compile and deploy. Developers compile and deploy the transformation web services using the regular compiler and deployment tools. The compiled plug-ins are placed in the proper directory for dynamic linking.

The figure also includes the following plug-ins as examples of transformation logic; these are the plug-ins implemented for the example stock broker application:

- *Basic Type Transformer.* Transforms basic types such as long, integer and short.
- *Data Transformer.* Transforms between different data code systems by using matching data from included code tables. In this example, we use this to transform stock and mutual fund symbols.
- *Data Generator.* Generates missing parameters that are required by the backup but not the primary. In this example, we generate time information using this plug-in.
- *Data Recorder.* The opposite of the above, it stores extra parameters that are required by the primary but not by the backup if they need to be restored for recovery.
- *Argument Decoder.* Analyzes structured text data and extracts parameters. In this example, we implement an XML decoder that extracts parameters from XML documents by specifying their XPath [12] definitions.
- *Argument Encoder.* The opposite of the above, it synthesizes structured text data from several parameters. In this example, we implement an XML encoder that synthesizes an XML document by specifying parameters and their XPATH definitions.

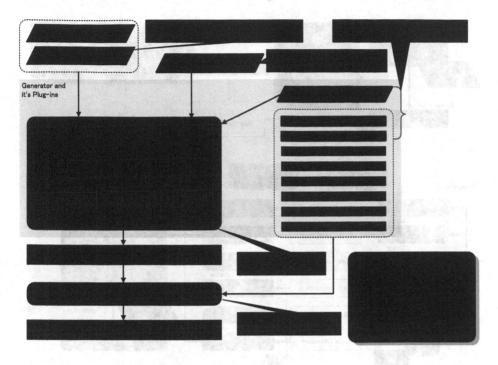

Generator and
it's Plug-ins

Fig. 6. Code Generation Process

In the above process, the two steps in which developers have to create data or provide code are the transformation flow definition and plug-in creation. Given that the former is especially important, we describe it in more detail in the following section.

4.2   Description of Transformation Flow Definition

The basics of the transformation flow definition process are explained using Fig. 7, which is again based on our example application. The transformation flow being defined in this figure is designed to mask the difference between these similar services related to the stock broker order functionality, including the differences shown above in Fig. 5. We explain the flow of this example below, with the step number corresponding to the numbers in the figure:

1. The generator extracts information about the parameters of the primary's interface from the appropriate WSDL definition. For example, in this case, the procedure name, number of parameters, type of parameters, and type of return value are extracted. Developers are required to specify the transformation flow for each extracted parameter. In this case, the parameter is a string value that contains XML text.
2. The Argument Decoder plug-in is put into the flow to parse the XML text. This plug-in extracts procedures by specifying the path of each procedure

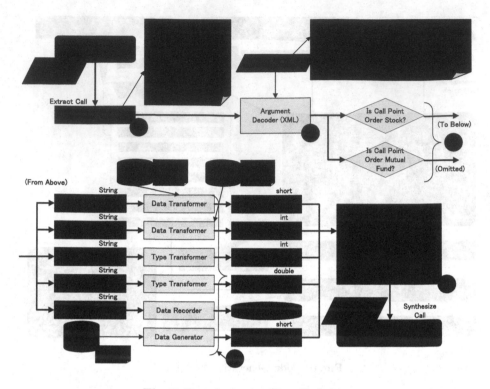

Fig. 7. Transformation Flow Definition

and its parameters using XPath expressions. In this case, the order procedure and its parameters are extracted by specifying the appropriate paths.

3. A branch mechanism is inserted to alter the control flow according to the type of the message. In this example, we implement a flow for stocks that connects to a proxy order function for stocks and another flow for mutual funds that just connects to a queuing function. Subsequent steps focus on the flow for stocks.

4. The proper plug-ins are placed into the flow to define the appropriate transformations for each parameter that was extracted. In this case, parameters that only require a simple type transformation, like amount and price, are transformed by including the Type Transformer plug-in. Parameters that require data code translations, like operation code or stock symbol, are transformed by including the Data Transformer plug-in; this plug-in exchanges data codes by specifying matching values in the data codes. Surplus parameters that are needed in order to later restore the value, like time, are stored to the local database by including the Data Recorder plug-in. Missing parameters, like currency code, are generated by including the Data Generator plug-in.

5. Code is generated to connect the transformation flow to the backup's interface based on the backup's WSDL definition.

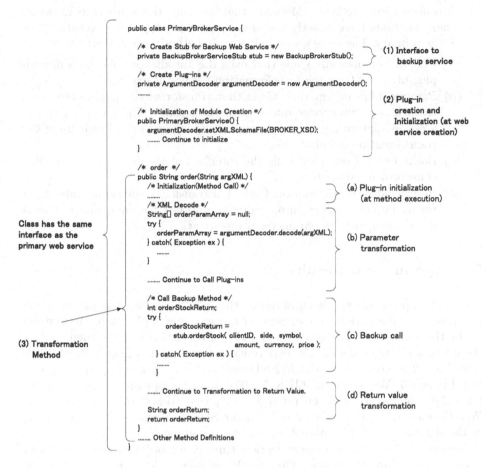

Fig. 8. Generate Code Example

The subsequent transformation flow needed for values being returned from the web service invocation would be defined in a similar way.

4.3 Generated Code

Figure 8 shows an example of the source code that the generator constructs—a class that has the same interface as the primary web service. We explain the contents of this class; the numbers correspond to the labels in Fig. 8.

1. Interface to backup service. Code that implements the mechanism to call the backup web service. In this example, this simply consists of code to create a stub that is defined in another class.
2. Plug-in creation and initialization. Code that creates plug-in instances. The generator also constructs code that calls their initialization methods when the web service is created.

3. Transformation Methods. Methods that actually transform the message. These methods have exactly the same parameter types and return types as the primary. The code generated in each method is described below.

   (a) Plug-in initialization. Code that calls the initialization methods of each plug-in at the time the transformation method is executed.

   (b) Parameter transformation. Code that transforms the parameters from the primary web service into that of the backup. The generator generates the appropriate runtime sequence of plug-in method calls using the transformation definition file.

   (c) Backup call. Code that calls the interface of the backup service with transformed parameters.

   (d) Return value transformation. Code that transforms the return value from the backup web service into a value appropriate for the primary. This is done analogously to parameter transformation.

5   Experimental Results

This section presents experimental results that illustrate the performance of the generated transformation web services for our example application. We first describe the performance in both normal and failover situations, and then analyze the overhead in more detail. The experiments were run on a Dell 2650 with two Intel Xeon 2.40 GHz CPUs with 512 KB caches and 1 GB memory running Red Hat Linux 7.3. We use Java[5] (JDK 1.5.02) as a development environment for both the implemented and generated code. Apache Tomcat 5.5.9 is used as the Web Container, Apache Axis 1.2 RC 3 as the SOAP[13] engine, MySQL 4.1.14[6] as the database, and Hibernate 3.0 as the O/R mapper.

Figure 9 shows the average execution time of an order transaction under normal and failure conditions. This graph represents the required round trip time for a client program that submits a stock order request to the broker. The broker forwards the order to the stock exchange web service and sends back a result. We measure the time with 1, 2, 4 and 8 clients continuously accessing the service in parallel. The time is the average of 100 trials. The differences between the two similar services are the same as those shown in Fig. 7.

The results indicate that the round trip time associated with invoking the backup is 801 ms longer than invoking the primary when only 1 client is accessing the service. These failure latencies increase to 917 ms, 3223 ms, 6393 ms and 7303 ms when the number of simultaneous clients are 2, 4, 6 and 8, respectively.

Figure 10 shows the detail of the overhead in the failover scenario. These times are measured when one client is accessing the backup broker via the transformation web service. The times enclosed in braces in the figure are those that were actually measured; the communication times from the client to the transformation web service and from the transformation web service to the backup

---

[5] Java is a trademark of Sun Microsystems, Inc.

[6] MySQL is a registered trademark of MySQL AB.

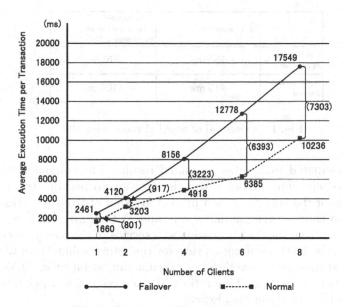

Fig. 9. Execution Time per Transaction

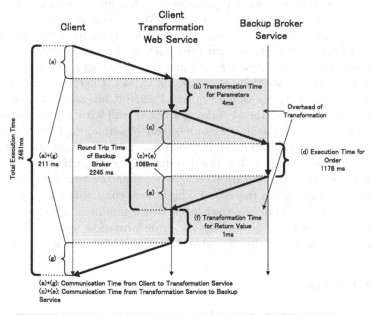

	Ratio of Transformation Logic Execution Time (b)+(f)/(b)+(c)+(e)+(f)	Ratio of Communication Time (c)+(e)/(b)+(c)+(e)+(f)
Division of Transformation Overhead	0.47 %	99.53 %

Fig. 10. Execution Time Detail

	Zero Parameter	7 Parameters (Same number as Performance Test)
Call from Java Application	150 ms	570 ms
Call from Web Service	415 ms	1100 ms

Fig. 11. Overhead of SOAP Procedure Call

service are calculated from other measured results. The communication time includes SOAP encoding/decoding time in addition to network transfer time. The overheads of the transformation process are sum of (b) 4 ms, which is the transformation time for the parameters, (c and e) 1069 ms, which is the communication time from the transformation web service to the backup service, and (f) 1 ms, which is the transformation time for the return value. From this result, we can see that most of the overhead is the communication time, 99.53% of the total in this particular case. This ratio will, however, vary depending on the complexity of the transformation logic.

Additionally, we measured the overhead of SOAP procedure calls by comparing the normal procedure (with 7 parameters) with a null procedure (with zero parameters) that simply returns a static value. We measured four specific cases: when the null procedure is called from a Java application, when the null procedure is called from a web service, and then each of the same experiments with the normal procedure with 7 parameters like the brokering example. From the results in Fig. 11 we can see that, as one would expect, the time increases when the procedure is called from a web service and when it has more parameters. In particular, note that the overhead of doing a SOAP call with 7 parameters from a web service—the same scenario as our broker example—is 1100 ms, almost the same as the time measured for the example for the communication time (c)+(e). These results suggest that the dominating factor in the end-to-end latency tends to be the communication cost rather than the transformation time, which is not surprising given the use of a high-level communication mechanism like SOAP. Note also that our approach keeps this communication time overhead to a minimum by statically generating the transformation web services rather than attempting to dynamically assemble the required functionality at runtime.

6   Conclusions

This paper has described an approach to improving the availability of web services by exploiting the existence of similar, but not identical, web services and using a strategy of cooperative fault tolerance. We realize the necessary failover mechanism by using a semi-automated approach to generating transformation web services that mask the differences between the similar services. In contrast to automatic web service composition work that is based on a general mechanism that dynamically gathers transformation web services to construct new services, our approach addresses the necessary state sharing and recovery issues, and focuses on statically synthesizing the transformation logic between a given pair of cooperating services. This minimizes the runtime overhead, and opens the door to performing further optimizations on the transformation service itself.

One area of future work is reducing the amount of human guidance needed to generate a transformation flow definition. Strategies that we will pursue include developing a GUI-based definition tool that can generate the transformation flow XML document automatically and exploring the use of meta expressions to indicate the meaning of parameters like ontology descriptions.

References

1. Christensen, E., Curbera, F., Meredish, G., Weerawarana, S.: Web Services Description Language (WSDL) 1.1. W3C. (2001) http://www.w3.org/TR/wsdl.
2. OASIS: Web Services Reliable Messaging TC WS-Reliability. (2004) http://docs.oasis-open.org/wsrm/ws-reliability/v1.1/.
3. Liang, D., Fang, C.L., Lin, C.C.: Fault Tolerant Web Service. In: Proceedings of the 10th Asia-Pacific Software Engineering Conference (APSEC'03). (2003)
4. Birman, K., Renesse, R., Vogels, W.: Adding High Availability and Autonomic Behavior to Web Services. In: Proceedings of the 26th Annual International Conference on Software Engineering (ICSE 2004). (2004) 17–26
5. Chandrasekaran, S., Madden, S., Ionescu, M.: Ninja Paths: An Architecture for Composing Services over Wide Area Networks. In: UC Berkeley, CS262 class project writeup. (2000)
6. Richards, D., van Splunter, S., Brazier, F.M., Sabou, M.: Composing Web Services using an Agent Factory. In: Proceedings of Workshop on Web-Services and Agent-based Engineering(WSABE2003). (2003)
7. Fujii, K., Suda, T.: Dynamic Service Composition using Semantic Information. In: Proceedings of the 2nd International Conference on Service Oriented Computing (ICSOC2004). (2004) 39–48
8. Sirin, E., Hendler, J., Parsia, J.: Semi-Automatic Composition of Web Services using Semantic Descriptions. In: Web Services: Modeling, Architecture and Infrastructure in ICEIS2003. (2003)
9. Ankolekar, A., et al: DAML-S: Semantic Markup For Web Services. In: Proceedings of the 1st International Semantic Web Conference (ISWC2002). (2002)
10. W3C: OWL Web Ontology Language Overview. (2004) http://www.w3.org/TR/owl-features/.
11. Sussman, J., Marzullo, K.: The Bancomat problem: an example of resource allocation in a partitionable asynchronous system. Theoretical Computer Science $291(1)$ (2003) 103–131
12. W3C: XML Path Language (XPath). (1999) http://www.w3.org/TR/xpath.
13. W3C: Simple Object Access Protocol (SOAP) 1.1. (2003) http://www.w3.org/TR/soap/.

Reducing the Recovery Time of IP-Phones in an H.323 Based VoIP System

Sachin Garg[1], Chandra Kintala[2], and David Stott[3]

[1] Avaya Labs, Basking Ridge, NJ
[2] Motorola India Labs, Bangalore, India
[3] Lucent Technologies, Warren, NJ

Abstract. In large deployments of H.323 based Voice-over-IP (VoIP) systems, achieving the desired availability is a major challenge. A major factor in determining the availability is the resilience of the recovery mechanisms in the H.323 protocol suite against server and network failures. In this paper, we focus on the "registration" aspect of the H.225 protocol in H.323 suite. Specifically, we tackle the registration-flood problem which occurs after a server or network failure, when more IP Phones attempt to register with the VoIP server than the server can handle. The most significant ramification of overload is longer registration times resulting in lower overall availability of the VoIP system. Existing solutions to mitigate registration-floods are either server centric or network centric. In this paper, we propose a complementary end-point based technique using random back-off. Discrete event simulation based evaluation shows that the proposed technique can yield significant reduction in the recovery time thereby increasing service availability. We also compare the performance of existing solutions with the proposed technique, particularly the relative effect of network delay and loss on the performance of the techniques.

1 Introduction

While the users have come to expect very high availability ("five nines") from legacy circuit-switched telecom networks, achieving comparable service availability in Voice-over-IP (VoIP) systems remains an on-going challenge. VoIP systems' underlying IP based network (hardware and software), which is shared amongst voice and data, is one of the primary reasons for the lower availability. In comparison, the legacy systems enjoy dedicated infrastructure to transfer voice between communicating end-points. Since the use of IP and the cost benefits of convergence is what is driving the VoIP adoption, a high availability solution for these systems needs to account for the inherent un-reliability of the shared IP infrastructure. Building resilience against network failures needs to be a key design driver in these systems. The above can be effectively rephrased in terms of the classical availability formula, A = MTBF / (MTBF + MTTR). In VoIP systems, knowing that MTBF is inherently smaller than in the legacy systems, reducing MTTR is of paramount importance if comparable service availability is to be achieved.

D. Penkler, M. Reitenspiess, and F. Tam (Eds.): ISAS 2006, LNCS 4328, pp. 92–105, 2006.

In this paper, we present a technique which aims to reduce the MTTR, and hence increase service availability for one specific problem known as the "registration flood". While the context in this work is built using H.323, an analogous problem exists in other VoIP protocols as well including SIP. Accordingly, the proposed solution in its essence is applicable to these as well. The rest of the paper is organized as follows. Section 2 contains a brief overview of H.323 based VoIP systems, a description of the problem and relevant technical background. Section 3 outlines solutions that are currently used to mitigate the effects of registration overload. In Section 4, we describe our end-point based proposal for improving service availability. We note that the proposed solution is complementary to the existing solutions and can be used in conjunction.

2   Background

H.323 is an ITU.T standard protocol suite, which specifies the architecture and protocols for signaling and media transfer between communicating entities. It is the most widely used standard for commercial VoIP systems. Figure 1 shows the basic architecture diagram and protocols in an H.323 VoIP system, which is composed of primarily three components; 1) End-points 2) Gatekeeper (server) and 3) Gateway. The end-points are IP based devices (IP phones, PCs etc.) used by end-users to communicate between each other and with other non-IP based devices on the PSTN network. A Gateway facilitates media translation between IP based end-points and PSTN and typically also includes what is called a Multi-control unit (MCU). The MCU's primary responsibility is mixing audio streams to enable multi-party conferences. The corner-stone of the architecture is the gatekeeper, which is also referred to as "Media Server", "Call Manager" or "Communication Manager". We shall use the terms *gatekeeper, media server* or simply *server* interchangeably in this paper. The server is responsible for controlling all aspect of a VoIP call including call setup, mid-call control and tear down. The binding and translation between phone numbers and IP address, digit collection and processing when users press phone buttons and all call associated features such as call forwarding, conferencing, caller-id etc. are provided and controlled by the server. The network connectivity between the phones, the server and the gateway(s) is provided by an IP network.

With respect to protocols used to deliver VoIP, the H.323 suite defines the signaling part. As shown in figure 1, H.225 and the H.245 protocols are used between the end-points and the server. The H.245 protocol is used for "call control". H.248 is used primarily between the server and the gateway and is used by the server (gatekeeper) to control the gateway in allocating resources for voice calls. RTP and RTCP protocols, which carry the media and media quality information respectively, are employed between communicating end-points, which might include only IP-phones or it might include the Gateway and the phones, if one of the call participants is on the PSTN network. The H.225 protocol, is subdivided into two parts, one is called "RAS" (Registration, Admission, Signalling) and the other is "call signalling". Although not required by the standard, the

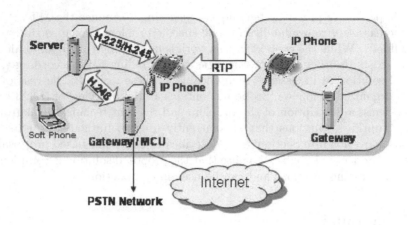

Fig. 1. H.323 VoIP Architecture and Protocols

call signaling part is implemented over TCP and the RAS part is implemented over UDP.

The RAS protocol comes under focus in this paper. Network connectivity failures, resulting from benign or malicious faults between any of the entities have the potential to cause service disruption. Specifically, loss of connectivity to and from the end-points is directly and immediately visible to the end-user as service un-availability. It is for this reason that H.225 and RTP/RTCP protocols need to be highly resilient against such failures. In the absence of redundancy, efficiently re-establishing broken socket links and state re-synchronization between the server and the endpoint(s) is vital to reducing the MTTR once the network outage is resolved.

2.1   Registration Overload Problem

In H.225 based systems, the end-points undergo what is called the "discovery and registration" procedure, which is necessary before an endpoint is ready to make or receive VoIP calls. The message exchange that happens between the server and the end-point enables them to establish each other's identity and capabilities. For instance, the phone sends to the server, its extension number, IP address, codec capabilities, desired calling features etc. The server acknowledges and stores the necessary bindings and state in its database. In this paper, we focus on a specific problem in the RAS part of H.225 called "registration overload" or "registration flood", which prolongs the time interval of the endpoints in becoming operational causing higher service unavailability.

Figure 2 depicts the exact sequence of messages received and sent by the server for a single successful end-point registration. Typically the messages are sent over UDP.

1. Gatekeeper request: Also called a "GRQ" message, this packet is sent by the phone to the server as the first message in starting the registration (recovery).

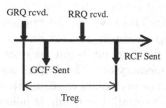

Fig. 2. Successful registration sequence at the server

It includes the end-points identity such as the extension number and the IP address. The server, upon receiving a GRQ allocates resources and proceeds with sending a confirmation to the end-point.

2. Gatekeeper Confirm: Also known as the "GCF" message, it is sent by the server to the endpoint in response to a GRQ, if the server is responsible for this endpoint. If not, the server responds by sending a Gatekeeper Reject (GRJ) message.

3. Registration Request: Also called a "RRQ" message, this is sent by the endpoint to the server after it has received a GCF from the server accepting its identity and request to proceed with registration. An RRQ message contains more capability information about the end-point.

4. Registration Confirm: After receiving the RRQ, the server sends a "Registration Confirm (RCF)" message to the end-point, again, after some bookkeeping operations. If the capability set sent with the RRQ message is not compatible with the server, the server sends a registration reject message to the endpoint. Once the phone receives the RCF message, it is ready to make/accept phone calls.

The server allocates resources including CPU, memory (both real and persistent) to serving registration requests from the time of receiving a GRQ till the time it sends out an RCF (T_{reg}). A common problem seen is that a flood of GRQ messages arriving at the server cause the server to overload which results in delayed completion of the message sequence for some or all endpoints. This translates to longer service unavailability for some or all users. In normal operation, the gatekeeper serves GRQs when a configuration change happens in the system such as a new endpoint is installed or a phone number changes etc. However, in certain situations many endpoints (which can be thousands) attempt to register simultaneously causing a GRQ flood at the server. These include:

- Server failure
- Network failure
- Scheduled Maintenance
- Global Configuration changes

The underlying reason in all of the above is the loss of connectivity between the server and the end-points, which results in a service outage. Once the connectivity is restored, the service remains unavailable until the endpoints complete the registration sequence. It is imperative, therefore, that the registration procedure be completed quickly. This is where the "registration flood" is problematic. Since in the above outage scenario, the recovery involves all endpoints trying to register, the ensuing flood might result in excessive queue buildup due to lack of resources (CPU, memory etc.), leading to lost GRQ messages. Since the protocol calls for retries, the endpoints continue to resend GRQs, which further compounds the problem. Overall, the result is delayed recovery and longer unavailability of the VoIP service. Further, since the server needs to keep some state information between receiving a GRQ and sending an RCF, the longer this duration (T_{reg}, see Figure 2), the easier it is to cause the flooding. In other words, the server is more susceptible to the flood problem if the round trip times between itself and the endpoints are longer. In this paper, we propose a simple, yet novel solution to mitigating the registration flood problem.

As mentioned before, while the context in this paper is around H.323 based VoIP systems, similar problem exists in SIP based systems. The end-points (referred to as clients in SIP terminology) undergo an analogous exchange with the SIP registrar, which faces the potential of registration floods. The proposed solution is equally applicable to these systems.

3   Prior and Related Work

Mainly two classes of solutions exist to mitigate the registration flood problem.

1. Network Centric: In this approach, the notion is to throttle the flood of GRQs before they reach the server. While the rate limiting could be done anywhere along the path from the endpoint(s) to the server, typically, it is done closer to the server via filtering GRQs in a router/firewall type device. The genesis of throttling GRQs to tackle registration flood problem lies in the well known and standard approach of rate-limiting capability employed by firewalls to thwart DoS attacks [2]. Preventing GRQs from reaching the server, however, has drawbacks. First, the IP phones, unaware of the imposed rate-limiting begin to operate under the assumption that the GRQs are lost and depending on the implementation, might start more aggressive re-sending of GRQs, which worsens the problem requiring continued rate-limiting. Under pathologic conditions and improper rate-limit thresholds, the net result might be longer registration times for phones causing even higher service unavailability.

2. Server Centric: In this approach, when the server receives a GRQ message, it first does an internal check to determine if it has the resources to process the complete sequence. This might include checking current registration requests being served, the CPU load, state of its network queues etc. The heuristic to determine if the request should be accepted or not is implementation dependent. In any case, if the server decides not to start the registration sequence, it sends out a "Request-in-progress" (RIP) message back to the IP phone. The RIP message indicates a time duration which the phone must wait before sending out a repeat GRQ message. In effect, when the server

determines itself to be in overload or nearing overload, it starts sending out RIP messages to registration requests asking IP phones to wait. It continues to send RIPs until the resources become available. This solution is part of the H.225 [3] standard from ITU. It is a generic solution for message sequences other than registration and can be used by the server and the gatekeeper [4]. This approach, while more effective than the network centric approach, also suffers from certain drawbacks. First, the server does need to process the first message (i.e. the GRQ packet) and generate the RIP message. That itself takes a certain amount of resources and depending on the available resources and the amount of overload, might result in undesirable behavior such as GRQs getting dropped. Second, the RIP message is vulnerable to network congestion and might be lost before reaching the IP Phone. In this case, the phone would behave as in the network centric approach and continue to send out GRQ messages. In its favor, though, this approach allows the server to tailer sending out RIP messages based on its current and anticipated resource usage, both instantaneous and average.

4   Proposal for Reducing the Recovery Time of IP Phones

The primary contribution in this paper is the proposal of a technique which complements both the network centric and the server centric approaches. In order to sketch the basic idea behind this proposal, we first outline the failure and recovery process in H.323 based IP phones. As mentioned earlier, the IP phones register themselves with the server using the H.225 RAS protocol, before they are operational and available for making phone calls. Further, each IP phone periodically probes for connectivity with the server using heartbeat messages. If a phone detects that there is no connectivity to the server, it can no longer be used to make calls since the server is responsible for call setup and control. Thus, it must attempt to re-register with the same or an alternate redundant server[1] and continue to do so until registration is successful.

Figure 3 depicts the recovery process assuming that the RIP based solution is present. The figure shows the time on the horizontal axis. Events from typical IP endpoints are depicted as symbols with legends. The GRQs are generated at the endpoints and are received at the server within a short span of time. While the first few GRQs grab the available resources at the server and engage in the registration sequence, any subsequent arrivals receive a RIP message back.

4.1   Local Random Backoff at the IP Phones

We propose that each IP endpoint should perform a local random backoff after detecting a connectivity failure but before starting the recovery process, i.e., before it sends out the GRQ message to begin the (re)-registration sequence.

---

[1] Typical VoIP architectures allow for multiple types of redundant servers including warm and hot standby. The IP address of the backup server is known a priori to the IP endpoints and is part of system provisioning and configuration.

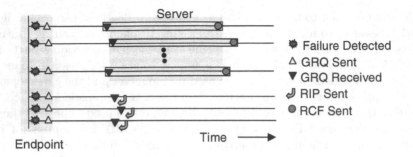

Fig. 3. Registration procedure basics and bottleneck

Obviously, the idea is to stagger the GRQ messages in time such that the registration flood is prevented. Before we delve into the specifics of the random backoff technique for H.323 based VoIP systems, we note that in any distributed system, where multiple clients access a single resource, random backoff is a fairly standard technique for handling access contention and fairness. The carrier sense protocols used in networks, such as CSMA/CD based Ethernet [5,6,7] which employs exponential backoff to tackle collisions and CSMA/CA based wireless LANs [8,9], which employ random backoffs to ensure fairness in channel access are prime examples. The technique has the benefit of not requiring any central coordination, which makes it efficient.

For H.323 based VoIP endpoints, the local random backoff ensures that the server does not get overloaded with GRQ flood. Note that if the server is not overloaded and an IP phone under recovery still performed a backoff, its recovery time will be longer than without the backoff. In other words, if the IP phone could recognize recovery situations which are likely to cause overload, this could be avoided. There are many potential ways to accomplish this, which are dependent on the cause of failure. In the simplest case of server outage due to scheduled maintenance, the server itself can indicate (by piggy-backing on the heartbeat messages) that the IP phones perform backoff before recovery. In another case, if the TCP sockets between the server and an IP phone are "RESET", the phone should perform the backoff since most likely, the server underwent a failure. The IP Phone can also perform periodic `ping` and `traceroute` to estimate the extent of failure and decide to perform the backoff. For instance, if the router interface to the server is unresponsive, the other IP-phones should also have lost connectivity to the server.

Here on, we assume that in most cases, it is possible for the IP phone to make such a distinction. Even otherwise, while the service outage at that IP phone is lengthened, it does not negate the benefit since it is the lengthening of the collective outage which causes bad user experience rather than one or two IP phones being unavailable.

Figure 4 illustrates the random local backoff proposal, including the possibility that RIP messages might still need to be sent back to the IP phones, although at a much reduced level.

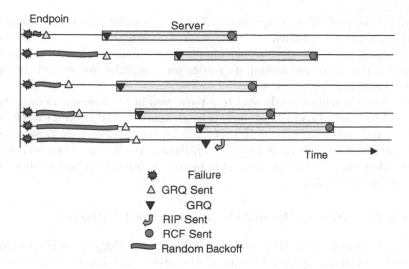

Fig. 4. Random local backoff before registration

While the use of RIP works on the principle of fault-tolerance, the underpinning in the proposed technique is that of "fault-prevention". In that sense, the combined use of the proposed technique and the known ones is intuitively more effective. For instance, while the use of RIP messages reduces the mean recovery time of a large VoIP system compared to when no RIP messages are sent, with the proposed technique, the recovery time is reduced further. Alternatively, depending on configuration parameters, far fewer RIP messages need to be sent by the server. An indirect, but desirable side-effect is the increase in robustness of the IP phone state machine, which, on an average is not as susceptible to lost RIP messages. There are several potential benefits of preventing registration floods, which are qualitatively listed below:

1. Generating RIP messages consumes CPU cycles at the server. The use of local backoffs reduces the contention for CPU at the server and more CPU horsepower is available for registration processing and call processing since the need for generating RIPs is reduced. This enables the server to serve more voice calls while a subset of the endpoints undergo recovery.

2. Endpoint recovery is less susceptible to loss of RIPs as there are less number of RIPs to begin with. This is especially true of deployments where the server and IP phones are separated via lossy links such as the public Internet or wireless networks, both local and wide-area. Obviously, prevention is better than having to tolerate faults. The performance analysis in the following section quantifies this benefit.

3. GRQ messages from the IP phones are queued at various interfaces within the server before processing completes. These include the network interface, the multiple network stack layer buffers, application processes etc. It is possible in a sudden burst of GRQs for some queue to overflow resulting in the loss of GRQ before it is processed. The local backoff at the phone substantially

reduces the probability of queue overflow by controlling the GRQ rate at the source, i.e., the IP phone.

4. In general, the recovery state machine is more robust as there is less probability of the phone exhausting its retries on a available server and therefore trying another one on the list.

5. The above benefits directly lead to a reduction in the average recovery time of an IP Phone in a situation where a large number of IP phones lose connectivity and try to re-register. In other words, the total average time it takes for the phones to recover is lower in comparison to the case when no random backoff is used by the phones. This benefit is quantified and explained in detail in Section 5.

4.2   Configuration of Backoff Duration at the IP Phones

If the mean backoff at the IP phones is too large, the GRQs get scattered more than necessary resulting in idle time at the server and longer service outage at the phones. On the other hand, a small mean backoff would not sufficiently stagger the GRQs causing flooding and hence longer outage. Obviously, the IP phones need to draw random samples with the optimum mean backoff (say M_{opt}) which, as we show in the following section, can be empirically obtained via simulation. When the registration procedure is started, the phones would draw a random sample between 0 and M_{opt} and wait for that many seconds before sending out GRQs. In practice, the IP phones need to be configured with the optimum value (say M_{opt}) a priori. Given that M_{opt} depends on the number of phones registered with the server and the CPU capacity of the server platform, one way to notify/configure the endpoints is via the server. For instance, during the initial boot and/or registration procedure (where the default backoff of 0 seconds is used), the server indicates the value of M_{opt} to the phone. This value is then statically configured in the server by an administrator. It is also possible for the phones to obtain the value of M_{opt} from a DHCP server in one of the optional parameters. The DHCP server, in turn, could be administered manually with the value.

5   Performance Evaluation

The performance of the local random backoff in terms of reducing the recovery time of VoIP phones is evaluated using discrete event simulation. The simulation includes the endpoints, local area network where the server resides, a wide area network between the server and the IP Phones and the server itself. Each element has certain settable parameters such as the amount of time needed to process each particular message type. The recovery process at each endpoint was simulated beginning with the start of the recovery process. It was assumed that the failure detection at the endpoints is staggered with a mean value of 5 milliseconds. Obviously, a perfectly synchronized connectivity failure detection at all the endpoints is unrealistic. In other words, failure detection lends an inherent "randomness" in starting the recovery process at the IP phones. For this reason, in the experimental runs, the mean backoff was not set to 0, rather started from 5 milliseconds. The time to complete the registration sequence once a GRQ is accepted and processed by the server was kept fixed for all experiments. In distinct simulation runs, 1000 and 2000 IP endpoints were simulated.

The sets of simulation trials that only varied the mean backoff at the endpoints were grouped into *runs*. In each run, the mean backoff was set at 5ms, 10ms, 20ms, 40ms, 75ms, 100ms, 150ms, and 250ms respectively. Because one of the primary advantages of the backoff solution is that the server spends less time generating RIP messages, intuitively, the RIP message processing time should be a factor for the effectiveness of the strategy. The time to process a RIP message was varied at 2.5ms, 5ms, and 15ms.

In order to compare the performance of the proposed backoff solution with the network centric solution, namely the throttling of GRQs, the runs were repeated with rate-limiting being simulated. Similarly, we expected the backoff to be more useful when there was high packet loss between the endpoints and the server since the RIP messages might be lost. To explore this hypothesis, the runs were repeated with a 5% packet loss probability. Then, the experiments were repeated with 2000 endpoints to see how the number of endpoints registering affects the registration time. *In the following discussion, the terms registration time and recovery time of an IP phone are used interchangeably.*

5.1   Experimental Results

The simulation results may be graphed in any of a few ways. Figure 5, for example, graphs the number of endpoints registered (on the vertical axis) versus the time (on the horizontal axis). Each curve represents a different mean backoff. Figure 6, on the other hand, graphs the same data results to show the amount of time required to recover the endpoints (on the vertical axis) as a function of the mean backoff value in milliseconds (on the horizontal axis). Figure 5 shows the cumulative number of endpoints registered as a function of time for various mean backoff values. Note that the first registration does not occur until after 30 seconds because a deterministic constant time is assumed to incur after the failure detection, which includes the time for internal state checking done by the phones, initializing parameters internally or from a DHCP server etc. The value for this interval is assumed to be 25 milliseconds. The RIP message processing time was set to 10ms for this graph. In general, the time required to register the endpoints (which equates to the system recovery time) decreases as the mean backoff value decreases until it passes an optimal value (near 150ms). Beyond the optimal value, the server begins to be idle while waiting for the phones to attempt to register.

For the largest mean backoff value of 250ms, the curve is completely linear, because the server was always free to process the next request. The second highest value of mean backoff (150ms) turned out to be slightly lower than the optimal mean backoff value. A few requests needed to be retried, resulting in an inflection point for the last 40 or so endpoints. The curves for smaller

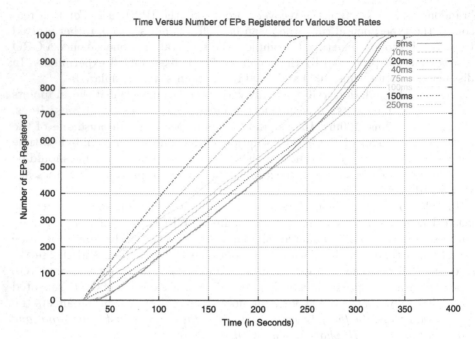

Fig. 5. Time to Register 1000 Endpoints

mean backoff values have an inflection point around 40 seconds before the first few endpoints could be registered. This suggests that the server was completely overwhelmed until after the RIP message processing has spaced out the requests. For example, it is likely that the GRQ messages were being dropped due to the limited length input queue on the server.

For the smallest mean backoff value of (5ms), the phones took a total of 338 seconds to register (in other words, system recovery time was 338 seconds), which is slightly better than the 360 seconds required for next higher backoff value (10ms). This counterintuitive effect had been observed in each of the experiments. With the extremely small backoff values, it is likely that many GRQ requests, which would otherwise force the server to process a RIP reply, got dropped at the server's input queue. In other words, the server itself served as a point where GRQs were throttled.

In the worst-case (10ms mean backoff), the phones required 360 seconds to register. The best-case (150ms mean backoff) required only 247 seconds. Setting the Local Random Backoff rate to 150 seconds, the registration time could be reduced by 113 seconds from the worst case. *The proposed technique, for these sets of parameters, resulted in decreasing the recovery time (MTTR) by more than 30%.*

Effect of Rate Limiting. Figure 6 shows the effect of rate limiting at the WAN router. Rate limiting was only effective in certain situation. For example,

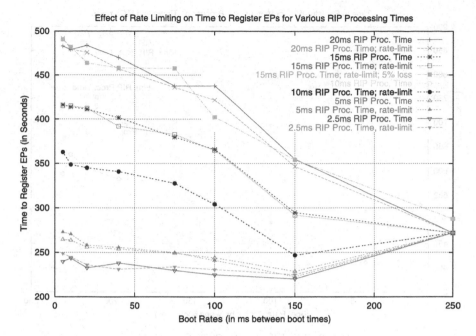

Fig. 6. Effect of Rate Limiting

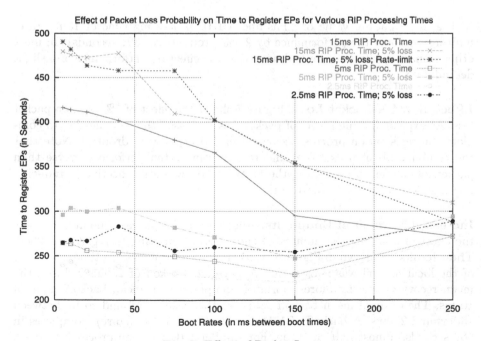

Fig. 7. Effect of Packet Loss

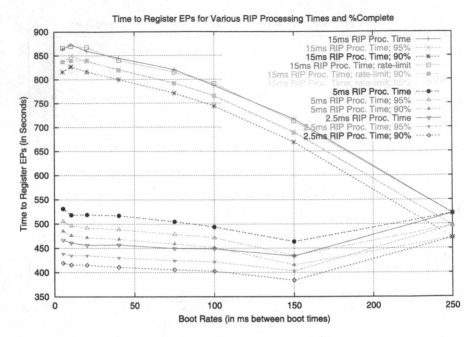

Fig. 8. Tail-Effect with 2000 Endpoints

with a mean backoff value of 40ms and a RIP processing time of 15ms, rate-limiting improves the performance by 2.5% (from 401 to 391 seconds). In most other scenarios, rate-limiting had no noticeable effect on performance or a slight degradation.

Effect of WAN Packet Loss. Figure 7 shows the effect of 5% random packet loss. As expected, a high level of packet loss increased the time needed to complete the registration process because useful packets were dropped. Note that the combination of packet loss and rate-limiting often performed worse than packet loss alone. In each case, the local backoff was still effective in reducing the completion time compared to the best-effort case.

Increased Number of Endpoints. Another set of runs was simulated to show the effect of doubling the number of endpoints attempting to register to 2000. These results are shown in Figure 8. With a 15ms RIP processing time, the effect of the local backoff was substantial. An average backoff of 250ms reduced the mean recovery time by more than 40% compared to a mean backoff value of 10 ms. The optimal mean backoff value, in this case was found to be between 150ms and 250ms. A backoff of 175ms (not shown in the figure), completes in 462 seconds, almost half the time. For smaller RIP message processing times, the local backoff may improve the registration time, but not as significantly as with the larger RIP message processing time.

6   Conclusions

In this paper, we dealt with a specific problem in a VoIP system, that of registration floods, which causes the IP phones to take longer to recover resulting in lower availability of the system. We proposed an endpoint based technique to alleviate the flood problem thereby increasing availability. We also compared the effectiveness of the proposed technique with existing techniques which are either network centric or server centric. For the example set of parameters, substantial reduction in recovery time of the system (30%-50%) was observed even when the existing techniques are used.

References

1. Packet Based Multimedia Communication Systems, *ITU-T Recommendation H.323*,1998.
2. W. Cheswick, S. Bellovin, A. Rubin, "Firewalls and Internet Security: Repelling the wily Hacker", Second Edition, Addison-Wesley, 2005.
3. Call signalling protocols and media stream packetization for packet-based multimedia communication systems *ITU-T Recommendation H.225.0*, 1998.
4. Understanding H.323 gatekeepers, Cisco document ID 5244, http://www.cisco.com/warp/public/788/voip/understand-gatekeepers.html, 2005.
5. Takagi, H. and L Kleinrock, "Throughput Analysis for Persistent CSMA Systems", IEEE Transactions on Communications, Vol. COM-33, No. 7, pp. 627-638, July 1985.
6. F. Tobagi and V. Hunt, "Performance Analysis of Carrier Sense Multiple Access with Collision Detection," Computer Networks, Vol. 4, pp. 245- 259, 1980.
7. http://standards.ieee.org/getieee802/802.3.html
8. L. Kleinrock and F. Tobagi, Packet Switching in Radio Channels, Part 11, IEEE Transactzons on Communications, Vol. COM-23, No. 12, pp. 1400-1433, 1975.
9. 1. S. Garg, M. Kappes, "Can I add a VoIP Call?" In Proc. of International Conference on Communications (ICC 2003), Anchorage, Alaska, May 11-15, 2003.
10. Radhika R. Roy, "Distributed Gatekeeper Architecture for H.323-Based Multimedia Telephony," 24th Annual IEEE International Conference on Local Computer Networks (LCN'99), 1999.
11. Control Protocol for Multimedia Communication Systems, *ITU-T Recommendation H.245*, 1998.

Hardware Instruction Counting for Log-Based Rollback Recovery on x86-Family Processors

Daniel Stodden, Hubert Eichner, Max Walter, and Carsten Trinitis

Technische Universität München
{stodden, eichnerh, walterm, trinitic}@cs.tum.edu

Abstract. Log-based recovery protocols enable process replicas in distributed systems to replay a computation up to the point where a previous computation failed. One fundamental assumption underlying these protocols is the piecewise deterministic (PWD) execution model, stating that recovery must not execute, but simulate the execution of nondeterministic events in order to maintain consistency.

One such source of nondeterminism are asynchronous events triggering software signal handlers, an issue known to be solved by instruction counters. Efficient implementations in software have been shown to be practical, but require significant changes to applications and system software. Hardware counters, in contrast, allow running software unmodified. A number of processors implementing the Intel x86 instruction set architecture provide monitoring registers with properties similar to a true instruction counter.

Designed for application profiling, these facilities reveal a number issues to be resolved when utilized for applications like the PWD model, which demands for a maximum in precision during replay. We discuss some of the most prominent problems faced when using performance counters for protocols satisfying the PWD model. We present additional hardware mechanisms, eliminating inconsistencies in counter interrupt delivery, based on standard processor debugging facilities, and at the expense of a small number of additionally generated exceptions.

1 Introduction

1.1 Log-Based Rollback Recovery

Rollback recovery protocols [1] in distributed systems use checkpointing at regular intervals, replaying process execution on backup systems from the last available checkpoint and beyond the point where a failure occurred. If implemented transparently, these techniques supplement fault tolerance for applications running otherwise unaltered, saving costly intervention through an application programmer.

Enforcing an execution model satisfying the *piecewise deterministic* (PWD) assumption [1][2], processes can be actively replicated. Assuming execution can be monitored in a way that any nondeterministic event occurring during process execution will be identified, recovery of a computational state before a failure

D. Penkler, M. Reitenspiess, and F. Tam (Eds.): ISAS 2006, LNCS 4328, pp. 106–119, 2006.

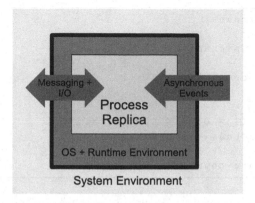

Fig. 1. Process replica interacting with a nondeterministic environment

is achieved by *replaying* original events based upon the results of a primary computation. This procedure limits the amount of communication required to achieve consistency to a set of *determinants* [1], comprising the information necessary for replay of nondeterministic events. *Log-based* rollback recovery is a conceptual subclass of rollback recovery, where the log comprises such a sequence of determinants [1].

Managing Nondeterminism. Figure 1 depicts the conceptual model a single process replica interacting with an initially nondeterministic environment. There are essentially two sources of nondeterminism during program execution:

Nondeterministic instructions. Nondeterministic instructions are a subset of those instructions interacting with a system's environment. Their effect on computational state may vary with differing environment state due to different result values.

Asynchronous event handling. Software signal handling enables variable interleaving of memory accesses. This is due to threads being interrupted for asynchronous execution of a respective event handler.

Depending on the system layer on which code subject to replay is operating on, nondeterministic instructions are typically system calls (calling an operating system), hypercalls [3] (calling a virtual machine monitor) or I/O instructions (interacting with devices).

In general, the precise mechanism chosen depends on the layer upon which a respective recovery protocol is implemented [4][1]. For the purpose of this paper, it will be sufficient to consider a single process on top of a commodity operating system environment.

Nondeterminisms through asynchronous events are ultimately due to hardware interrupts delivered to a processor. In multitasking operating systems, interrupt delivery drives preemptive thread scheduling, and thereby ultimately determines the timing of any asynchronous inter-process communications [5].

```
 1    int count;
 2
 3    void sighandler()
 4    {
 5        count = count * 2;
 6    }
 7
 8    for (i = 0; i < 100000; ++i)
 9        count = count + 1;
10
11    return count;
```

Fig. 2. A simple example program sensitive to asynchronous events. A transition induced by the signal handler will depend on global state. For several instances of the same program, process state will diverge if signal delivery is not virtually synchronized among replicas.

As a result, asynchronous event sources in a processor's hardware environment entail nondeterminism at any considerable software layer, unless precise replay is enforced through some software mechanism. Figure 2 shows a simple program whose state and ultimate result would be immediately affected by a signal handler triggered through an asynchronous event.

Accomplishing deterministic timing for signal delivery implies delivery on each replica precisely after a common number of state transitions. An appropriate mechanism may count any event which can be precisely mapped to a point in the progression of computational state during process execution. Both the event occurrence and the state where it needs to be delivered are then added to the log, and need to be replayed during recovery.

Counting Instructions. One mechanism eliminating nondeterminism occurring due to asynchronous events are hardware instruction counters [6]. Since transitions in computational state are – assuming proper isolation – immediately bound to instruction execution, there is an unambiguous mapping from the number of instructions executed to a corresponding process state reached [1]. Implemented as a hardware register, interrupt generation upon a desired number of instructions can be implemented as well [6].

A large number of publications have called for instruction counter registers for debugging and profiling purposes [7]. For the purpose of this document, we focus on instruction counting as a means for tracing and replaying process state transitions in order to implement log-based rollback recovery in fault-tolerant, distributed systems.

1.2   Related Work

A survey covering the subject of rollback-recovery in message-passing systems is given by Elnozahy et al. in [1].

One protocol eliminating nondeterminism of software signal delivery has been developed by Bressoud and Schneider [2]. The protocol implements a fault-tolerant virtual execution environment for two or more instances of a guest operating system, one *primary* and one or more *backups*, each running on top of a virtual machine monitor (VMM) in a *distributed* fashion, i.e. on separate processors with a standard network interconnect. Implementing a system VM [4], the VMM receives hardware interrupts and deliver signals to guest operating systems in a replayable manner. Since

- signal delivery to a hosted system is backed by software, and
- progress of virtual machine execution is controlled by the VMM

a VMM is enabled to delay signal delivery to any point during guest execution, assuming the necessary instrumentation is available.

With respect to asynchronous event handling, the protocol operates roughly as follows:

- Subdivide execution of the guest system into *epochs* comprising a defined number of instructions to execute.

  Execution of an epoch at the backup system is delayed by one epoch with regard to execution on the primary, i.e. while a primary executes an epoch E_{n+1}, a backup executes epoch E_n based upon determinants received from the primary system.
- At the primary processor, signals for a guest system occurring during an epoch E_n are locally buffered and logged through message passing to the backup system.
- During execution of epoch E_n at the backup processor, locally occurring signals for a virtual machine are silently ignored. Messages received from the primary, logging execution of E_{n+1}, are buffered.
- Upon termination of any epoch E_n, at equal computational state, both primary and backup system deliver the buffered set of signals during that epoch.

Note that this protocol employs instruction counting satisfying *preemption* in the same sense an operating system scheduler is driven by timer intervals, i.e. there are upper and lower bounds on the time spent in process execution until a given number of events has occurred. This is to make epoch lengths selected by instruction count approximately equal in time span. In fact, the epoch length is subsequently tuned to optimize system performance with varying I/O loads. Furthermore, epoch lengths define the timeout interval for detecting failure of the primary [2].

The protocol above has been implemented with hardware instruction counting support in the form of a *Recovery Register* on Hewlett Packard Precision Architecture (PA-RISC) processors.

Mellor-Crummey and LeBlanc demonstrated that instruction counters can be implemented in software as well [7]. Efficiency is maintained by taking advantage of the fact that any computational state can be identified solely by the number of backward branch instructions performed. However, such an approach still requires code instrumentation and therefore fails if recompilation or binary translation cannot be applied. Slye and Elnozahy have shown that the approach can be applied to replay multithreaded applications by tracking timer signals driving scheduler decisions [5].

2   Setting Epoch Boundaries on x86-Family Processors

2.1   IA32 and x86-64 Performance Monitoring

Modern x86-family processors often support a number of event counter registers. Designed for monitoring system events and code optimization, the IA32 *Performance Counters* [8] implement a flexible means for counting events during regular process execution, relevant to users wishing to optimize code efficiency, i.e. system and compiler performance. Counting is non-invasive, i.e. event sampling does not affect regular program execution, and does not require code instrumentation or statistical sampling as employed by many profiling applications, e.g. the UNIX *prof* or *gprof* utilities [9]. Consequently, low run time performance penalty is induced by their use [10].

In contrast to the ISA (Instruction Set Architecture) they implement, modern microarchitectures for IA32 are typically not CISC-machines, but implemented as RISC cores, executing so-called micro-ops (μOps), embedded into an IA32 decoder front-end. This affects performance counters in a way that they typically select from a number of event classes at the microarchitectural level, as opposed to the processor model system software was compiled for.

Processor microarchitectures tend to evolve over time. Their design and implementation is subject solely to vendor decisions. Therefore, event selectors mostly feature vendor-specific event types, spanning a given set of functional units. Examples are MMU operation, multi-level caching or μOp processing for integer and floating-point operations [8].

Processor support currently comprises the following:

- P4: Intel Pentium 4 and Xeon (Intel Netburst Architecture)
- P6, e.g. Intel Pentium Pro and later, most prominently including current Pentium M processors.
- K7: AMD Athlon, Athlon 64 and Opteron Processor (K8) families

Performance monitoring is a model-specific processor facility, although operating roughly equivalent across different microarchitectures. Architectures supporting monitoring extensions implement them through a set of model-specific registers (MSR) which are accessible exclusively to system software operating at instruction privilege level of 0 (i.e., the kernel). A *Performance Monitoring Counter* (PMC) is a register which can be preset to a desired value by system software. It is incremented by one on each monitored event once it occurs. PMCs on 32-bit Intel systems are typically limited to a range of 40 significant bits [8], AMD64 processor families implement 48 bits [11].

Event selection for each register is controlled through a set of one or more associated control registers. On Intel Pentium 4 and Xeon Processors, an ESCR (*Event Selection Control Register*) configures event filtering for a PMC, while an additional CCCR (*Counter Configuration and Control Register*) controls counter operation, e.g. the instruction privilege level to which counting shall be limited (i.e. user space versus kernel space instructions). P6-based architectures limit PMC control to one single *Event Selection* Register per PMC, although one serving very similar purposes [8][12].

Counting *Instruction Retirements*[1] at the comparatively coarse-grained level of ISA instructions[2] is featured by any of these processor architectures. Furthermore, PMC control registers include the ability to request interrupt generation upon counter overflow [8][11].

Programming performance monitoring counters counting instruction retirements can then be implemented by system software, operating with kernel privileges, as follows:

1. Choose a PMC capable of counting instruction retirement and program requisite control registers to select retirement events accordingly. More precisely: for the purpose given, event selection is typically adjusted to solely count non-bogus instructions at a lower privilege level (CPL 1-3).

2. At the beginning of each epoch, initialize the counter with a negative value $-\texttt{interval}$, designating the desired number of instructions to perform.

3. Adjust the counter control register to generate an interrupt upon counter overflow.

4. Upon return to user context, the processor starts process execution, thereby counting instructions up to the point where the counter register in question wraps to zero. The generated PMI (*Performance Monitoring Interrupt*) will be delivered through a built-in local APIC (*Advanced programmable interrupt controller* [8]), directable to either a separate interrupt vector or signaled as a system management (SMI) or non-maskable interrupt (NMI).

---

[1] The term *retirement* applies to instructions executed and ultimately committed to architectural state [13][14]. The distinction from other types of instructions becomes necessary in microarchitectures performing speculative and out-of-order execution in order to improve overall processor performance. Intuitively, it corresponds to those instructions "actually executed" (*non-bogus*) from the perspective of a system programmer following program flow in a debugger.

[2] The question arises, whether counting e.g. μOp retirements represents a viable alternative to ISA instructions. As noted above, a RISC core embedded in modern IA32 architectures is a vendor-specific entity, as is the core instruction set and a corresponding front-end instruction decoder. Hence, counting at the μOp-layer would limit any composition of primary and backup processors to matching microarchitectures (and microcode revisions). Generally, less stringent requirements regarding the mixture of processor architectures are generally more flexible, and therefore more desirable. Further discussion will therefore stay limited to ISA instruction retirement exclusively.

2.2   A Testbed for Retirement-Driven Preemption

As outlined above, each of the above-mentioned architectures needs a model-specific driver to control program execution.

As an example, the Intel Pentium 4 processor family introduced a complete redesign of prior monitoring facilities, considerably different from its predecessor P6.

Performance monitoring on AMD Athlon and AMD64-Architectures was functionally derived from P6. However, MSR and event assignments differ. AMD architectures offer 4 separate PMCs [11], whereas the P6 architecture is limited to 2 PMCs. Pentium 4 systems feature 6 MSRs for *at-retirement* counting [8] of execution events.

Furthermore, there are differences in counter progression under certain conditions, as further discussed below, all of which need to be accounted for on a per-model basis.

Our experimental implementation of epoch boundaries for Intel architecture instruction counters is currently developed as a set of run-time loadable kernel modules for the Linux 2.6 kernel series. Consequently, sampled instruction streams are user space processes.

We focus on supervised process execution in time-slices defined by an alterable number of processor instruction retirements. Note that any regular, timer-driven preemption by an operating system scheduler remains unaffected by this procedure and continues to operate as it used to. We are using the *Kprobes* [15] facility included with recent Linux 2.6 kernels in order to interact with critical procedures executed during regular kernel operation, most notably task state switching and some additional points in the start and completion phases of process management.

Our module provides execution of arbitrary programs in one of two modes:

Trace. *Trace* mode corresponds to execution of the primary instance in a fault-tolerant execution environment.

Tracing implies running and interrupting processes in regular intervals, up to the point of regular program termination. At each point of interruption, process state information is saved to an in-memory database. This information comprises at least monitored retirement, i.e. performance counter values, as well as register file contents, foremost including the instruction pointer value marking the given point of preemption in program code.

The resulting trace file can be memory-mapped by utility software and, upon completion, stored to disk, either for analysis or later restoration for *Replay* mode, which operates as described below.

Replay. Like with tracing and trace file generation, *replay* mode executes processes in the same sequence of epochs. Replaying, however, corresponds to the mode of operation a backup system in a fault-tolerant execution environment would conduct.

Seeking replay consistency, each point of interruption during replay must consequently match the interruption point (and thereby computational state) exactly as experienced during the original execution in trace mode.

Note that, since we are focusing on the subject of signal replay in log-based recovery, we make no attempt yet at eliminating instruction-level nondeterminism, e.g. tracing and replaying system calls. Hence, replay consistency depends on user space code carefully crafted to avoid any opportunity for state transitions not exactly matching the transition sequence underlying the original trace file.

Our experiments are based upon the following test programs:

- A short x86-assembly program, performing a simple loop with a fixed number of iterations.
- A version of the Ackermann-Function written in assembly.

In order to avoid any potential source of instruction-level nondeterminism, programs were built standalone, i.e. without any references to the C runtime libraries or the support code usually added by compilers.

2.3   Compensating Interrupt Latencies

Fully consistent with some predictions which can be drawn from [8], the results of implementing retirement-driven preemption as outlined above seem, at first sight, discouraging. The reason is that, due to latencies between event generation and actual suspension of process execution through interrupt delivery, the point of interruption does not follow the point of counter overflow precisely. As a consequence, execution progress tends to exceed the targeted number of instruction retirements. For the purpose of this document, we refer to this effect as *interrupt lag*.

Interrupt lag can be determined precisely from PMI service routines through simple inspection of counter values. While execution continues for a number of additional instructions before entering the interrupt handler, so does retirement event generation and counter propagation.

While the amount of lag for a given epoch is neither constant nor predictable, it is just due to latencies at the microarchitectural level [8]. It is therefore fair to assume that the number of instructions executed beyond counter overflow is limited by some upper bound. On the other hand, the maximum amount of lag to be tolerated is not documented and therefore has to be derived from observation. Lag boundaries we experienced so far are listed in table 1, e.g. for a Pentium M at 1700 MHz, a model-specific upper bound max_lag of up to 84 instructions has been observed[3].

Interrupt lag adds imprecision to the exact position of a computational state at which an epoch boundary can be inserted. However, we note that this amount of imprecision does not disqualify its usability for the type of applications we are seeking. Assuming the ability for a precise replay on a backup system remains unconstrained, eventual extension of an epoch length by numbers of additional retirements as small as the ones experienced so far is perfectly negligible.

---

[3] We assume these values will differ with individual processor models and steppings (revisions) (as shown in Column 3 of table 1). They may be subject to future refinement.

Table 1. Interrupt lag experienced for some x86 processor models

Model	Processor	Fam./Mod./Step.	max_lag
P6	Intel Pentium M @ 1700 MHz	6/9/5	84
Pentium 4	Intel Pentium 4 @ 2400 MHz	15/2/5	49
K7	AMD Athlon @ 1200 MHz	6/4/2	98

Tuning counter adjustments. We propose a considerably simple procedure based on the processor's standard debugging facilities to correct impending offsets between the amount of instructions executed on a primary and the amount actually replayed on a backup.

In our scheme, the primary dictates the number of instructions to be executed in epoch E_n as the number $\texttt{interval}_P$ of instructions targeted, plus the amount of lag $\texttt{lag}_{P,n} \in [0; \texttt{max\_lag}]$ experienced at the actual preemption point terminating that epoch. As a result, the number $\texttt{retired}_n$ of instructions to be retired in E_n will fall within a fixed range as follows:

$$\texttt{retired}_n = \texttt{interval}_P + \texttt{lag}_{P,n} \in [\texttt{interval}_P; \texttt{interval}_P + \texttt{max\_lag}] \quad (1)$$

Assuming, the amount of lag actually occurring as being arbitrarily distributed[4], the number of instructions retired on the backup for the same counter adjustment $\texttt{interval}_P$ may differ from $\texttt{retired}_n$. For our purposes, two cases need to be distinguished:

$\texttt{max\_lag} \geq \texttt{lag}_{P,n} - \texttt{lag}_{B,n} \geq 0$ A backup interrupts a replayed process up to $\texttt{max\_lag}$ instructions *before* $\texttt{retired}_n$, if $\texttt{lag}_{B,n} < \texttt{lag}_{P,n}$.
Hence, the backup preempts the process earlier within the executed sequence of instructions. For the purpose of the following discussion, we refer to such differences in the resulting preemption points as backup *overpreemption*.

$-\texttt{max\_lag} \leq \texttt{lag}_{P,n} - \texttt{lag}_{B,n} < 0$ A backup interrupts a replayed process up to $\texttt{max\_lag}$ instructions *after* the primary, if $\texttt{lag}_{B,n} > \texttt{lag}_{P,n}$.
We refer to this case as backup *underpreemption*.

The latter case of underpreemption must be avoided under all circumstances, since underpreemption implies a progression of state transitions on the backup system beyond the one dictated by the primary. Since there is no rollback mechanism available to revert these instructions, a fully deterministic replay of events would fail irreversibly at this point.

Given upper and lower bounds in interrupt offsets as $[-\texttt{max\_lag}; \texttt{max\_lag}]$, reliable avoidance of underpreemption can easily be implemented by adjusting the initial counter value, per epoch, on a backup accordingly:

$$\texttt{interval}_{B,n} = \texttt{interval}_P + \texttt{lag}_{P,n} - \texttt{max\_lag} \quad (2)$$

---

[4] For loop constructs, executing certain blocks of code a significant number of times, a tendency to finally deliver counter overflow repeatedly at one and the same position, e.g. following a branch instruction, can be observed. As a result, equal distribution may not even be the case. This may in fact turn out as an opportunity for optimizations, although one which has not been explored yet.

While this approach provokes permanent overpreemption, and thereby makes the computationally cheap, "coincidentally" immediate match in actual retirement counts highly improbable in practice, we assume this is the only option available to reliably eliminate replay failures due to underpreemption on a backup instance.

Dealing with overpreemption. Given some amount of overpreemption, backup systems are left at a state preceding the one dictated by the primary. They need to execute $\text{lag}_{P,n} - \text{lag}_{B,n}$ additional instructions, up to the point where a pending retirement offset and thereby impending differences in computational state drop to zero. We refer to this transient state of monitored process execution as a *catchup phase*.

The determinant gathered from the primary computation essentially consists of the following parameters:

- The number retired_n of instructions to be retired in E_n.
- The program counter PC_n, marking the point of termination of E_n.

Different approaches can be chosen in order to accomplish a catchup phase. The latter value can be used simplify monitoring process execution during catchup significantly.

Supported by virtually all processor architectures are standard debugging facilities, one of which resuming execution in single-step mode, provided for program debugging[5]. The approach is comparatively inefficient, since it implies a switch to a debug exception service routine on every single instruction to be executed within the given retirement offset.

Another approach is insertion of a breakpoint instruction [8] at the targeted code position PC_n. An advantage of this method over single stepping is that the catchup phase is interrupted only at code positions matching the targeted computational state. A second advantage is that it does not require allocation of debug registers, which are possibly subject to acquisition by user code.

The downside is that, given any number of instructions large enough to step across a branch, the need to repeatedly execute the original breakpoint position may arise before the epoch boundary has been reached. In that case, the original instruction would have to either be prematurely restored, executed, and immediately overwritten again, or to be interpreted. Both approaches are comparatively time-consuming.n

The most straightforward alternative, and the one currently employed by our prototype, is utilization of breakpoint registers. Both 32- and 64-Bit x86-families support up to 4 address-match breakpoint conditions [8]. Like breakpoint instructions, this narrows the amount of additional process interruptions

---

[5] Performance monitoring in Pentium 4 and Xeon processors provides a similar facility, by setting a control flag for the respective PMC, forcing interrupt generation not only on overflow but any counter increment. This facilitates improved reporting precision, but otherwise remains equivalent to single stepping, degrading performance to a fraction of normal execution.

to breakpoints at the targeted code position. The downside is that a debug register needs to be allocated. Whether this disqualifies the approach may depend on the amount of transparency desired for a given application.

The catchup phase during replay then operates as follows:

1. Set an execution breakpoint on the targeted program counter PC_n.
2. Continue program execution until the anticipated breakpoint exception occurs.
3. Compare the counter value read from the local PMC to the number of instructions dictated by the primary.
   If the program location PC_n is part of a loop construct, the numbers may differ (with a counter reading less than $retired_n$). In that case, return to step 2. Otherwise, if the numbers match, the targeted program state is known to be found.

2.4 Further Implications of PMI Lag

While we have shown so far that the implied imprecision can be solved at the arithmetic level, we should point out that there are additional side effects implied, which need to be addressed when implementing recovery protocols like the ones described above. Monitoring software will typically run in supervisor mode (CPL 0). Event filtering will exclude instructions executed at that level, in order to not let the execution of runtime system and monitoring software interfere with event counting.

However, virtually any system will provide entry points (*gates*) between application code monitored and system code implementing the runtime environment. In context of a customary operating system, these entries are system calls and exception handlers, both of which in turn again can be suspended by hardware interrupts, including a PMI signaling counter overflow.

As a consequence, conditions like the following can occur: application code may perform an entry to supervisor mode just after counter overflow, but before the point of interruption, into a processing context not subject to replica monitoring. It is therefore not suitable to serve as an epoch boundary. The preferable boundary is the instruction preceding the original entry point, which reflects replica state as indicated by the current counter reading. However, without substantial, therefore undesirable changes to the existing operating environment, determination of that point from interrupt context turns out to be hard.

Again, we found that during the primary computation, these states can be recovered by using processor debug facilities:

1. Adjust the respective tasks debug registers to *single stepping* mode (as opposed to the breakpoint facilities employed above).
2. Continue execution of interrupt service routines from the given processing context.
3. After return from the original entry, the monitored process will fault to an additional debug exception, on the instruction boundary following the original entry point. This processing state can be safely chosen as the epoch boundary for any pending signal delivery.

Note that this exception occurs before, not after the first replica instruction following the entry point, and therefore does not need be accounted for in table 1.

3 Conclusion

We presented some methods for using available performance monitoring facilities as a replacement for a true instruction counter on a subset of currently available IA32-based platforms, suitable for log-based rollback recovery protocols. We are currently not aware of any other work, prior or ongoing, in that specific area.

We identified the problem of *interrupt lag* to be the most prominent issue in using hardware monitoring mechanisms to gain preemption points at the precision log-based rollback recovery demands for. We found overflow and subsequent process interruption suffers from nondeterministic, but nonetheless bounded delays.

We have shown that processor debugging facilities can provide effective means to solve these issues. Sections 2.3 and 2.4 both describe considerably simple algorithms for that purpose, which can be implemented with standard processor facilities available on virtually any implementation of 32- and 64-bit x86 architectures.

It must be noted that, due to additional hardware exceptions generated, these mechanisms add additional overhead not experienced with other processor designs, e.g. the PA-RISC platform employed by [2].

There may be a lesson to be learned here. Event counting at the granularity of process state transitions is confined to events at the target instruction set. Current x86 families of processors, in contrast, are not. Instead, event counting is mostly bound to a RISC-based processor core operating on a μOp layer, which in turn is largely beyond the degree of precision asked for. On the other hand, counting events at that level is not desirable. Even within the same processor model, across processor steppings the microarchitecture may become a source of nondeterminism practically impossible to handle.

Due to some design limitations with log file generation within our prototype, discussed in section 2.2, we have not made any attempts yet at replaying x86 code between different processor families. However, experience of interrupt lag turned out to be largely vendor-neutral one, which suggests that process replays with catchup phases as discussed in section 2.3 may be carried out across different microarchitectures as well, and efficiently.

4 Future Work

Regarding the state of our prototype implementation, a future revision will implement a determinant log based upon ring buffers, in order to eliminate present limitations in log file size and, consequently, process runtime. Executing trace and replay modes in parallel, more confidence in the applicability of a catchup phase as described in section 2.3 may be gained. Furthermore, this step will enable us to measure the performance implications of the proposed overpreemption approach with real-world applications.

The Intel architecture manual [8], as at the time of this writing, lists two conditions for the P6 architecture where instruction retirement counting suffers from undercount. These events are due to hardware interrupt delivery occurring in combination with specific instructions being in execution at that point, and therefore qualify as nondeterminism in counter propagation. AMD documentation for K7 models reveals similar opportunities for underpreemption [16], though ones which seem deterministic ones, i.e. not bound to asynchronous events.

Inspired by prior work in developing software counting mechanisms [7], hardware counting of taken branches instead of single instruction retirement may be an option. Branch counting has not been explored yet within our testbed. The approach seems promising since, judging from its nonappearance in processor errata [17] [16], it appears more robust against consistency hazards implied by nondeterministic counter inconsistencies, as outlined above.

References

1. Elnozahy, E.N.M., Alvisi, L., Wang, Y.M., Johnson, D.B.: A survey of rollback-recovery protocols in message-passing systems. ACM Comput. Surv. **34**(3) (2002) 375–408
2. Bressoud, T.C., Schneider, F.B.: Hypervisor-based fault tolerance. ACM Trans. Comput. Syst. **14**(1) (1996) 80–107
3. Barham, P., Dragovic, B., Fraser, K., HAND, S., Harris, T., Ho, A., Neugebauer, R., Pratt, I., Warfield, A.: Xen and the art of virtualization. In: SOSP '03: Proceedings of the nineteenth ACM symposium on Operating systems principles, New York, NY, USA, ACM Press (2003) 164–177
4. Smith, J.E., Nair, R.: Virtual Machines: Versatile Platforms for Systems and Processes. Morgan Kaufmann Publishers, San Francisco, CA, USA (2005)
5. Slye, J.H., Elnozahy, E.N.: Support for software interrupts in log-based rollback-recovery. IEEE Trans. Comput. **47**(10) (1998) 1113–1123
6. Cargill, T.A., Locanthi, B.N.: Cheap hardware support for software debugging and profiling. In: ASPLOS-II: Proceedings of the second international conference on Architectural support for programming languages and operating systems, Los Alamitos, CA, USA, IEEE Computer Society Press (1987) 82–83
7. Mellor-Crummey, J.M., LeBlanc, T.J.: A software instruction counter. In: ASPLOS-III: Proceedings of the third international conference on Architectural support for programming languages and operating systems, New York, NY, USA, ACM Press (1989) 78–86
8. Intel Corporation: IA-32 Intel Architecture Software Developer's Manual, Vol. 3: System Programming Guide. (2005) http://developer.intel.com/design/Pentium4/manuals/253668.htm.
9. Graham, S.L., Kessler, P.B., McKusick, M.K.: gprof: a Call Graph Execution Profiler. In: SIGPLAN Symposium on Compiler Construction. (1982) 120–126 http://citeseer.ist.psu.edu/graham82gprof.html.
10. Intel Software Network: Intel VTune Performance Analyzer. (2004) http://developer.intel.com.

11. Advanced Micro Devices: BIOS AND Kernel Developer's Guide for AMD Athlon 64 AND AMD Opteron Processors. (2005) http://www.amd.com/.
12. Intel Corporation: AMD64 Architecture Programmer's Manual. (2005) http://www.amd.com/.
13. Intel Corporation: IA-32 Intel Architecture Software Developer's Manual, Vol 1: Basic Architecture. (2005) http://developer.intel.com/design/Pentium4/manuals/253665.htm.
14. Hinton, G., Sager, D., Upton, M., Boggs, D., Karmean, D., Kyler, A., Roussel, P.: The Microarchitecture of the Pentium 4 Processor. Intel Technology Journal **Q1** (2001) http://www.intel.com/technology/itj/q12001/pdf/art_2.pdf.
15. Panchamukhi, P.: Kernel debugging with Kprobes. IBM developerWorks (2004) http://www-128.ibm.com/developerworks/library/l-kprobes.html.
16. Advanced Micro Devices: AMD Athlon Processor Model 10 Revision Guide. (2003) http://www.amd.com/.
17. Intel Corporation: Intel Pentium 4 Processor Specification Update. (2005) http://developer.intel.com/.

Improving Robustness Testing
of COTS OS Extensions*

Constantin Sârbu, Andréas Johansson, Falk Fraikin, and Neeraj Suri

Computer Science Department - Technische Universität Darmstadt,
Hochschulstr. 10, 64289 Darmstadt, Germany
{cs, aja, fraikin, suri}@informatik.tu-darmstadt.de
http://www.deeds.informatik.tu-darmstadt.de

Abstract. Operating systems (OS) are increasingly geared towards support of diverse peripheral components, both hardware (HW) and software (SW), rather than explicitly focused on increased reliability of delivered OS services. The interface between the OS and the HW devices is provided by device drivers. Furthermore, drivers have become add-on COTS components to support the OS's capabilities of widespread device support. Unfortunately, drivers constitute a major cause of system outages, impacting overall service reliability. Consequently, the testing of drivers becomes important. However, despite the efforts to develop appropriate testing methods, the multitude of possible system configurations and lack of detailed OS specifications makes the task difficult. Not requiring access to OS source code, this paper develops novel, non-intrusive support for test methods, based on ascertaining test progress from a driver's operational state model. This approach complements existing schemes, enhancing the level of accuracy of the test process by providing test location guidance.

Keywords: Software testing, robustness testing, COTS, operating system, device driver.

1 Introduction

Device drivers[1] are commonly written to provide OS support for new computer peripherals in an commercial environment where time-to-market and low cost are key aspects. However, producing high quality drivers typically requires deep knowledge and understanding of OS internals and a proper testing strategy. Unfortunately, the details of the intricate internal structure are not available for many COTS OSs. Deadline pressure also reduces the time allocated for testing, creating a need for systematic and effective testing strategies.

Drivers are software components typically running in privileged mode, i.e., within the operating system kernel. Most COTS operating systems available today run kernel-mode device drivers.

---

* This research has been supported, in part, by Microsoft Research, EU FP6 NoE ReSIST and EU FP6 IP DECOS.
[1] "Drivers" in Microsoft Windows, "modules" in Unix / Linux.

D. Penkler, M. Reitenspiess, and F. Tam (Eds.): ISAS 2006, LNCS 4328, pp. 120–139, 2006.

If something goes wrong with the driver and the OS kernel is not able to properly handle the exception situation, the error can propagate across the OS, causing instability and potentially crash the entire system. Also, if the driver is the recipient of a faulty command issued by the kernel (for instance, as a result of an application request), a driver with no (or improper) error handling capabilities can crash, reducing the system's ability to use the related piece of hardware. All the scenarios described above lead to reducing (or even refusing) the level of service provided by the system.

Assuming the monolithic architecture of current COTS OSs, drivers are difficult to test due to the complex OS kernel structures they deal with. During normal operation of an COTS OS, a large number of running processes can interact in unforeseeable ways, mainly due to the unpredictable set of active processes.

For instance, testing an operating system under different loads may lead to completely different results as the operational context is different each time. To ensure a controllable testing process and repeatability of experiments, we need an accurate definition of how the tested operating system performs under certain, reproducible conditions.

Our work represents an effort to capture the functional execution patterns of a COTS driver under test, despite the non-deterministic behavior that characterizes its observable activity. The presented approach is based on architectural specifications of the communication between OS kernel entities and drivers, as defined by the Windows Driver Model (referred throughout this paper as *WDM*) [1]. We considered the Microsoft Windows operating system drivers as a case study, but our approach is general enough to be applied to other COTS operating systems with minimal changes (i.e., no modifications are required to the OS kernel or drivers), as long as the specification of the communication interface between OS and the tested driver is available.

Overall, the approach entails developing and identifying a driver state model, and locating relevant test states. Moreover, in this paper we are not trying to identify proper test cases. Instead, we provide guidance for existing test methodologies to better localize the current execution of the driver under test and monitor test progress. Therein, the development of a non-source code based and reproducible driver robustness testing support represent the contributions of this paper.

The paper is organized as follows: Sect. 2 presents the robustness problem we intend to solve. Section 3 localizes our work in the related research context. Section 4 introduces our system model and Sect. 5 explains the technical background of the considered drivers. Section 6 describes our approach in detail while Sect. 7 discusses the proposed testing coverage metrics. Section 8 presents the experimental work and Sect. 9 discusses various aspects related to them. We summarize presenting conclusions and future work in Sect. 10.

2   The OS Robustness Problem Statement

Currently, OS kernels have reached a certain design maturity and are now diminishing as the main cause for system failures. With numerous hardware producers rapidly introducing new peripherals onto the market, many new drivers are developed and installed onto the OS every day. These constitute relatively "immature" software compared to the rest of the OS kernel. Therefore, many faults can be present in the driver source code. High defect density combined with the fact that, for instance in Linux, about 70% of the total of lines of code are driver code [2], indicate a high likelihood that a driver-related fault is the cause of the overall system failure.

Additionally, the set of loaded drivers is likely to be different across computer systems. This aspect limits testing's effectiveness, given the difficulty to ensure representativeness of the test setup (in the driver development stage).

Testing of a COTS component, such as a driver, can be performed in different phases, either by the *component-provider* in the design/development phase or by the *component-user* in the system implementation phase [3]. Test campaigns of the component-provider may require access to the component's source code, whereas the component-user is usually limited to a black-box testing approach. This paper focuses on the latter case, considering that the component-user (i.e., system designer) wants to assess (and later improve) the robustness of a given driver in the context of a known system, without having knowledge about its implementation details. The only information assumed available for the driver under test is the interaction with the OS kernel (see Sect. 4).

In this paper the source code is considered not accessible. Therefore, we use a black-box testing approach, meaning that the only available information is the binary, i.e., the executable form of the driver, and the OS ⇔ driver interface specification. As driver implementations vary considerably, the usage specification provided to the component-user along with the COTS driver is not required or used in the approach presented throughout this paper.

3   Related Work

Since the 1970s, the software testing research community has pursued determining the relative effectiveness between partition and random testing. Myers [4] considered random testing an inefficient method for finding faults. Later, Hamlet and Taylor [5] claimed that partition testing is successful "only when sub-domains with a high failure probability can be identified". In the early 1990s, Möller and Paulish [6] showed that software faults have a tendency to concentrate in certain parts of the code, so splitting the test inputs into sub-domains matching the most defective partitions of the code seems to be the right thing to do. Weyuker and Jeng proved analytically in [7] that partition testing effectiveness strongly depends on the failure rate associated with each sub-domain. If these failure rates can be obtained, partition testing can be very efficient in finding faults. Though, when testing is targeting COTS components (i.e., source code is not available) this task is non-trivial.

In this paper we present an empirical method to divide the operational behavior of a driver into partially overlapping sub-domains. The method attempts to solve the COTS component robustness problem and relies on the functional specifications of the driver (rather than the source code). The testing progress can be evaluated based on the operational behavior of the driver under test under an expected workload, as in [8].

A similar approach was proposed in [9]. The paper introduces a load testing technique called Deterministic Markov State Testing for describing the operational model of a telecommunication system. The incoming and completion of five types of telephone calls define the state of the system. However, as the work was driven by the necessity to test the given telecommunication system, detailed knowledge of the system internals was required. This obviously limits the usability of the method for a different black-box system. In contrast, our approach makes no assumptions about the driver under test.

In the area of OS error propagation profiling, Johansson et. al [10,11] used a different level of the OS ⇔ driver interface in their experiments (i.e., the specification of functions imported / exported by the targeted driver). In this paper we use a shared memory communication scheme used by the OS ⇔ driver interface as defined in Sect. 5. As the two methods are complementary, we intend to extend our approach in the future to include both of them.

4   System Model

Our system model is illustrated in Fig. 1. It describes the structure of a computer system equipped with a COTS OS acting both as a hardware resource manager and as an execution platform for applications. By *COTS OS* we mean any monolithic operating system, designed for general purpose and not for specialized needs (i.e., real-time, safety-critical or highly-available systems). We currently use Microsoft Windows XP as a case study, and extending this approach to other operating systems is part of our ongoing work.

The system model is divided into three layers: (a) user space, (b) OS kernel space and (c) hardware space. The two dashed lines represent communication interfaces between two neighboring layers. For instance, an application in user space might want to read the content of a file stored on the local hard-disk.

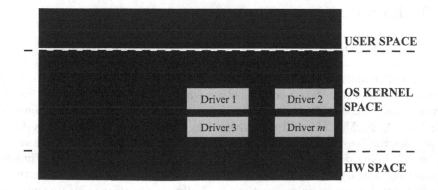

Fig. 1. A system featuring a COTS OS with m drivers

The request will be passed to the OS by means of standardized calling methods defined in the *System Services* layer. Further on, the command is handled by the *I/O Manager*, which will transform it into a command for one of the system's *device drivers*. In this specific example the command is passed to the driver associated with the local hard-disk. The driver will access the hard disk by instructing the reading heads to move to the proper position on the magnetic disk, will store read data in a memory buffer which will be made available to the application that initially issued the `read` request. Our focus is on the communication between the I/O Manager and the drivers.

We consider a driver as a collection of functions designed for controlling hardware. For Windows, drivers are implemented as Dynamic Link Libraries (.DLL or .SYS files). The files containing driver code, follow the Microsoft PE (Portable Executable) format and, therefore, publish a list of functions imported and/or exported from/to other libraries. The "import" list contains functions used by the driver, and the "exported" functions are entry points available to other software entities. We will refer to this level of interaction between drivers and OS as *software communication interface*. This functional behavior is captured in [10,11].

Another level of interaction between these two entities is the *WDM (Windows Driver Model) communication interface* and will be detailed further in Sect. 5.1. In short, this is a shared memory communication scheme. Two participants communicate with each other by accessing specialized shared data structures and by notifying their counterpart after operating changes to these structures.

A third communication scheme exists, in which the driver/OS kernel is responding to events generated by the hardware, however this is not addressed in this paper.

Alternatively, we consider that each request from the I/O Manager will trigger the execution of a piece of driver code associated with the request type. The execution is finished when the driver returns the request back to the I/O Manager, together with a result and a status flag. The driver is *processing* a given request if the request was received and not yet returned to the caller.

5   Technical Background

5.1   Windows Driver Model and WDM-Compliant Drivers

To standardize and simplify the OS ⇔ driver communication inside kernel space, Microsoft created a unified communication framework, called WDM (Windows Driver Model) [1]. WDM is a definition of the interface between the Windows OS kernel (NT4, 2k, Me, XP) and the drivers designed for these operating systems. It specifies the way that drivers are supposed to use certain structures inside the kernel, being developed mainly for forward-compatibility among Windows versions. By sharing this communication framework to the driver manufacturers, Microsoft establishes an unified method for building new drivers for its emerging OS versions. At the same time, WDM represents an attempt to standardize the

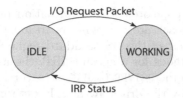

Fig. 2. Basic processing of a WDM-compliant driver

way drivers execute in privileged kernel space, without harming the functionality of the operating system.

A *WDM-compliant driver* has to follow certain rules for design, implementation, initialization, plug-and-play, power management, memory allocation etc. A benefit of this approach for driver developers is the feature-set partitioning that WDM brings to focus: the driver must implement several standard routines, the rest of the code being application dependent. This is not always beneficial from a robustness viewpoint, as programmers tend to reuse large pieces of code when building new drivers (assisted by modern programming languages and IDEs) for reducing development time. This practice typically creates residual functionality that is not present in the specifications, decreasing the coverage of existing testing techniques applied by the component-user (who does not have access to the source code and thus cannot measure code coverage).

After a WDM-compliant driver code is loaded into memory and all the kernel structures related to that driver are initialized, it is ready to accept commands. These commands are issued by the I/O Manager (see Fig. 1), as a result of an application request. Such commands are called *I/O Request Packets* (IRP) and are OS kernel structures which contains a request code and all the necessary parameters needed by the driver to service the particular IRP request.

The driver receives the request and, following its processing, a result of the operation is returned to the caller. This data flow is depicted in Fig. 2.

5.2   WDM Kernel Structures

There are three structures defined in the WDM guidelines which are important for our approach. These structures are DRIVER_OBJECT, IO_REQUEST_PACKET and IO_STACK_LOCATION.

The former one, DRIVER_OBJECT, contains pointers to dispatch functions inside the driver code, every function being responsible for dealing with a specific IRP command. The latter two structures contain standard parameters of the request (IO_REQUEST_PACKET) and additional fields for parameters, respectively.

IO_REQUEST_PACKET and IO_STACK_LOCATION are strongly related and, therefore, when using the term *IRP* we refer to both of them, jointly.

a) DRIVER_OBJECT: This is a structure used by the operating system for publishing relevant information about a driver. Each driver is associated with an instance of this structure when the driver code is loaded to the kernel's memory. After loading, a standard method of the driver is executed (*DriverInit*) and the structure is populated with information published by the driver. Relevant to our approach are the pointers to functions inside the driver's code for managing each of the OS standard requests (IRPs). If the driver does not provide methods for a specific IRP, the associated pointer is set to NULL. Looking into the DRIVER_OBJECT structure, one can find out which IRPs are supported by the driver by simply determining the value of the associated pointer.

b) IO_REQUEST_PACKET and IO_STACK_LOCATION: These structures represent the trigger that makes the driver change its runtime mode from IDLE to WORK-ING (Fig. 2) and back. The receipt of an IRP by a driver initiates execution of a specific functionality. Whenever the result of the execution is available, the driver returns the two structures to the originator, after filling them with the result and setting a status flag. The current WDM version defines 28 IRP types, each of them associated with a particular operation supported by the driver (e.g., CREATE, READ, WRITE or CLOSE).

6   State Space and Operational Profile

From a robustness testing perspective it is important to accurately pinpoint what the system under test is processing at any chosen time instance. Therefore, the software testing community identified an increased demand of proper methods to precisely define the "state" of the system under test. In the case of static (deterministic) systems this task is relatively simple but for operating systems this is non-trivial. OSs are complex and dynamic, and often perform in a non-deterministic manner, mainly as a result of user input. A complete definition of the state must include information related to (a) the values of all used variables and (b) the functionality currently in execution.

In this paper we consider the total *state space* of a driver being infinite, therefore testing all states is infeasible. However, a driver is a special software component and can only be utilized by the user applications in a restricted manner (defined by the WDM interface). This means that a workload applied to the driver produces a particular operational behavior which triggers visiting only a certain state space subset. In our work we refer to this subset of the state space as the *operational profile* of the driver. As long as the operational profile of a driver (related to a given workload) is known, we can concentrate the testing only to this subset of states. The main reason behind our approach is to avoid spending resources on testing functionalities that will likely not be exercised in the field. Consequently the testing effort is better focused on the more likely operational states.

Obviously, this approach can primarily be used in component-users' testing scenarios (i.e., testing campaigns performed by COTS driver users) when the set of applications exercising the driver can be precisely determined. For instance, our approach is particularly useful for testing embedded systems using COTS operating systems. In this type of environments, the set of applications and the way they use the driver under test can be precisely determined, leading to an accurate outline of the driver's operational profile.

Nevertheless, our approach can prove itself useful to component-providers, too. For instance, their testing can make use of different user profiles to define sets of applications and characterize independent operational profiles for later guidance of their testing methods.

6.1   Driver State in Our Approach

As we assume a black-box driver under test, we try to provide state identification methods only with regard to the accessible communication interface. To avoid confusion with "driver state", we use the term "driver mode" in this paper. The *driver mode* is defined at a specific instance in time, with respect to the IRP requests the driver is executing at that moment. Thus, we use the information provided by ongoing functionality for guiding focused and reproducible testing campaigns of a driver.

6.2   Driver Mode

The I/O Manager serializes the IRPs that need to be sent to a driver D though some can be concurrently processed by the target driver. Hence, D can start processing the next request(s) received from I/O Manager, before a result of the current operation is available. Therefore, we represent the *mode* of the driver as follows:

Definition 1. *The mode of a driver D is defined by a tuple of predicates, each assigned to one of the n IRPs that the driver supports:*

$$M_D : \quad < P_{IRP_1} \; P_{IRP_2} \; P_{IRP_3} \; .. \; P_{IRP_n} >,$$

where P_{IRP_i} $(1 \leq i \leq n)$ shows if the driver D is performing or not the functionality associated with IRP_i, as below:

$$P_{IRP_i} = \begin{cases} 1, & \text{if } \textbf{performing} \text{ the functionality triggered by } IRP_i \\ & \text{(the } IRP_i \text{ was received by the driver and the driver} \\ & \text{did not yet return a result to the caller)} \\ 0, & \text{otherwise} \end{cases}$$

At any instant in time, a driver can be processing multiple different IRPs. Therefore, we can build the complete set of tuples (as binary strings of length n) that represent all the different modes a driver can be in, the complete *state space* of the driver under test. Transitions between modes are triggered either by receipt of an IRP or by finishing the execution of an IRP.

6.3   Driver Modes and Transitions Between Modes

Let us consider a simple example of a driver supporting four different IRPs (Fig. 3), i.e., CREATE, READ, WRITE and CLOSE. After the driver is loaded, it will be in an IDLE mode (no IRP requests are currently processed), i.e., $< 0000 >$. The driver will stay in this mode as long as no IRP requests are issued. Let us assume that the driver receives a READ request. This request is associated with the second bit in the tuple, and therefore the driver switches to $< 0100 >$. We assume that the driver receives and finishes execution of the functionality associated with IRP requests in a sequential manner, i.e., only one bit from the bit string describing current mode can flip at a time. Therefore, from the mode $< 0100 >$ the driver can only switch to :

(a) $< 0000 > \rightarrow$ READ operation finished; driver returned to IDLE mode;
(b) $< 1100 >$ or $< 0110 >$ or $< 0101 >$ (any of the modes containing two set bits and having 1 on the second position) $\rightarrow$ READ operation not finished and another IRP was received.

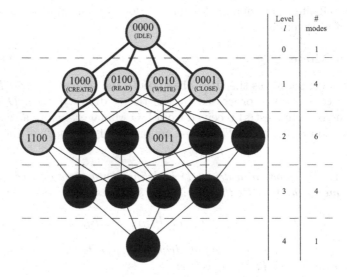

Fig. 3. The *state space* of a WDM-compliant driver in our model. The modes depicted in gray are the ones visited (using the bold edges) under a certain workload, so they represent the *operational profile* of the driver with respect to the given workload. Note: all lines represent bi-directional edges.

In our model, the size of the state space (the total number of modes) is $N = 2^n$, since a mode is defined as a binary string of length n. We represented the set of modes in a layered form (i.e., the modes represented by tuples containing l number of ones are on level l), having N_l modes on the l-th level, where

$$N_l = \binom{n}{l}, \; with \; 0 \leq l \leq n \tag{1}$$

The number of modes accessible from a current mode is restricted to a limited subset of modes. Assuming the IRPs are sent to a driver in a serialized manner, the driver can switch from a mode located on the level l to only few of the modes located on levels *immediately* above or below. More precisely, a driver can switch

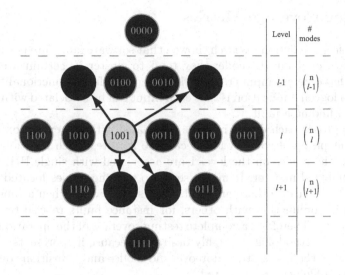

Fig. 4. A mode on level l ($< 1001 >$) can only switch to selected modes on level $l - 1$ or $l + 1$

from the current mode *only* to modes whose tuples are at the Hamming distance of 1.

This behavior is represented in Fig. 4. Supposing that the driver under test is currently in mode $< 1001 >$, on level l (in this example $l = 2$) it can switch only to the highlighted modes on the levels $l - 1$ and $l + 1$. These modes are $< 1000 >$, $< 0001 >$, $< 1101 >$ and $< 1011 >$. Observe the fact that these modes differ from the current mode only by a single digit.

Table 1. Number of transitions from a mode located on level l

Current mode on level l	Can *only* switch to:	
	Modes on upper level $(l \rightarrow l{-}1)$	Modes on lower level $(l \rightarrow l{+}1)$
0	0	n
1	1	n − 1
2	2	n − 2
⋮	⋮	⋮
l	l	$n - l$

The number of transitions from a l-level mode is given in Table 1. Since a transition implies changing one digit in the mode, there are n possible transitions from a mode located on every level l in the model. Therefore, the total number of transitions that need to be covered in our model is

$$T = n \cdot N = n \cdot 2^n \tag{2}$$

7   Testing Coverage Metrics

Software defect prediction research showed that software faults are not uniformly distributed throughout the code; they tend to cluster in certain areas [6,12]. Assuming that different inputs to the driver trigger different functionalities inside the driver, a logical implication is that each input can be associated with a certain likelihood of finding a fault.

In our approach each driver mode is associated with the execution of one or more disjoint pieces of code. A tester can use it to test each functionality separately (i.e., the modes on the level 1 are associated with single IRP requests) and in a combined manner. It makes sense to test the modes located on levels below 1 ($l \geq 2$) because there are faults that surface only when a functionality is executed in conjunction with others, for instance faults related to accessing shared resources. Therefore, a complete testing coverage of the operational profile defined by our methodology is highly desirable because it represents a quantifiable measure of the test status. Moreover, no modes and transitions outside the operational profile need to be tested.

As long as a driver is in a certain mode, it can only switch to a limited number of neighbors, located on the immediately upper and lower levels. A testing campaign aimed at transition coverage must exercise the entire set of transitions from a given mode, for all accessible modes. Ensuring traversal of all transitions in the operational profile can reveal errors that occur at entering or exiting a driver function. For instance, mode $< 1000 >$ in Fig. 3 can be visited even if the transition $< 0000 > \rightarrow < 1000 >$ was never traversed (i.e., only the path $< 0000 > \rightarrow < 0100 > \rightarrow < 1100 > \rightarrow < 1000 >$ was followed). Intuitively, this means that some of the transitions between modes might never be traversed, even if all the modes were visited, so *transition coverage* is more complete than *mode coverage* testing but is still not complete enough.

As drivers use memory to communicate and store variables while processing IRP-related functionalities, the sequence of IRP requests that put the driver in a certain mode is relevant for the testing process, too. In the example above, one should be aware of the fact that the two paths between $< 0000 >$ and $< 1000 >$ may lead the system to two different states (i.e., having different memory contents). Our method cannot capture the whole driver state (see Sect. 6), but is useful from a testing viewpoint because it can capture the effect of input sequences, i.e., ordering of requests. Knowing the paths between two modes (from inspecting the mode graph), a tester can develop test cases to traverse all of them to discover faults that occur as a result of certain input sequences. For instance, assuming the initial mode being the same, the sequence READ, CLOSE might work fine in contrast to the sequence CLOSE, READ that might yield an error.

For complete test coverage of our operational model, a testing process should ensure that (a) mode coverage, (b) transition coverage and (c) path coverage are satisfied at the same time [4].

7.1 Mode Coverage (MC)

Our approach improves the granularity of the testing process: the WORKING mode of a driver in Fig. 2 is split into several refined modes (see Fig. 3, all modes located on levels $l \neq 0$). Using our method, one can precisely pinpoint which functionality the driver is executing at a given instance, with regard to the received IRP requests. Moreover, the approach captures the concurrent execution of several requests, so a testing campaign can identify faults in procedures that only surface when the driver is executing them in conjunction with other procedures (modes on level 2 to n in Fig. 3).

If complete mode coverage is intended, a testing process can use a set of test cases which put the driver under test into every mode, thus implying that all the functionalities were executed at least once, separately *and* in conjunction with all other ones.

Definition 2. *A testing technique having 100% mode coverage (MC) ensures that every mode of the operational profile is tested.*

The mode coverage of a testing procedure can be quantified by relating the tested modes and the total number of nodes which form the operational profile, as defined below:

$$MC = \frac{|\text{tested modes} \cap \text{operational profile modes}|}{\# \text{ of operational profile modes}} \tag{3}$$

7.2 Transition Coverage (TC)

Since the state space is not large (WDM defines 28 distinct IRPs, see 5.2), covering all of it is feasible, given that a set of test cases capable of putting the driver into each mode can be devised. However, the mode coverage metric only ensures the execution of IRP-related functionalities, in all possible combinations, without considering the ways a driver can leave the current mode. Therefore, we need a more comprehensive coverage metric and we can use the concept of transition coverage.

Definition 3. *A testing technique with 100% transition coverage (TC) ensures that for each mode which belong to the operational profile all outgoing transitions (traversed under given workload) are tested.*

$$TC = \frac{|\text{tested transitions} \cap \text{operational profile transitions}|}{\# \text{ of operational profile transitions}} \tag{4}$$

Satisfying complete transition coverage requires a larger number of test cases than mode coverage, but it is a better measure of testing completeness and it implies also 100% mode coverage.

7.3   Path Coverage (PC)

The concept of path is used in our approach to express a sequence of IRP requests that lead the driver under test from an initial mode to another. For instance, in Fig. 3 are two 2-hop paths from mode $< 1000 >$ to $< 1110 >$ (an infinite number if we consider cycles and multi-hop paths):

1. $< 1000 > \rightarrow < 1100 > \rightarrow < 1110 >$;
2. $< 1000 > \rightarrow < 1010 > \rightarrow < 1110 >$.

Definition 4. *Path Coverage (PC) denotes traversing all the paths between two different modes of the operational profile, over any number of hops.*

We consider that the number of paths in our model is infinite, but one can use path coverage to compare the influence of following two different paths between two modes, assuming that the parameters which are different can be captured. For instance, if a value at a memory location associated with the tested driver is different for the two paths, this might be an indication of a fault.

Our approach can be used for pinpointing the execution behavior of a driver, combined with other tools for monitoring other parameters of the runtime environment. Together, they can provide insightful information, helpful for debugging or robustness evaluation of different drivers.

8   The Serial Driver - A Case Study

To validate the presented approach, we have conducted experiments to monitor the flow of IRP requests sent to a targeted driver. We determined the relative size of the operational profile in contrast with the complete state space of the driver.

We considered the serial driver provided together with Windows XP Professional SP2 operating system. The file containing the executable code of the driver was `serial.sys`, version 5.1.2600.2180. As an indication that it successfully passed Microsoft's quality tests, the driver was digitally signed by Microsoft. The tests used to test the driver are available in the HCT (Hardware Compatibility Tests) and in the DDK (Driver Development Kit) and include reliability and stress tests.

For our experiments we utilized two Pentium4(HT)@2.80Ghz machines with 1Gb of RAM and an 56k external serial modem (Devolo Microlink 56k Fun II). To monitor the IRP request flow we used `IrpTracker.exe v2.1`, a free tool from Open Systems Resources Inc. This tool is capable of logging all the communication that takes place at the targeted driver interface. Both the receipt of an IRP and the return of the completed IRP to the originator are logged.

The experimental setup is depicted in Fig. 5. For each of the two experiments we present in this paper, a different application was used to generate relevant workload for the targeted driver. The workload generates IRP requests (via the I/O Manager) that triggers mode switches of the driver. We assume the driver is already installed in the OS kernel and initialized, so each experiment started

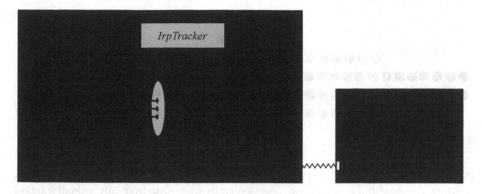

Fig. 5. The experimental setup. The workload application exercises the serial driver (via I/O Manager) by communicating data through the serial port to a second party. IRP requests are captured and logged by `IrpTracker`.

with the driver in *idle mode*. After the IRP requests were captured and saved, the log files were sequentially parsed and processed and mode graphs similar to the ones presented in Sect. 6.3 were built.

8.1   Experiment 1 - Modem Diagnostic Driver-Usage Pattern

In this experiment we used an external modem, connected to the serial port. As workload we used `ModemTest v1.3`, a diagnostic test from PassMark Software. `ModemTest` sends data packets which are echoed back by the modem. Before sending any data, `ModemTest` first checks the serial port settings and then the modem itself. Any data received is verified to ensure its completeness and correctness. We have chosen this diagnostic tool to generate workload which is representative for modems and thus for serial port usage. At the same time, we used the diagnostic tool as it generates a repeatable workload, which was one of the requirements in order to ensure the repeatability among different runs of the same experiment.

The observed behavior of the serial driver under this workload is represented by the mode graph in Fig. 6. For readability reasons, only the transitions between visited modes were depicted. Details can be observed in Fig. 7, which shows only the operational profile (visited nodes and traversed transitions).

The experiment issued a total of 186 IRP requests (issued and returned) using 7 distinct IRP requests (in order of appearance: CREATE, POWER, DEVICE_CONTROL, WRITE, READ, CLEANUP and CLOSE,). With a state space of 128 modes and 896 transitions, only 9 modes and 16 transitions were actually visited, forming the operational profile for the considered workload. This means that 7% of the modes and 1.8% of transitions were traversed. Therefore, for properly testing the driver's robustness under the given workload, one has to focus only onto very few modes and transitions.

We executed the same experiment five times, each time using different baud rates (4800, 14400, 19200, 57600 and 115200). The other COM port settings

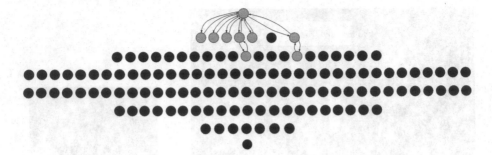

Fig. 6. An experiment using `ModemTest`. The visited modes and the traversed edges (defining the *operational profile*) are represented in gray. Note that only a small fraction of the graph was visited.

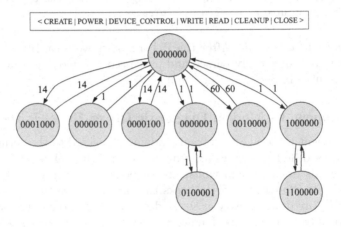

Fig. 7. An experiment using `ModemTest`. Edge label indicate the number of traversals. The upper box shows the corresponding IRP names.

were the default ones (8/N/1/no flow-control). Every time the observed flow of IRPs was identical and produced the same graph of visited modes (Figures 6 and 7). Moreover, the number of IRPs issued was also identical each time.

This fact indicates that the workload application is following a pattern, with each execution generating the same sequence of IRP requests. Additionally, the serial driver under test performed in a deterministic manner (responded to requests in the same manner every time). If a single IRP request would have been dropped or the driver would have finished executing the associated code in a different period of time (so that the driver would have started processing another IRP request), the graph would have had a completely different conformation.

Given the identical behavior of the serial driver in our experiments (under similar workloads), we assume that a system designer planning to use COTS drivers in a system can utilize our framework as a complement to an existing testing strategy. If the operating system, drivers and the set of applications to be used on the designed system are known (or at least a subset of them), the system designer can first build behavioral patterns that describe the manner the OS and the installed applications exercise a driver (the *operational profile*), as sets of visited modes and traversed transitions. If needed, one can associate counters to each node and transition, to observe which are frequently visited or, respectively, traversed. In the following experiment we show that this kind of information is useful for robustness testing.

8.2   Experiment 2 - Aggregated Workload

Under the assumption that the system designer has identified the set of applications to be used on the future system, we collected a set of applications (see Table 2) which we used to generate a workload for the targeted driver, the serial driver.

Table 2. The set of applications used to generate relevant workload for the serial driver

Application	HW at COM port	Description
A1: BurnIn Test Pro v4.0	Loopback serial cable	Reliability and stability test; RTS, CTS, DTR, DSR test, cycling all the baud rates
A2: DirectX Diag. Tool v9.0c	Computer (via serial cable)	DirectPlay test; text messages exchanged between machines
A3: HyperTerminal v5.1.2600.0	Computer (via serial cable)	Exchanged messages and 50k files
A4: ModemTest v1.3	External modem	See 8.1
A5: Win XP modem diagnostics	External modem	Windows XP queries the modem to check its capabilities
A6: Win XP Device Manager	External modem and COM port	Device Manager scans for hardware changes; the serial port and the modem are queried
A7: Dial modem off	External modem	Tried to dial a number when modem is off

Similar to the previous experiment, we built the operational profile of the serial driver, for the selected application set. Table 3 contains the results of the aggregated workload experiment, as well the results for each application.

107456 requests were issued in total, out of which 10 were distinct, thus modes are represented by 10 bits. The full graph (not shown here for space reasons) has 1024 modes and 10240 transitions. Only 17 nodes and 35 transitions were visited, which corresponds to 1.66% of modes and 0.34% of transitions.

This result shows that even for a set of varied applications (some of them serial port benchmarks!) only a very small percent of modes and transitions is visited, even if a large number of IRP requests is issued. A second observation is the huge difference between the number of times transitions and modes were visited (see Fig. 8).

Table 3. The results of considered applications, one by one and together (aggregated)

Application	IRPs		Total (from which (%) visited)	
	Issued	Distinct	Modes	Transitions
A1	98398	7	128 (7.03)	896 (1.78)
A2	220	8	256 (4.68)	2048 (1.07)
A3	6704	7	128 (7.81)	896 (2.12)
A4	187	7	128 (7.03)	896 (1.78)
A5	1326	8	256 (3.90)	2048 (0.87)
A6	146	8	256 (4.68)	2048 (0.92)
A7	476	8	256 (4.29)	2048 (0.97)
Aggregated:	**107456**	**10**	**1024 (1.66)**	**10240 (0.34)**

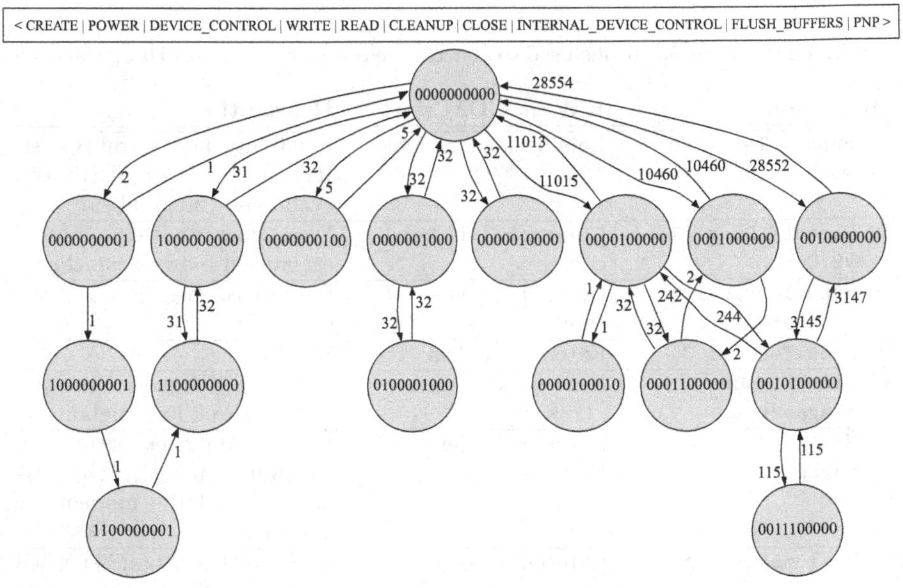

Fig. 8. An experiment using the aggregation of applications described in Table 2

We observe that the modes located on lower levels in our model are not visited; we have only two visited modes on level $l = 3$. This can be an indication of the low degree of IRP interlacing, i.e., not many IRPs are permitted by the driver's design to execute concurrently.

9   Discussion

Operational Profile Size: Our experiments showed that the operational profile is only a very small part of the driver's mode graph. This has significant implications on testing coverage. First, it indicates the modes and transitions that have a high likelihood to be reached in the field (the set of applications considered in the second experiment exercise most of the serial port capabilities). Second, we observed that few IRP requests are executed concurrently (the deepest visited level is $l = 3$). This may disclose internal constraints on how requests can be executed concurrently. The total number of test cases used by a test campaign can be reduced dramatically, since not all modes are reachable. Third, assuming that a testing technique starts in idle mode, the length of the sequence needed to bring the driver into the mode of interest for testing is very short.

IRP Sequences: Generating the IRP sequence necessary to put the driver in a mode of interest for the tester can be difficult, as the receipt and return of a request are events occurring in asynchronous manner. For visited nodes and transitions, the sequence of incoming requests can be saved (as they are structures in the kernel memory, see Sect. 5.2) and reproduced for the testing campaign. If testing is aimed at completeness (all modes / transitions to be tested), many request sequences may be unachievable. Therefore, we suggest using the following technique for testing.

Wave Testing: By monitoring how the driver under test performs under a relevant workload, two parameters that quantify the testing progress can be obtained:

1. the number of visited modes together with the values of the counters associated with each mode;
2. the number of traversed edges in the graph and their access counters.

"Wave testing" is now possible. In the first wave, the visited modes should be tested, accessing the same traversed edges. Obtaining a relevant workload for this step was discussed above. One can even split this wave in smaller units, i.e., first test the modes and transitions with the higher counter value.

After finishing the first wave, a set of modes accessible via one hop from the visited modes are identified. The problem of building an IRP sequence to reach next-hop modes is solved by appending a new IRP request to the sequences already available. The testing process continues by testing these modes and related transitions until no transitions can be traversed.

Limitations: While developing the presented approach, we aimed at generality of its applicability. Unfortunately, there are exceptions and drivers are as different in nature as the hardware they deal with. At the current stage, our method cannot deal with drivers that concurrently process several instances of the same IRP request type. On the same line, the transitions in our model are limited between modes located on neighboring levels; this means that no two or more IRP requests can start or finish their execution at exactly the same moment. Ongoing research includes experimental monitoring of different types of drivers on multiprocessor machines. Though, if such behavior is observed, the method presented in this paper can be extended accordingly.

10   Conclusions and Future Directions

Overall, our contribution provides means to quantify the test progress of already existing techniques for black-box testing of COTS drivers. The presented experiments show that only a small subset of the driver modes are actually exercised by several commercial applications (benchmarks) used to generate workload for the driver monitoring sessions. This result is important, indicating a relevant location to focus a testing method (i.e., put high priority on modes and transitions visited in the field). Therefore, this approach represents a significant improvement over random testing, given the tendency of faults to concentrate in specific areas of the code [6].

Moreover, we can now determine an operational profile of the driver under test, associating with each mode and transition a probability of occurrence in the field, as proposed in [8]. Additionally, the method is non-intrusive, requiring no access to the source code of the operating system and the COTS driver under test.

Future Work: We intend to further develop our method to embody more information which is observable from outside of COTS drivers. For instance, we will incorporate into our model the OS ⇔ driver interface discussed in [10,11]. As modes represent execution of driver code, the functionality associated with some of them may call methods defined in other software libraries of the OS kernel. We consider that the driver under test might fail as a result of a fault in the external functions, not only due to faults in the own code. Therefore, the tester of the COTS driver can take advantage of the new, aggregated insight.

Another direction of future work will include monitoring several drivers in conjunction with relevant applications. We intend to investigate if there are patterns of driver usage that are independent of the workload. This fact might facilitate associating traversal probabilities with each mode and transition. Using this patterns, testing campaigns could concentrate on the modes and transitions accessed more frequently.

Acknowledgments

We would like to thank all DEEDS group's members for the valuable discussions, comments on early versions of the paper and feedback.

References

1. Oney, W.: Programming the MS Windows Driver Model. Microsoft Press, Redmond, Washington (2003)
2. Swift, M.M., Bershad, B.N., Levy, H.M.: Improving the reliability of commodity operating systems. ACM Transactions on Computer Systems. **Volume: 23** (2005) 77–110
3. Harrold, M.J.: Testing: A roadmap. In: International Conference on Software Engineering. (2000) 61–72

4. Myers, G.J.: The Art of Software Testing. 2nd edn. Wiley & Sons, inc. (2004)
5. Hamlet, D., Taylor, R.: Partition testing does not inspire confidence. IEEE Transactions on Software Engineering. **Volume: 16 , Issue: 12** (1990) 1402–1411
6. Möller, K.H., Paulish, D.: An empirical investigation of software fault distribution. In: First International Software Metrics Symposium. (1993) 82–90
7. Weyuker, E.J., Jeng, B.: Analyzing partition testing strategies. IEEE Transactions on Software Engineering. **Volume: 17, Issue: 7** (1991) 703–711
8. Weyuker, E.J.: Using operational distributions to judge testing progress. In: ACM Symposium on Applied Computing, New York, NY, USA, ACM Press. (2003) 1118–1122
9. Avritzer, A., Larson, B.: Load testing software using deterministic state testing. In: International Symposium on Software Testing and Analysis. (1993) 82–88
10. Johansson, A., Sârbu, A., Jhumka, A., Suri, N.: On enhancing the robustness of commercial operating systems. International Service Availability Symposium (ISAS). **Springer Lecture Notes on Computer Science 3335** (2004) 148–159
11. Johansson, A., Suri, N.: Error propagation profiling of operating systems. In: International Conference on Dependable Systems and Networks (DSN). (2005) 86–95
12. Fenton, N., Neil, M.: A critique of software defect prediction models. IEEE Transactions on Software Engineering. **Volume: 25, Issue: 5** (1999) 675–689

Transparent Checkpointing for Applications with Graphical User Interfaces

Jan-Thomas Czornack, Carsten Trinitis, and Max Walter

Technische Universität München
Lehrstuhl für Rechnertechnik und Rechnerorganisation
{czornack, trinitic}walterm@in.tum.de

Abstract. Transparent checkpointing is a well known method to increase the dependability of long running applications. However, most known implementations concentrate on applications that do not use graphical user interfaces.

In this paper we describe common problems arising with transparent checkpointing of applications including their graphical user interfaces. We present a proxy that is able to store the window session of an application and compare our approach with an existing X-Server extension that serves the same purpose.

We also discuss the performance impact of both solutions and present performance and latency measurements that demonstrate the usability of the proxy.

Keywords: Checkpointing, X-Server, Proxy, GUI.
Category: Service infrastructures.

1 Motivation

Saving application relevant data on a regular basis is a well known method to avoid data loss and increase the dependability of an application. In case of hardware failures the application can be reset to the point where the *checkpoint* was saved. On the one hand, for many programs such mechanisms are desired, but, on the other hand, only few applications offer checkpointing. Especially desktop applications rarely make use of mechanisms to enhance their reliability. With some effort it is possible to add checkpointing mechanisms to existing applications, provided that the source code is available. Unfortunately, for most applications this is not the case. One way to circumvent this problem is *Transparent Checkpointing*. Such mechanisms allow application transparent saving of relevant data, and they are able to restore file descriptors (open files), sockets (network connections) and even graphical user interfaces. Since the application does not support this kind of checkpointing itself, the algorithms have to deal with much less information compared to other checkpointing mechanisms. For this approach several problems must be solved:

- Graphical User Interfaces (GUI) are difficult to save and restore because their state is not part of the process context. On Unix-Systems, most information about the GUI is stored within the X-Server. Since there is no easy way to retrieve this information, additional mechanisms are needed to obtain this data. Two possible solutions to this problem will be discussed in chapter 3 of this paper.

D. Penkler, M. Reitenspiess, and F. Tam (Eds.): ISAS 2006, LNCS 4328, pp. 140–148, 2006.

- The usage of Linux threads is getting more and more common with the further development of hyper threading and multi core processors [14] [19]. Especially high performance applications, but also common desktop applications make use of Linux threads to exploit the available processing power.
- Open files can be modified by other processes (or the application itself) after the application has been checkpointed. The file is then in an unexpected state after application restart. Typically a copy of the opened files is added to the checkpoint to avoid this problem. Consequently, this can result in very large checkpoints.
- The ability to restore network connections depends strongly on the protocol being used. Sockets can be restored from the file descriptor table. Usually a client will need to reconnect, especially if connection oriented protocols like for example TCP [11] are used. It is also possible to keep the connection alive while the application is restored. This is especially useful for server applications. However, the applications network state needs to be aligned after the restart.
- Since there is no support for the checkpointing mechanism from within the application, the mechanism tends to save a lot of unimportant information about the application process. This is one of the major drawbacks of most known transparent checkpointing mechanisms. The amount of checkpoint data can be reduced (a) with compression algorithms and (b) by only saving the differences between consecutive checkpoints.

1.1   Area of Application for Transparent Checkpointing Mechanisms

Naturally, one of the most important objectives of transparent checkpointing is the increase in dependability. By saving checkpoints of an application on a regular basis, it is possible to reset the application to an earlier point in execution. This is especially useful in case of hardware and some (but not all) software failures or when recovering from faulty user input.

Transparent checkpointing can also be used to achieve better load balancing within clustered systems. By process migration it is possible to systematically migrate processes from heavily used nodes to less occupied ones by transferring the checkpoint to the other machine. The application can be continued on the other node if operating system and hardware architecture match. In addition, the application's environment (files, services) must be available. But especially on clustered systems with network file systems this is often the case.

Another field of application is *application mobility*. Transparent checkpointing offers the possibility to interrupt applications and restart them later on the same or on another machine. The checkpoints of opened desktop applications can be transfered to other machines, and the user can continue his work at the same application state. Obviously, additional constraints must be met: It is not possible to continue the application on completely different hardware (processor architecture) or on another operating system.

Chapter 2 will discuss some technical fundamentals about transparent checkpointing. In chapter 3 we will discuss two ways to retrieve and restore the state of graphical user interfaces and present some measurements on their performance impact. The paper will finish with some conclusions and an outlook on future work.

2 Technical Details on Transparent Checkpointing

There exist different ways to create and restore checkpoints in an application transparent manner [16]. One possibility is to modify the Linux kernel and retrieve the process context from within the kernel space. While this is a clean and reliable approach, changes to the kernel need to be applied by every user of the checkpointing system.

It is also possible to retrieve the process context from within the user space. This solution is more complex, but its main advantage is, that every user can use the checkpointing mechanism without modifications to the kernel. Typical user space implementations are described in [12] and [20]. An extensive overview over several well known implementations was published in [16].

2.1 Saving Relevant Data

The task of creating a checkpoint can be split into three major parts:

1. First, the process has to be stopped. This is very important because otherwise it would modify itself while the checkpoint mechanism runs. This would of course lead to an inconsistent checkpoint file, and it would be impossible (or at least very difficult) to restart the process from this checkpoint.

   Since creating a checkpoint can take some resources/time (this depends strongly on the process and its memory usage) it is sometimes better to clone the process and create the checkpoint from the clone. Cloning the process does not imply copying the memory allocated by the process. Only write access to the cloned memory leads to additional allocation of memory.

2. After the process has been stopped, its context is saved on a reliable storage device (e.g. local hard disk or NFS). Such a checkpoint usually includes:

   - The file descriptor table. This is needed to restore opened files and sockets.
   - Allocated memory, registers, stack and process id.
   - Additional information, like e.g. the state of the graphical user interface.

3. The third step is to continue the stopped process or remove its clone.

2.2 Restoring the Process

The task of restoring a process can also be divided into three major steps:

First, an *empty* process needs to be created. This process will be stopped immediately after creation.

After that the process context needs to be restored. Files and sockets need to be reopened, and the graphical user interface needs to be rebuilt within the X-Server.

Finally the process will be continued, and, in the ideal case, does not notice any interaction of the checkpointing mechanism.

3 Implementation: Saving the Graphical User Interface (GUI)

Saving and restoring information about the graphical user interface (GUI) of an application is not possible in a straightforward approach because such information is not stored within the process context of the application. Hence, other ways to obtain this information have to be found.

The information about the state of the GUI is stored within the X-Server. The application communicates with the server via the X-Protocol. Communication does not need to take place on the same machine, in fact it is also possible to operate the application and the X-Server on different machines, since communication can be forwarded over a network connection.

We found two different approaches to retrieve the GUI state and will discuss their assets and drawbacks in the following sections.

3.1 Related Work: Retrieving the GUI State from Within the X-Server

The default Linux X-Server [8] does not support the retrieval of GUI state information. However, it is possible to enhance the server by using an X-Server extension that has to be loaded at X-Server startup. This extension offers the possibility to capture the window session of the application from within the X-Server [21].

The main advantage of this approach is, that the application and the X-Server need not be modified. There is no slowdown of the application before the checkpoint is being taken because the checkpoint mechanism hijacks [22] the application.

But there are also some disadvantages with this mechanism: First of all, the user has to reconfigure his X-Server and needs to restart it. The X-Server extension was designed exclusively for the XFree86 implementation of the X-Windows system. It does not work with other implementations (e.g. VNC [5] servers) and there may be a need to modify the extension for future releases of XFree86 or X.org [7] [8]. Apart from that, the application binary needs to contain symbol table entries for the window protocol stubs it calls.

The retrieval of the GUI state does take a noticeable amount of time (about 20 seconds). This is due to some performance problems when checkpointing the font state. However, this problem only occurs when detaching the GUI the first time [20].

3.2 New Approach: Eavesdropping the Communication Between Client and Server with a Proxy

The disadvantages when using an X-Server extension can be circumvented by using a proxy between the X-Server and the client application.

The proxy keeps a copy of the window session and updates this copy by eavesdropping the communication between client and server. With this approach no modifications to the X-Server need to be made, there is no need to change its configuration, and no extension needs to be loaded.

This results in a reduction of compatibility issues. Probably any X-Server that follows the X-Protocol will operate with this setup. Additionally there is no extra overhead when retrieving the GUI state, because it is available at any time within the proxy.

However, there are also some drawbacks with this solution. First, it is not possible to switch the proxy between an existing client - X-Server connection *after* the client has been started and the GUI has been created. Instead, the client has to connect to the proxy directly. This can be achieved by setting environment variables.

It also should be noted that the proxy adds additional latency that might result in a slower and less responsive application or user interface behavior. Our tests have shown that on modern machines the delay inflicted by the proxy is just a few milliseconds.

3.3   Combining the Proxy with a Checkpointing System

The system we want to implement consists of two major components: The first component is a standard checkpointing system for applications without graphical user interfaces. Since most known applications that make use of a GUI use threads, the checkpointing systems needs to support this. Possible solutions to this problem are described among others in [12] and [10].

The second component is a proxy that is switched between the client and the X-Server. This proxy keeps a copy of the applications window session. This information can be saved to disk.

Both, the checkpointing system and the proxy create a checkpoint for the application. From this checkpoint the application can be continued later. The size of the checkpoint depends strongly on the application's demand for memory. Tests with several applications have shown that the amount of data for the graphical user interface tends to stay within the range of several Kilobytes and about 2 Megabytes. This depends on the bitmap data an application uses. This data is kept within the X-Server in raw format. Thus, an image viewing program, even if it uses a very simple GUI, will probably need more disk space for the checkpoint than a word processing application.

The structure of the desired system can be seen in the Figure 1.

3.4   Possible Areas of Application for the X-Server Proxy

The main application for the proxy is the checkpointing of applications. But being able to continually write the the communication between client and X-Server to disk offers additional possibilities. It is possible to use the proxy to monitor an application and

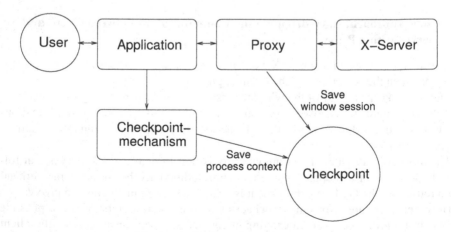

Fig. 1. Checkpointing system structure

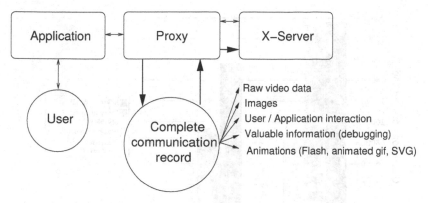

Fig. 2. Possible applications for the proxy

every interaction between user and application. The saved information can be used to extract valuable information that can be used to debug the application or log a users interaction. It is also possible to completely replay the the user's interaction with the application step by step.

It is also possible to capture videos or animations (as long as they don't use any hardware acceleration that circumvents the proxy). But since all bitmap data is stored in raw format on disk, even small movies will need a tremendous amount of disk space. First tests with a 6 megabyte Windows Media Video (WMV) file resulted in more than 400Mb uncompressed data. Also it has to be noted that the proxy is not fast enough to process this amount of data (the movie runs noticeable slower) and of course it does not save audio data.

The possible fields of application for the proxy are illustrated in Figure 2.

4   Results: Performance Impact

Test runs were carried out with the x11perf [6] test suite under different test environments. The used hardware was a VIA C3 system with 1GHz.

In a first approach, a VNC [5] server without proxy was used, and the performance when displaying 100x100 pixel rectangles and when displaying 80 characters in a row was measured.

In a second approach, the proxy between client and server without processing the data was used.

In a third approach, the data was written to disk during the test. This was carried out with and without gzip [3] compression.

Figure 3 shows operations per second for the different tests. As can be seen, the proxy itself does not significantly affect the performance, provided that only simple operations are conducted. However, with more complex operations, like e.g. displaying characters, there is a noticeable loss in performance. Writing the data to disk reduces the performance of the proxy by more than 50 per cent. Surprisingly, compressing the data before writing it to disk leads to a small, but reproducible performance increase.

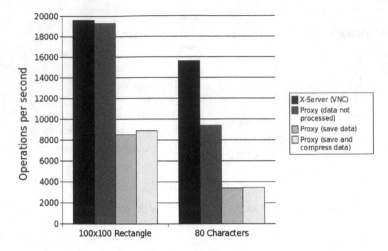

Fig. 3. Proxy performance measurements performed with X11Perf

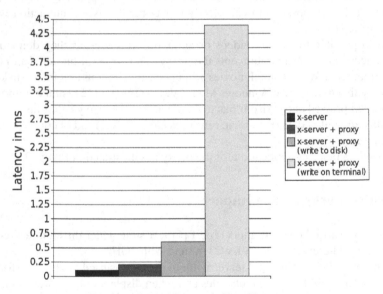

Fig. 4. Additional latency inflicted by proxy

This appears to happen because of the large amount of data that is produced during the tests. Compression reduces data from about 55Mb down to 680Kb and therefore reduces the load on the IO interface and the hard disk. The results of this performance measurements are shown in Figure 3.

4.1 Additional Latency Inflicted by the Proxy

Pure performance and throughput are definitely of high importance for complex user interfaces. In addition, what really makes an interface responsive and enables fluent work, is latency. Users expect applications to immediately react to their input. Even small delays in the range of 50 - 150ms result in a sluggish behavior. Therefore, additional tests were performed, with focus on latency, as opposed to throughput or performance. The tests were run on a VIA C3 with 1GHz running a VNC-Server [5] and a standard X-Server (X.org 6.8.2 [8]), which, in terms of latency, both behave almost identically.

The inflicted latency was always below 1ms. Tests with well known applications, like e.g. Firefox [1] or OpenOffice.org [4], did not show any significant latency problems. The test results are shown in Figure 4. The high latency values in the last column result from the slow terminal output. The terminal used was the gnome-terminal [2]. This is of course only useful for debugging reasons and has no practical benefit for the enduser.

5   Conclusions and Future Work

In this paper we presented an approach to checkpoint applications that use graphical user interfaces. We explained different application scenarios and demonstrated the usability of our solution with performance and latency measurements.

Future research will focus on combining different checkpointing approaches with the X-Server proxy. The goal is to checkpoint a wide range of applications, including those with graphical user interfaces. Additionally further possible applications for the proxy, like e.g. monitoring a user's interaction with an application or capturing animations or video data, will be subject to closer investigations.

References

[1] *Firefox Web Browser.* http://www.mozilla.com/firefox/central/.
[2] *The Free Software Desktop Project.* http://www.gnome.org/.
[3] *gzip.* http://www.gzip.org/.
[4] *OpenOffice.org - The Free Office Suite.* http://www.openoffice.org/.
[5] *Real VNC.* http://www.realvnc.com/.
[6] *X11PERF Manual Page.* http://www.xfree86.org/4.2.0/x11perf.1.html.
[7] *The XFree86 Project.* http://www.xfree86.org/.
[8] *X.Org Foundation.* http://wiki.x.org/wiki/.
[9] C. D. Carothers and B. K. Szymanski. *Linux Support for Transparent Checkpointing of Multithreaded Programs.* Department of Computer Science, Rensselaer Polytechnic Institute, August 2002.
[10] J.-T. Czornack. Transparent checkpointing. *Tagungsband zum Diskussionskreis Fehlertoleranz*, pages 23 – 28, Sept. 2005.
[11] DARPA Internet Program Protocol Specification.   *Transmission Control Protocol.* http://www.rfc-editor.org/rfc/rfc793.txt, September 1981.
[12] W. R. Dieter and J. E. Lumpp. *User-Level Checkpointing for LinuxThreads Programs.* Departement of Electrical and Computer Engineering, University of Kentucky, 2001.
[13] J. Glauber. *Checkpointing als Basis für transparente Service Migration unter Linux.* Institut für Systemarchitektur, Technische Universität Dresden, 2002.
[14] Intel. *Hyper-Threading Technology.* http://www.intel.com/technology/hyperthread/.
[15] J. S. Plank, M. Beck, G. Kingsley, and K. Li. *Libckpt: Transparent Checkpointing under Unix.* Department of Computer Science, University of Tennessee, 1995.

[16] E. Roman. *A Survey of Checkpoint/Restart Implementations*. Lawrence Berkeley National Laboratory, 2002.

[17] E. Solomita, J. Kempf, and D. Duchamp. Xmove: A pseudoserver for x window movement. *The X Resource*, pages 143 – 170, July 1994.

[18] G. Stellner. Cocheck: Checkpointing and process migration for mpi. *10th International Parallel Processing Symposium*, page 526, 1996.

[19] C. Szydlowski. Multithreaded technology and multicore processors. *Dr. Dobb's Journal*, May 2005.

[20] V. C. Zandy. *Application Mobility*. Computer Sciences Department, University of Wisconsin, 2004.

[21] V. C. Zandy and B. P. Miller. Checkpoints of GUI-based applications. *USENIX Annual Technical Conference*, pages 155 – 166, 2003.

[22] V. C. Zandy, B. P. Miller, and M. Livny. Process hijacking. *Eighth IEEE International Symposium on High Performance Distributed Computing*, page 32, 1999.

Performance Measurement and Tuning
of Hot-Standby Databases

Antoni Wolski and Vilho Raatikka

Solid Information Technology, Itälahdenkatu 22B, 00210 Helsinki, Finland
{first_name.last_name}@solidtech.com

Abstract. General-purpose, high-availability database systems have lately pro-
liferated to various network element platforms. In telecommunication, databases are expected to meet demanding availability levels while preserving the
required throughput. However, so far, the effects of various high-availability
configurations on overall database performance have not been analyzed. In this
paper, the operation of a fully replicated, hot-standby database system is presented, together with some performance tuning possibilities. To study the effect
of several database-tuning parameters, a telecom-oriented database benchmark,
TM1, is used. The experiments involve varying of the read/write balance and
various logging and replication parameters. It is shown that, by relaxing the reliability requirements, significant performance gains can be achieved. Also, it is
demonstrated that a possibility to redirect the log writing from the local disk to
the standby node is one of the most important benefits of a high-availability
database system.

1 Introduction

The goal of highly available (HA) systems is to make system or component failures
tolerable. The extent to which failures are tolerable is specified with the availability
measure A that is equal to the percentage of the time a service is operational, as related to the total time the service is supposed to be operational. Availability can be
derived from the maximum duration of an outage (equal to mean time to repair,
MTTR) and the frequency of outages (represented with mean time between failures,
MTBF), by using the following formula:

$$A = \frac{MTBF}{MTBF + MTTR} \bullet 100\% \tag{1}$$

To deal with failures, an HA system embodies redundancy both in hardware and
software, typically managed by a framework such as AMF (Availability Management
Framework) [1] of SA Forum[1].

In the simplest redundancy model, called 2N, the two units, active and standby,
make up a mated pair, and the redundant application components are organized in

---

[1] http://www.saforum.org

D. Penkler, M. Reitenspiess, and F. Tam (Eds.): ISAS 2006, LNCS 4328, pp. 149–161, 2006.

pairs in the corresponding units. Should a failure occur, the failed active unit (hardware or software) is quickly replaced with a corresponding standby unit. This operation is called a failover. The purpose of failover is to maintain the required service availability, in the presence of failures. The hot-standby technique described above allows achieving at least five nines (99.999%) availability required in the telecom systems.

The availability of the database services is maintained by using the very same approach. Various architectures of highly-available database management systems (HA-DBMS) have been proposed and implemented commercially [7]. In this paper, the focus is on the utility of a fully replicated hot-standby (HSB) HA DBMS. In such a system, a stream of transactions is continuously sent from the Active server to the Standby server, by way of a replication protocol.

A typical hot-standby database system can be configured in a variety of ways. Most important tuning parameters are the ones dealing with the synchrony of the log writing (the durability settings) and the synchrony of the database replication protocol (the safeness characteristics, first introduced in [2]). Typically, the goal of the HA-DBMS tuning is to achieve the best trade-off among the three characteristics: data durability, failover time, and performance.

The problem is that the usage of those parameters is often based on intuitive argumentation, without any experimental data to depend on. We are not aware of any published work shedding any light on the problem. In this paper, we report on experiments conducted using a real-life commercial HA-DBMS in a telecom setting. The purpose of the experiments was to find out what was the effect of the tuning parameters on the overall HA-DBMS performance. The product used in the experiments was Solid's HA-DBMS called Solid Database Engine with CarrierGrade Option [8]. For a case study on applying the product to a commercial telecom HA framework, see [11].

The obtained results support the general notion that increasing asynchrony improves performance. However, the comparison among the effects of different setting may not correspond to intuitive presumptions.

We summarize the HA-DBMS architecture in Section 2. Various configuration parameters are also introduced together with their intuitive purpose. Database benchmarking is discussed in Section 3, where also the TM1 benchmark is introduced. Test results are summarized in Section 4. We conclude with a summary of the results, and general guidelines for HA-DBMS users.

2   Tuning Highly Available Databases

An HA-DBMS based on the hot-standby principle is composed of the elements shown in Fig. 1.

A database (Active or Standby) server is a component that offers a database access service to applications, mostly by way of over-the-network connections. Transaction is an abstraction of a transaction processing thread. The DB (database file) is an abstraction of persistent storage of the data. In reality, one or more system-level files can be used for the purpose. Primary DB is a "live" database updated by the transactions running on the Active server. Secondary DB is kept up-to-date by way of a replication protocol. Secondary DB may be subjected to read-only load, if necessary

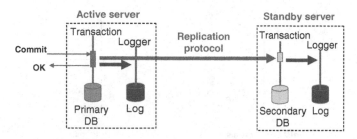

Fig. 1. Architecture of a hot-standby HA-DBMS

Logger is a thread that writes the Log. The Log represents one or more persistent files to store the effects of transactions as they are executed in the server. The Log is instrumental in making it possible to perform a startup database recovery. In the recovery process, the Log is scanned to ensure that the database is in a consistent state, by:

- removing the effects of uncommitted transactions, and
- re-executing committed transactions that have not been checkpointed to the database.

If we deal with a standalone database system (not hot standby), the recovery process preserves the Atomicity and Durability characteristics of the database over system failures and terminations [2].

The standard level of durability support is called strict durability. It requires that the commit record of a transaction is written synchronously to the persistent medium (disk) before the commit call is returned to the application. The technique is often referred to as WAL—Write-Ahead Logging. WAL processing is very resource-consuming and often becomes a bottleneck in the system. Therefore, whenever the durability requirement can be relaxed, it is done. Especially, in the telecom environment, in some applications like call setup, session initiation, etc., a service request is occasionally allowed to fail (and be lost) if the probability is not very high. In such a case, relaxed durability may be applied whereby the log is written asynchronously. This means that the commit call may be returned without the need to wait for the disk. This results in significant improvement in both the system throughput and response time. In this paper, an effort is made to quantify the effect of switching from strict to relaxed durability on total throughput.

In an HSB database, transactions are also sent to the standby server by way of a replication protocol. In order to preserve the database consistency in the presence of failovers, the replication protocol is built very much on the same principles as physical log writing: the transaction order is preserved, and commit records demarcate committed transactions. If a failover happens, the Standby server performs a similar database recovery as if a transaction log was used: the uncommitted transactions are removed and the committed ones are queued for execution.

Similarly to log writing, the replication protocol may be asynchronous or synchronous. To picture that, we use the concept of safeness level where 1-Safe denotes an asynchronous protocol and 2-Safe denotes a synchronous one [2]. The two safeness levels are illustrated in Fig. 2.

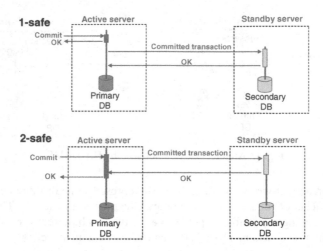

Fig. 2. Illustration of safeness levels

One may see that the benefit of 1-Safe replication is similar to that of relaxed durability: the transaction response time is improved, and the throughput may be expected to be higher, too. On the other hand, with 2-Safe replication, no committed transactions are lost upon failover. You might call this transaction characteristic standby-based strict durability, as opposed to log-based strict durability of a traditional DBMS. One immediate observation is that the log-based durability level has no effect on actual durability of transactions in the presence of failover. It is the standby-based durability that counts. The traditional log writing is relegated to the role of facilitating the database system recovery in the case of a total system failure. All other (more typical) failures are supposed to be taken care of by failovers. If a total system failure is unlikely (as builders of HA systems want to believe), a natural choice is to replace strict log-based durability with strict standby-based durability, that is, the 2-Safe protocol. Here, the gain is a faster log processing without really loosing strict durability (if only single failures are considered). To take the full advantage of the possibility, Solid's HA DBMS has an automated feature called adaptive durability. With adaptive durability, the Active server's log writing is automatically switched to strict if a node starts to operate without a Standby. Otherwise, the Active server operates with relaxed durability.

The possibility to transfer the log writing responsibility from the disk to the network is very tempting because, by a common perception, a message round trip travel over a high-speed network may be almost an order of magnitude faster than writing synchronously to the disk.

In addition to the choice between 1-Safe and 2-Safe replication, 2-Safe protocols may be implemented with different levels of involvement of the Standby server in the processing of the commit message. In [7], two levels were proposed: 2-Safe Received and 2-Safe Committed. In this paper, the following 2-Safe policy levels are defined:

- 2-Safe Received: the Standby server sends the response immediately upon receipt (as in [7]).

- 2-Safe Visible: the Standby server processes the transaction to the point that the results are externally visible (in-memory commit).
- 2-Safe Durable: the Standby process processes the transaction to the point that it is written to a persistent log (strictly durable commit).

The three policy levels are illustrated in Fig. 3.

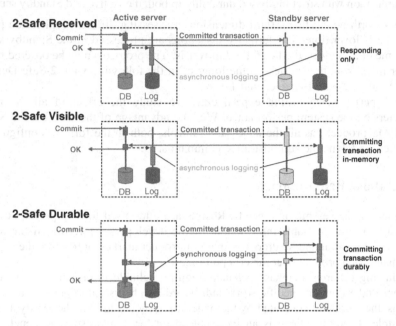

Fig. 3. 2-Safe policy levels

Of the three 2-Safe policy levels, 2-Safe Received is intuitively the fastest and 2-Safe Durable the most reliable. In a system with 2-Safe Durable replication, the database may survive a total system crash and, additionally, a media failure on one of the nodes. This comes, however, at a cost of multiple synchrony in the system.

The 2-Safe Visible level is meant to increase the system utility by maintaining the same externally visible state at both the Active and Standby servers. Thus, if the transactions are run at both the Active and Standby servers (read-only transactions at Standby), one-copy serializability [2] may be maintained over global transaction histories. The cost of maintaining this consistency level involves waiting for the transaction execution in the Standby server, before acknowledging the commit message.

To summarize, the intuitive rules for choosing the best trade-off between performance and reliability are the following:

1. To protect against single failures while allowing for some transactions to be lost on failover ➔ use 1-Safe replication with relaxed log-based durability.
2. To protect against single failures, with no transactions lost on failover ➔ use 2-Safe Received replication with relaxed log-based durability.

3. To protect against single failures, with no transactions lost on failover and a possibility to use the Primary and Secondary databases concurrently ➔ use 2-Safe Visible replication with relaxed log-based durability.
4. To protect against total system failure (in addition to single-point failures) ➔ use any 2-Safe protocol and strict log-based durability in the Active server.
5. To protect against total system failure and a media failure ➔ use 2-Safe Durable replication with strict log-based durability in both the Active and Standby servers.

It is also worth noting that a third dimension in assessing different replication protocols is the failover time. The further transactions are processed in the Standby server at the time of a failover, the faster the failover is. The protocols may be ordered by the failover time, from the shortest to the longest, in the following way: 2-Safe Durable, 2-Safe Visible, 2-Safe Received and 1-Safe.

In the performance testing experiments, we study the effect of all the above parameters on the system performance. We take advantage of the fact that the Solid's HA DBMS product has all the necessary controls, both in the form of configuration parameters and dynamic administrative commands.

3 Database Benchmarks

Benchmarking serves multiple needs. Results are often used to help product evaluation and they offer valuable information for the developers. Moreover, if the results happen to be good, manufacturers use them in product marketing to show the superior performance of a product over the competitors.

Evaluating different database products requires reliable information of their performance under domain-specific workload. In order to be useful in performance comparisons, the workload generated by the benchmark should imitate the reality as much as possible. Therefore, there is an inevitable need for domain-specific benchmarks. Furthermore, a benchmark is more likely to be widely accepted if its provided by a consortium consisting of wide range of independent participants than if its published and owned by a single organization. It is also assumed that a domain-specific benchmark must generate typical operations in that domain and measure them trustworthy. It must also be easily portable to different platforms. It should scale to systems of different sizes, too. Finally, it must be easily understandable to create credibility [4].

Wisconsin benchmark [3] measures the performance of a single-user database software and the hardware it runs on. It is generic, not domain-specific, but it is intuitive and the database scales in size. To get reliable results, the test must be conducted under certain conditions. For example, the database size must be at least five times the size of the buffer pool (page cache). Moreover, the effect of the buffer pool, which is one of the main performance makers in read-intensive operations, is intentionally eliminated by varying the queries of query sets.

AS3AP [10], which fills the deficiencies of the Wisconsin benchmark, is also general-purpose in its nature, but it provides both single-user and multi-user tests to measure the performance of a database system under "typical" OLTP[2], IR[3], mixed, and single-user workloads.

---

[2] OLTP = On-Line Transaction Processing.
[3] IR = Information Retrieval.

Nowadays, enterprise-oriented benchmarks come from the Transaction Processing Performance Council[4]. They deal with enterprise applications: order entry, decision support and web server applications.

The telecom field has been long in the need of a domain-oriented benchmark. The TM1 Benchmark started life as a special purpose benchmark used internally by a telecom equipment manufacturer. It was used to estimate the speed of various database management systems on different hardware platforms. In April 2004, the benchmark specification was published as part of a Master's Thesis at the University of Helsinki [9]. In November 2004, Solid published the entire benchmark description on their web site and made a benchmark kit available for free download[5]. The kit enabled any interested party to set up a test environment and run the TM1 benchmark. In February 2006, the corresponding Nokia's Network Database Benchmark was published[6].

Unlike the TPC benchmarks, the TM1 benchmark is based on a telco scenario, the Home Location Register (HLR). The HLR holds subscriber's identification information as well as other details of service provisioning. TM1 measures performance only. Maintenance or purchasing costs are not considered.

The benchmark uses four tables and a set of seven transactions that can be combined in different mixes (see the Appendix for more details on TM1). The most typical mix is denoted as "R80W20" meaning 80% of read transactions and 20% of modification transactions. In the experiments reported here, we used both the R80W20 and R20W80 mixes.

4   Testing Results

4.1   Test System

The system under test (SUT) consisted of two database servers both running on Linux Fedora Core 2. One server played the role of an Active database server while the other was a Standby database server. The configuration of both the Active and Standby servers remained the same during the tests excluding the logging modes. That is, the durability level and the safeness level of the servers varied. The workload was generated by TM1 benchmark, which ran simultaneously on two separate Windows 2000 computers. All four computers shared an isolated one gigabit network. More specific description of the test environment is presented in the table below:

Table 1. Test system configuration data

Role	CPU/MHz	Memory/B	disks	OS
Active server	1800	4096	2xSCSI	Fedora Core 2
Standby server	1800	4096	2xSCSI	Fedora Core 2
TM1 client host	2x1666	1024	IDE	Win2000 SP4
TM1 client host	2x1666	2048	2xSCSI	Win2000 SP4

---

[4] http://www.tpc.org
[5] http://www.solidtech.com/tm1
[6] https://hoslab.cs.helsinki.fi/savane/projects/ndbbenchmark/

The results of the tests were stored into the Test Input and Result Database (TIRDB), which was located on its own computer.

Tests started by copying a fresh database file to the working directory of the Active database server, disabling the write-ahead caches of both SCSI devices, and starting the server. In those tests where the Standby database server was used, it was started in the similar way, and the database of the Active server was replicated to it. According to the TM1 specifications, each test run was divided to ramp-up time and measured run time. We used 10 minutes ramp-up time followed by 20 minutes run time.

TM1 measures mean qualified throughput (MQTh) and response times for each transaction type. MQTh is a sum of successfully executed transactions from all clients divided by the duration (in seconds) of test run. The result is the average transaction rate per second.

We used 10 database client instances in each TM1 client host to create the workload. In TM1, clients are represented by separate processes and each client retains its own data structure for result data

The workload consisted of write and read intensive transaction mixes. In write intensive workload 80% of transactions included writes and 20% included reads only. In read intensive load the share between write and read transactions was the opposite.

The distribution of different transactions is presented in the following table:

Table 2. Transaction mixes for two kinds of load

write-intensive load	*read-intensive load*
GET_SUBSCRIBER_DATA 9	GET_SUBSCRIBER_DATA 35
GET_NEW_DESTINATION 2	GET_NEW_DESTINATION 10
GET_ACCESS_DATA 9	GET_ACCESS_DATA 35
UPDATE_SUBSCRIBER_DATA 8	UPDATE_SUBSCRIBER_DATA 2
UPDATE_LOCATION 56	UPDATE_LOCATION 14
INSERT_CALL_FORWARDING 8	INSERT_CALL_FORWARDING 2
DELETE_CALL_FORWARDING 8	DELETE_CALL_FORWARDING 2

The TM1 HLR database size is determined by the number of rows in the SUBSCRIBER table. The population used consisted of 500 000 subscribers, 1.25 million rows in ACCESS_INFO, 1.25 million rows in SPECIAL_FACILITY and 1.9 million rows in CALL_FORWARDING. The database file size was about 840MB.

4.2 Result Summary

We ran three kind of tests in which emphasis was on the log write mode (log-based durability) of the Active server, the log write mode of the Standby server and the safeness level of the replication protocol. Every test was run with both read-intensive and write-intensive workload. A set of tests was run on a standalone server first, to quantify the effect of durability settings on the general performance. The results are shown in Fig. 4.

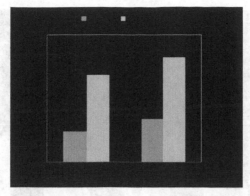

Fig. 4. Effect of the durability level on performance of a standalone database server

The comparison above shows that using asynchronous log writing in a standalone server increases the throughput of the system with read and write intensive workload by 20-40%, respectively. In the hot-standby configuration, a question may arise whether to use strict log-based durability in the Active server or not. The difference is illustrated in Fig. 5.

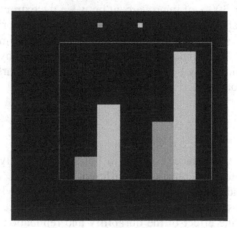

Fig. 5. Effect of the durability setting on performance of an HSB database using 2-Safe Received protocol

The results shown suggest that, by using relaxed durability in the Active server (that is, "delegating" the log writing to the Standby), a significant (70-250%) increase in the system throughput can be gained. In the case of the presented 2-Safe Received replication protocol, the Standby node runs with relaxed durability, in any case. Since logging affects the write transactions only, the benefit especially materializes with write intensive workload.

When looking at the comparison of all the replication protocols (all of which run with relaxed durability in the Active node, except for 2-Safe Durable), one can see that the earlier intuitive conjecture is verified: the more asynchrony there is in the system, the more throughput can be achieved (Fig. 6).

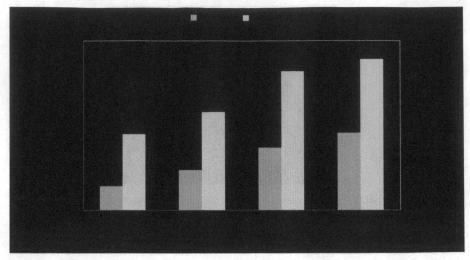

Fig. 6. Comparison of all HSB database replication protocols

The difference in performance is most significant for the write-intensive loads: there can be more than 300% of improvement between the extreme ends. On the other hand, the modest benefit of the 1-Safe protocol comes as a surprise. The explanation may be that, in the presence of high concurrent load, other optimization mechanisms (like group commit [159]) compensate for the lack of asynchrony, with 2-Safe protocols. Another explanation may be that another bottleneck appears in the system with the speed-up of the protocol.

5   Conclusions

We have conducted performance testing of a hot-standby highly available database, using a telecom-oriented benchmark and different load mixes. The obtained results provide quantitive guidance to developers of HA systems, needing to configure the databases properly. In seeking a right trade-off among the required reliability, failover time and throughput, the effect of the durability and replication settings on the performance is the most important factor in making the decision.

The results support the intuitive conjecture that increasing asynchrony leads to more throughput. The reported significant gains in throughput should encourage the developers to select asynchronous processing modes as much as they are not restricted by other requirements.

References

1. Application Interface Specification, SAI-AIS-B.02.02, December 2005. Service Availability Forum, available at http://www.saforum.org.
2. Bernstein, Ph. A.; Hadzilacos, V.; Goodman, N.: Concurrency control and recovery in database systems. Addison-Wesley Publishing Company, 1987, ISBN 0-201-10715-5.

3. Bitton, D., DeWitt, D.J., Turbyfill, C.: Benchmarking Database Systems A Systematic Approach. VLDB 1983: 8-19.

4. Gray, J. (ed.): The Benchmark Handbook for Database and Transaction Processing Systems. Morgan Kaufmann Publishers, 1993, ISBN 1-55860-292-5.

5. Gray, J. and Reuter, A.: Transaction Processing Systems, Concepts and Techniques. Morgan Kaufmann Publishers, 1992, ISBN 1-55860-190-2.

6. Brossier, S., Herrmann, F., Shokri, E.: On the Use of the SA Forum Checkpoint and AMF Services. Proc. ISAS 2004, May 13-14, 2004 Munich, Germany. Springer-Verlag Lecture Notes in Computer Science, Vol. 3335, ISBN: 3-540-24420-4.

7. Drake, S., Hu, W., McInnis, D.M., Sköld, M., Srivastava, A., Thalmann, L., Tikkanen, M., Torbjørnsen, Ø.,Wolski. A.: Architecture of Highly Available Databases. Proc. ISAS 2004, May 13-14, 2004 Munich, Germany. Springer-Verlag Lecture Notes in Computer Science, Vol. 3335, ISBN: 3-540-24420-4.

8. Solid High Availability User Guide, Version 4.5, Solid Information Technology, June 2005, available at http://www.solidtech.com.

9. Strandell, T.: Open Source Database Systems: Systems study, Performance and Scalability. Master's Thesis, University of Helsinki, Department of Computer Science, May 2003, 54 p. (http://www.cs.helsinki.fi/u/tpstrand/thesis/)

10. Turbyfill, C., Orji, C.U., Bitton. D.: AS^3AP - An ANSI SQL Standard Scaleable and Portable Benchmark for Relational Database Systems. In [4].

11. Wolski, A. and Hofhauser, B.: A Self-Managing High-Availability Database: Industrial Case Study. Proc. Workshop on Self-Managing Database Systems (SMDB2005), April 8-9, 2005, Tokyo, Japan. http://research.solidtech.com/publ/wolhof-smdb05-ha-case.pdf.

Appendix. TM1 Specifications

Because of lack of space, only general descriptions are included here. For a full benchmark description, see http://www.solidtech.com/tm1.

The purpose of the benchmark is to derive a maximum performance that can be achieved in a database system under a certain load. The SUT (system under test) is composed of target equipment and a database system being tested. In the case of HSB tests, two target computers are used. The load is generated in a separate computer (TM1 client host) where distinct processes emulate user applications. The detailed description includes specifications for the test duration, the database scaling and population rules, transactions mixes and user loads.

TM1 Database Schema

The TM1schema models an HLR (Home Location Register) structure found in all mobile telephone systems. The schema is composed of the four tables shown below.

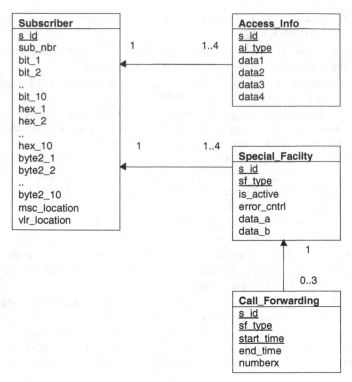

Fig. A-1. Schema of TM1

TM1 Transactions

The purpose of the transactions is to emulate typical HLR activities in call set-up and provisioning. The transactions are listed below.

```
GET_SUBSCRIBER_DATA {
        SELECT s_id, sub_nbr, bit_1, bit_2, bit_3, bit_4, bit_5, bit_6, bit_7, bit_8, bit_9, bit_10, hex_1, hex_2,
            hex_3, hex_4, hex_5, hex_6, hex_7, hex_8, hex_9, hex_10, byte2_1, byte2_2, byte2_3, byte2_4,
            byte2_5, byte2_6, byte2_7, byte2_8, byte2_9, byte2_10, msc_location, vlr_location
        FROM subscriber
        WHERE s_id = <s_id rnd>;
}
GET_NEW_DESTINATION {
        SELECT cf.numberx FROM special_facility AS sf, call_forwarding AS cf
        WHERE (sf.s_id = <s_id rnd>
                AND sf.sf_type = <sf_type rnd>
                AND sf.is_active = 1)
                AND (cf.s_id = sf.s_id
                AND cf.sf_type = sf.sf_type)
```

```
                    AND (cf.start_time \<= <start_time rnd>
                    AND <end_time rnd> \< cf.end_time);
}
GET_ACCESS_DATA {
        SELECT data1, data2, data3, data4 FROM access_info
        WHERE s_id = <s_id rnd>
        AND ai_type = <ai_type rnd>;
}
UPDATE_SUBSCRIBER_DATA {
        UPDATE subscriber
        SET bit_1 = <bit rnd>
        WHERE s_id = <s_id rnd subid>;

        UPDATE special_facility
        SET data_a = <data_a rnd>
        WHERE s_id = <s_id value subid>
                    AND sf_type = <sf_type rnd>;
}
UPDATE_LOCATION {
        UPDATE subscriber
        SET vlr_location = <vlr_location rnd>
        WHERE sub_nbr = <sub_nbr rndstr>;
}
```

A Simulation-Based Case Study of Multi-cluster Redundancy Solutions

Maria Toeroe

Ericsson Canada Inc., 8400 Decarie Blvd., Town of Mount Royal, QC, H4P 2N2, Canada
maria.toeroe@ericsson.com

Abstract. The paper discusses the requirements of high-availability that vendors are facing today in the telecommunication area, and some of the solutions that shall be considered to provide such highly reliable systems.

Through simulation, we compare multi-cluster redundancy models, namely, configurations of hot standby and load-sharing clusters using Ericsson's TSP clusters as a basis. The TSP cluster simulator is extended to provide the necessary features. Then through examples of simulated processor crashes, cluster failures and reconfigurations we demonstrate some of the issues that need to be taken into account when such systems are designed and dimensioned for fault tolerance.

Keywords: simulation of computer clusters, high-availability, performance evaluation, fault tolerance, recovery procedures.

1 Introduction

In telecommunications systems, the high-availability requirements demand that the system should be up and running for the 99.999% of the time. This permits approximately 5 minutes of downtime per year that includes the regular maintenance, operating system, application and hardware upgrades [1]. To achieve this level of availability, telecom systems often are cluster-based systems, such as Ericsson's TSP platform [2] that deploys simple redundancy of mainly commodity hardware complemented with software features that provide fault management and fault tolerance. These systems have proved to be scalable in the sense that with an addition of hardware any higher performance requirement is achievable. They are also multi purpose platforms; that is, they can run a wide range of applications.

These larger configurations, however, create new problems. As the size of the system grows, the risk of multiple failures within the system increases. This raises the question whether the same scalability and high-availability can be maintained for larger and possibly heterogeneous configurations running both telecom and datacom applications. Whether the solutions used today are appropriate for those future systems.

To answer this question, we investigate several aspects of such systems. One of the directions is building a performance simulation tool for clusters that allows one to experiment with new software and hardware configurations. Such a tool has the immediate use of dimensioning of these complex systems. It also has the advantage to be easily extendable and modifiable to experiment with new designs.

D. Penkler, M. Reitenspiess, and F. Tam (Eds.): ISAS 2006, LNCS 4328, pp. 162–176, 2006.
© Springer-Verlag Berlin Heidelberg 2006

In this paper, we present a simulation-based study of fault-tolerance related features based on Ericsson's proprietary clusterware, TelORB [3] that lies at the core of the TSP platform [2]. TelORB is a CORBA compliant and scalable distributed processing environment for mission critical, soft real-time applications.

First, we introduce briefly the simulation model used in our study. Then, we discuss the simulation of multi-cluster solutions similar to those offered by TSP that introduce additional redundancy at cluster level. We look at the simulation of the normal operation of such multi-cluster configurations and their behavior in emergency cases such as a recovery from processor failures. We compare a more traditional hot standby solution with a cost-efficient load-sharing configuration.

2 Simulation Model

In the past years, we have built a simulator for performance evaluation of applications running on TSP clusters. The model was implemented in a proprietary simulation framework that supports event-driven simulation and permits run-time user interventions.

The tool is based on a high-level model of the TSP system. According to this, the simulator is split into four major parts: the hardware and the software simulation components, the distribution mechanism and the traffic generators. A detailed discussion of the model can be found in [4], [5]. Here we present a short summary.

2.1 Baseline Model

Initial requests (Fig. 1) to the system are produced by traffic generators that typically represent external traffic – one that is served by the system; but they can also be used to reflect internal traffic, such as database recovery procedures. Each request is interpreted as a process invocation request in the system.

The software components of the model provide a user interface to specify process and data types. Instances of process types are invoked by requests generated by traffic generators or by other process instances. Each process invocation is represented in the model as a separate entity. Instances of data types compose an in-memory database that can be accessed by process instances. Data instances are not represented as separate entities.

A process type describes the run-time requirements of its instances (e.g. CPU time, memory allocation, etc.) and their interactions with the rest of the modeled application (i.e. invocation of other process instances). A process invocation request is first parameterized according to the user's current setting for the requested process type. Subsequently, the request is passed to a distributor that dispatches it to a processor for consumption – simulation of the execution of the process instance.

The components of the distribution mechanism – the distributors implement the *rules* according to which the database access and process invocation requests are distributed in the system to processors. The distribution rules are partially determined by TelORB itself and partially by the application designers. The designer controls such details as the distribution pool (i.e. the set of processors on which a data or process type is distributed), the redundancy model and the granularity of the distribution

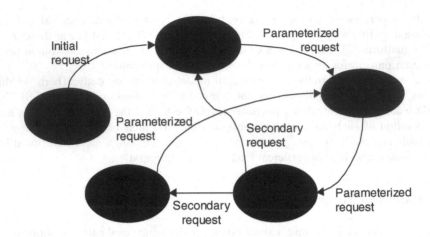

Fig. 1. Collaboration of the model components

(i.e. the number of the so called distribution units). Each process and data type is assigned to a distributor. This calculates the destination processor for each invocation request of the assigned types based on its own settings and parameters of the request.

The hardware simulation components: the processors and the interconnecting links and switches compose a *queuing* system in the model. Links and switches are simple delaying queues. Processors are priority queues controlled by its operating system's scheduling scheme.

As the distributor forwards an invocation request to a selected processor, depending on the communication path between the source and the destination of a request, it passes through links and switches that introduce delays that model the delay in the real communication media. Once the request reaches the destination processor, it is placed into the processor's scheduling queue as a process instance. Process instances of the scheduling queue gain access to the processor's CPU according to the modeled operating system's scheduling scheme. As instances consume CPU time, their CPU time requirement parameter is updated - decremented. A process instance remains in the scheduling queue until it is granted all the time it requested.

Besides using the CPU, process instances may access the database and invoke other processes while being served. For either case they generate secondary invocation requests that go through a similar cycle as initial invocation requests as it is shown in Fig. 1. For database accesses the data type user interface object holds the information necessary for the parameterization of the secondary request and the distributor may dispatch multiple invocations depending on the requested operation and the number of effected replicas. Note that message exchanges between process instances are also implemented via process invocations. However, there is no additional parameterization provided for them. Their significance is in taking into account the communication and the scheduling delays that takes place at inter-process communication.

Secondary invocations can be synchronous (blocking) or asynchronous (non-blocking) invocations with respect to the initiating process instance. A blocked process instance will not be granted any CPU time until it is released by the instances holding the block, for example, until the instance representing the data access terminates.

The verification of the tool implementing this baseline model revealed that for our benchmark application, the performance characteristics produced by the simulator were within 5% error rate compared to the real system [5]. These results encouraged us to enhance this baseline model with features modeling multi-cluster configurations designed to increase the system's fault tolerance.

2.2 Modeling of Fault Tolerance Mechanisms

In TSP, there are a number of features providing fault tolerance. Some of these features were included in the baseline model since they are part of the system's basic operation and have immediate impact on the system performance. For example, a database update operation affects all the data replicas existing within a cluster, so the number of the replicas determines the system performance.

Other features that are not part of this basic operation needed for self-healing (e.g. repair after a processor crash) therefore they were left out from the baseline model. However, they are significant when it comes to dimensioning highly available systems, since when it becomes necessary the system must have enough capacity to carry out these repair and recovery procedures without interrupting or even degrading its normal services.

As mentioned earlier, TSP offers increased reliability based on multi-cluster configurations where remote clusters serve as standbys for each other. Therefore we extend our model the following way:

A container object is introduced to allow grouping of hardware components into different clusters. New links are defined to connect these clusters with each other that represent remote Internet connections (as opposed to local switch fabric connections). For these, the speed and capacity parameters need to be specified for each direction for each pair of connected clusters (for local connections we made the simplification of assuming homogeneity). The actual delay introduced by such a link then calculated from these parameters and the size of each packet sent through the link. The traffic passed through these links is the update information sent by the primary cluster to the appropriate standby. Thus, the distribution mechanism is also modified to dispatch these updates. Also, the distribution pool needs to be extended for all clusters, i.e. the set of processors where a given type is distributed is configured for each cluster participating in the cluster redundancy.

To model the recovery procedures we need further modifications.

First of all, for each processor and each cluster we need to maintain the state information whether they are in working condition, or not; and if they are, whether they are serving the traffic or recovering from a failure. The simplified state machine is presented in Fig. 2. Note that this model allows for a single processor failure in a cluster, the state changes to "*Processor reload*". The failure of the second processor while the first one is still recovering results in a cluster failure ("*Cluster reload*") that switches the traffic over to the standby cluster. If a failed processor cannot be recovered, the cluster is reconfigured by excluding that processor from the cluster (state becomes "*Cluster reconfiguration*" after a single crash or user initiated processor removal; and "*Pending processor*" during reconfiguration or cluster reload), and the failure condition is cleared that way.

The recovery procedure itself can be looked at as a special type of traffic internal to the system. Therefore we model it via traffic generators that are automatically created and removed from the simulation model. The amount and the type of the traffic that needs to be generated are determined by the current content of the failed component that triggered the mechanism. Once this traffic is served, the generator terminates, and the state of the associated component returns to the normal working condition.

To trigger these mechanisms at any time, we added a user action of a processor crash. Repeating the crash action on the same processor while it is recovering is interpreted as failure of the repair that triggers a cluster reconfiguration.

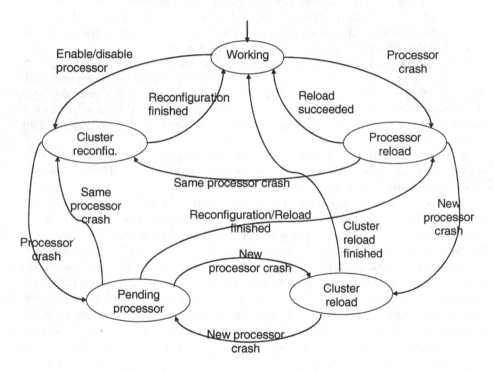

Fig. 2. Simplified state machine for system recovery

Most of the required changes could be achieved by introduction of specialized entities of the existing simulation components, such as special process types (i.e. system processes) that are dispatched under certain conditions. Thus, the user does not need to specify these invocations. In fact, many of them were tested first by defining the appropriate traffic generators and process types through the normal user interface. Only if that resulted in the expected behavior were they introduced to the tool.

3 Simulation of Multi-cluster Configurations

3.1 Hot Standby Redundancy

One way to enhance the system's reliability is to use hot standby redundancy (it is often referred as 2N redundancy). This is a traditional telecom solution: In this case, a primary cluster has a geographically separated back-up system, a hot standby cluster, which is regularly updated and synchronized with the primary cluster. This standby system is ready to take over the traffic of the primary system any time an emergency requires. Such a solution protects against losses caused by natural disasters such as earthquakes or floods, when the entire primary system may go down. Fig. 3 shows the simulation of the normal behavior of such a system.

The simulation model consists of three clusters that contain nine, eight and ten processors. The processor loads for each of the clusters appear in the top row of diagrams of Fig. 3. In this configuration, cluster #1 is the primary system (top leftmost chart) and cluster #2 (top middle chart) is the hot standby for it. The third cluster is not used in this configuration. Appropriately, the processor loads in cluster #1 that runs the application serving the traffic, are around 30% of their total capacity. Once cluster #2 is assigned as the first cluster's standby, load appears on its processors and this load stabilizes at around 2% as this cluster executes only updates of the standby replicas.

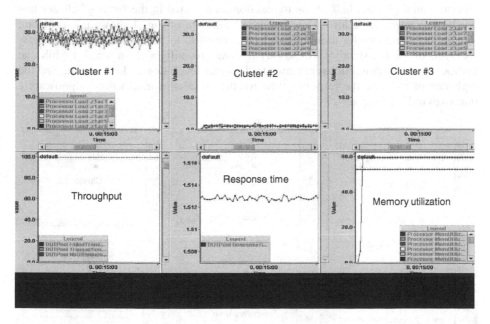

Fig. 3. Hot standby redundancy

The bottom three charts of Fig. 3 show the following from left to right:

- The number of initiated, served and failed requests: In this case, the number of initiated requests is 100 requests per second all of which are served successfully.

- The response time in seconds: For the modeled application, the average response time is 1.513 seconds.
- The memory utilization: For the processors of the primary cluster, the utilization is around 52%. Since the standby cluster contains fewer processors, there the memory utilization is higher. It reaches 60%.

The problem with this solution is cost-efficiency: Under normal circumstances, the second cluster is hardly ever used resulting in a cost-inefficient system.

3.2 Load-Sharing Clusters

In a different solution the clusters share the load while also serving as backup systems for each other. To limit the response time, a restriction is imposed on this solution: No transaction containing a database write-operation is allowed to cross cluster boundary. This implies that all the data necessary for an update (or any write related) operation must be located in the same cluster where the transaction is initiated.

In the first scenario shown in Fig. 4, initiated requests are randomly placed in the system, i.e., the location of the data is not taken into account at the distribution among the clusters. As the simulation results show that with load-sharing the processor loads in all clusters drop below 10% (between 5% and 8%) and the memory utilization is between 30% and 40% depending on the size of the cluster. However, because of the random initial placing, half of the transactions are started in the "wrong" cluster that results in transaction failure. The bottom left diagram of Fig. 4 shows this problem: the number of successful transactions drops from 100 to 50 (compared to the measurements of the hot standby redundancy that was reconfigured on the fly) while the number of failed transactions increases to the same level. Due to load sharing and the high rate of failures, the response time for the successful transactions significantly improves to 1.510 seconds.

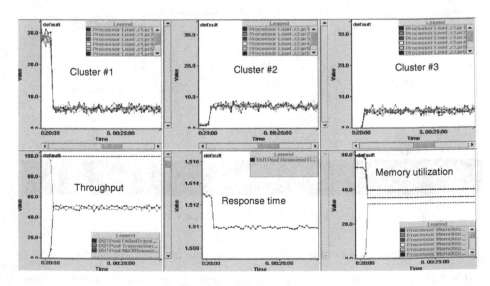

Fig. 4. Load sharing clusters

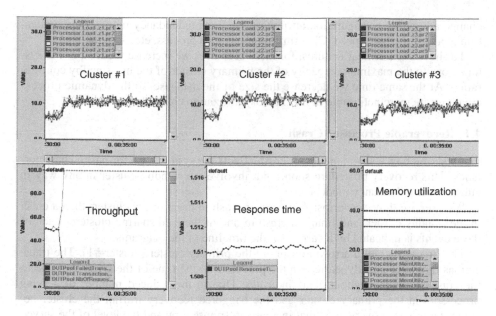

Fig. 5. Load sharing clusters with correct cluster selection

Thus, a real load-sharing system of this type must assess the data location before placing a request and it must direct the transaction to the appropriate cluster. In the simulation model as we mentioned earlier, we do not represent data object instances. Instead, the correlation between a given traffic and a set of distributors can be specified. For instances distributed by these distributors the cluster selection assumed to be based on the data location.

The simulation results of Fig. 5 show that with this adjustment all the requests succeed, as expected. The processor load increases in the clusters to 10-12% depending on the cluster size. The response time also slightly increases close to 1.511 seconds.

4 Simulation of Processor and Cluster Failures

To simulate the recovery mechanism triggered by cluster failures as mentioned earlier, we introduced a state model for the different components (see Fig. 2).

In the case of a processor crash, it is recovered by restarting the persistent processes lost due to the crash and restoring the data stored in the memory of that processor from the replicas existing in the system. This procedure is interpreted in the simulation as an internal traffic generated by the system itself to initiate the necessary invocations. This traffic generator automatically ceases to exist when all the lost instances are recovered.

In the following, we present different crash scenarios for both hot standby and load-sharing clusters. The processor load and memory utilization charts show clearly when we switch between these two redundancy models. (The simulator allows one to change any of the configuration attributes – such as redundancy model, data replication model, processor speed, CPU time required by a process, etc. – on the fly.)

To show some critical features, for these scenarios we increase the load of the system close to the maximum capacity of the primary cluster of the hot-standby configuration. At the same time we decrease the size of the database, so the dynamic process creations are more noticeable in the memory utilization charts.

4.1 Recoverable Processor Crash

Fig. 6 shows how a single processor crash affects the system's performance characteristics. This recovery procedure should not involve the standby cluster in any way in either of the redundancy models.

We exercise three scenarios: A processor crash in the primary cluster; then a crash in the standby cluster; and finally a crash in one of the load sharing clusters. Each of these events is indicated by an arrow on the timeline of the diagrams.

The first crash (solid arrows) occurs in the primary cluster (cluster #1). The transactions that have already started on the processor at the time of the crash, fail due to the crash as the throughput chart indicates. Due to the reduced number of serving processors in the primary cluster and the triggered recovery traffic, the cluster becomes temporarily overloaded that increases response time and the level of the served requests drops in the system. The processor load slightly increases in all but the crashed node of the primary cluster. Once the crashed processor recovers and starts to serve the traffic, the system gradually returns to its normal operation. That is, the response time decreases and the rates of initiated and served requests become equal. Since the process creation is more significant in this configuration compared to the database size, we also see an oscillation of the memory utilization parameter of the primary cluster. This reaches a higher level when requests are queued longer during the recovery.

Once the primary cluster recovers, we trigger a crash in the standby cluster (dashed arrow). This results in no other significant change for the system performance, than the recovery procedure of the crashed processor in the standby cluster. This creates a peak load (80%) in the recovering node and increases the load on the other processors (15%) as the lost replicas are restored from the copies existing on those.

Finally, we change the system configuration to share the load among the three clusters and we trigger a crash in cluster #3 (dotted arrow). In this case, again, we see a slight increase of the load in the processors of the affected cluster and a peak in the crashed processor as the recovering processor uses the copies existing within the cluster on other nodes to restore its state. However, the two other clusters are not affected at all. The transactions in progress on the crashed processor fail.

These scenarios show that in the case of a single processor crash, the most important issue is whether the rest of the cluster remains stable and balanced after the crash. Since after the crash the normal and the recovery traffic are served using the remaining copies of the data, an inappropriate replication could result in an uneven load of the remaining processors. This can overload some of them, and in a worst case scenario, can trigger a system collapse through a chain of processor failures.

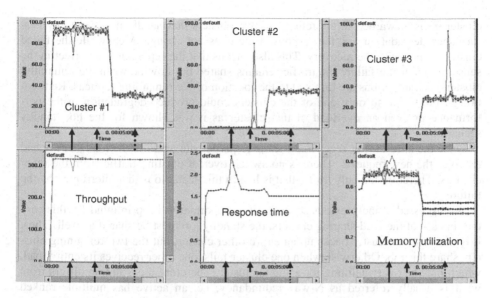

Fig. 6. Simulation of single processor crashes

As mentioned earlier, a traffic generator is created in association of the crashed processor. Since the generated traffic depends on the content of the processor at the moment of the crash, this is the first factor that determines the recovery time. The second factor is the speed at which the rest of the system can serve these requests. So for different applications and different traffic, we get different recovery times.

4.2 Cluster Failure

Once we can simulate a single processor crash, we are able to trigger a cluster failure by initiating multiple processor crashes within a cluster according to that state model of Fig. 2. Fig. 7 shows such scenarios. These scenarios again compare the configuration of the hot standby redundancy with load-sharing clusters.

The solid arrows in the diagrams indicate the failure of the primary cluster (#1) of the hot-standby configuration. As a result the standby cluster (#2) takes over the traffic: The processor loads drop sharply in the failed primary cluster and rise steeply in the standby. The former primary cluster immediately starts the recovery that prevents the processor loads from dropping to zero. Since the standby cluster contains fewer nodes than the primary, the traffic is overwhelming for it that causes a steady 100% processor loads, an increasing response time, and a significant queuing of requests shown by the increase in the memory utilization. These phenomena mean that cluster #2 was under-dimensioned for this traffic load.

Once the failed cluster #1 recovers the traffic is given back to it (indicated by the dashed arrows) to remedy the situation. However, this causes that all the transaction queued in cluster #2 fail as ongoing transactions cannot be transferred between clusters.

Compared to the hot-standby model, load-sharing clusters handle the failure of cluster #3 rather smoothly (marked with dotted arrows). The traffic of the failed cluster #3 is forwarded to the remaining two clusters that handle it without any performance degradation, i.e. the response time does not change. Meanwhile the failed cluster is busy with the recovery. This also means that the replication is correct in the sense that after the failure the traffic remains shared but now between the remaining clusters as transactions are directed to the location of the remaining replicas. Redirection of the traffic to only one of the clusters could produce degradation in the performance or even an overload of that cluster as it was shown for the hot-standby scenario.

Once the third cluster recovers, it starts to participate again in the load sharing and receives the new requests. There is no switch over of existing traffic from the other clusters. Therefore the only traffic that is lost in this scenario is that interrupted by the failure.

As discussed at the previous scenario, it is important to keep in mind for this case that in case of the load-sharing clusters, the standby job must be shared as well. Thus, it is not that one cluster backs up an entire other cluster, but the two remaining clusters share this job. Otherwise when one cluster fails, one other receives its entire load, which may be overwhelming for a single cluster. Therefore this solution differs from what is usually referred as N-way redundancy, i.e. an active has multiple ranked standbys from which the highest ranking takes over the traffic in case of the failure of the active. While N-way redundancy generally works within a cluster, in the demonstrated case it would create an imbalanced system.

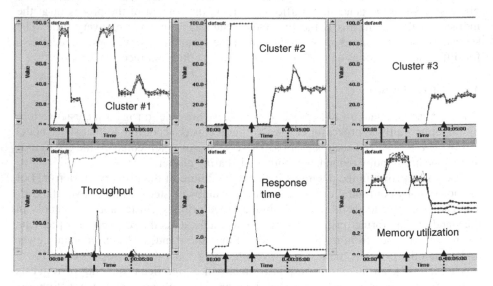

Fig. 7. Cluster failures

4.3 Fatal Processor Crash

In the above scenarios, the crashes are not fatal in the sense that the processors recovered after the crash. However, this may not always be the case. The next scenarios show as the clusters reconfigure themselves after fatal processor crashes.

These scenarios are simulated again through internal traffic generators. However, in this case once it is determined that the processor cannot recover, the initial traffic generators that simulate the recovery of the lost instances in one processor, are replaced with new generators. These imitate the traffic of a total reconfiguration of the cluster appropriate for the reduced number of processors. This procedure recovers the lost replicas as well as re-balances the system.

For these scenarios, we choose cluster #3 as the primary cluster of the hot standby redundancy since it contains ten processors. As we have already shown, eight processors cannot cope with the traffic for an extended period.

The top-right diagram of Fig. 8 shows the first processor crashing in the primary cluster (solid arrows). Since it cannot recover (the crash is triggered second time in the processor while it is trying to recover – this is interpreted as fatal failure according to Fig. 2), the load and the memory utilization on the failed node drops to zero (the short delay is due to the manual trigger of the repeated crash). At the same time, the remaining processors start the reconfiguration that increases their load: Even though the processors loads before the crash are around 80%, during the reconfiguration they become 100% that causes the response time to grow steadily. The throughput diagram (bottom left) shows that during the reconfiguration the serving rate is below the initiated rate. However, once the reconfiguration is completed the remaining processors are able to cope even with the backlog and the cluster fully recovers. This exercise demonstrates that the 20% free capacity available in the system is not enough for seamless system reconfigurations for the modeled application even though even less was enough for processor recovery.

The second fatal crash (marked by the dashed arrows) is triggered in the standby cluster #2 after the primary recovered. As expected, it does not affect the system

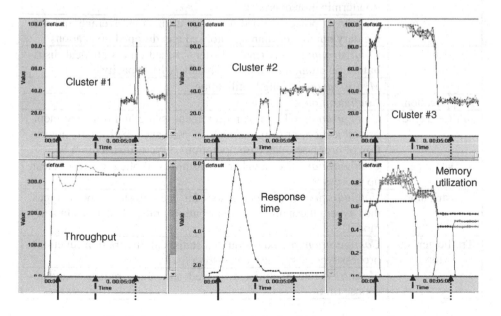

Fig. 8. Automatic reconfiguration after fatal processor crash

performance but it generates an average 35% additional load on the processors of that cluster. This explains why the 20% free capacity in the primary cluster is not sufficient for reconfiguration.

Finally, the third crash is exercised in a load-sharing system (dotted arrows). It is triggered in cluster #1. An initial peak in the crashed processor's load shows that the attempt of restarting the processor is made that fails as the fatal crash is triggered. This deems the processor to be removed from the system and starts the reconfiguration. The reconfiguration affects only the cluster of the failed processor. Like in the other cases, the reconfiguration creates and additional 35% load, however for a shorter period since there are less data replicas in the cluster and there is no overload. As a result, the reconfiguration does not effect the response time or the throughput.

5 Simulator Controls

The presented scenarios showed that the simulation results were similar to those expected from such systems. However, the situation changes in complex systems such as heterogeneous clusters (different processors within a cluster, and clusters of

Table 1. Configuration attributes and measurements for the different simulation components

Simulation components	Configuration and measured attributes
Cluster	*Configuration*: list of processors, inter-cluster connections
Processor	*Configuration*: speed, RAM size, hard drive speed/capacity, input links, scheduling time slot, scheduling and process instantiation/termination overhead
	Measured: processor load, memory utilization, average and momentary number of running, blocked and dropped invocations
Link	*Configuration*: delay (intra-cluster – based on a statistical distribution function; inter-cluster – bandwidth), capacity
	Measured: queue length/utilization
Application	*Configuration*: distributors
Process type	*Configuration*: CPU time requirement, static and dynamic memory allocation, priority, number of messages exchanges, invocation of processes, database operations, timers, distribution type
Data type	*Configuration*: size, number of instances, replication type, clean up process
Distributor	*Configuration*: list of processors for each cluster, process types, data types, the number of distribution units, cluster redundancy model
Traffic generator	*Configuration*: period (through a statistical distribution function), process type, distributor correlation list
	Measured: rate of initiated, served and failed requests, and response time

different sizes), running collocated applications, with different distribution schemas of processes and data. One needs a tool to be able to properly design a site, to carry out similar analysis as shown for the sample application in these small clusters.

To appreciate the power of the simulator, Table 1 lists the most important configuration attributes and measurements for the different simulation components. From this list one may see that a wide variety of systems can be simulated.

The simulator runs on a Windows PC. The engine and the model are written in C++ while the GUI is in Java.

6 Conclusions

We presented a simulation-based case study of multi-cluster redundancy configurations that can provide higher fault tolerance than that of the base cluster. We used simulation as a mean of investigation and presented a variety of scenarios that we carried out to understand better the system behavior and to pinpoint possible problems.

These exercises taught us what needed to be taken into consideration at the system and application design to support fault tolerance. They have also shown issues that have to be taken care of each time a new site is designed (e.g. reserve capacity for the case of unplanned reconfigurations) to enable these recovery features.

Traditionally, engineers would use rules of thumb to handle these issues. However, with the increased complexity of new systems and the expanding range of applications one cannot rely any more on rules of thumb. There is a need of reliable methods and tools to answer these questions. Simulation is one of the options and our study demonstrates that it offers a great help in all aspects: system, application and site design. In addition, it is an invaluable training tool for staff maintaining these complex systems.

We exercised up to two processor crashes in a cluster, and the simulation showed system downtime in none of the cases. In some scenarios ongoing user requests were dropped due to the failure or switchover. This was more significant in the hot standby configuration.

For load-sharing clusters our solution differs from the one usually referred as N-way redundancy, as the clusters share the standby roles: Each is standby only for a partition of each other cluster. As a result, when a cluster fails its load is not switched to a single standby cluster as that would double its load and therefore can be overwhelming. Instead, it is distributed among the remaining clusters according to the standby partitions so the system remains balanced during the recovery of the failed cluster.

Carrying out this study made us realize many aspects of such systems that were not obvious at first glance. It also gave us a deeper understanding of the different mechanisms that will help us in the future design and development of transaction oriented high availability clusters and to tune application and site configurations to their best but still safe performance.

References

1. Harry Singh, Distributed fault-tolerant/high-availability systems, white paper, Trillium Digital Systems, Inc., 2001
2. V. Ferraro-Esparza, M. Gudmandsen, K. Olsson, Ericsson Telecom Server Platform 4, Ericsson Review No.3, 2002
3. Lars Hennert and Alexander Larruy, TelORB —The distributed communications operating system, Ericsson Review No.3, 1999
4. Maria Toeroe, Performance simulation of the Jambala platform, 35th Annual Simulation Symposium, San Diego, April 2002
5. Maria Toeroe, Performance Simulation of Cluster-Based Asynchronous Soft Real-Time Systems, Kluwer Academic Publishers, Cluster Computing 6, pp. 315-324, 2003

Inconsistency Evaluation in a Replicated IP-Based Call Control System

Thibault Renier, Erling Matthiesen, Hans-Peter Schwefel, and Ramjee Prasad

CTIF, Aalborg University, Niels Jernes Vej 12,
9220 Aalborg Ost, Denmark
{tr, evm, hps, prasad}@kom.aau.dk

Abstract. The Session Initiation Protocol has been chosen for controlling multimedia sessions in the IMS part of UMTS infrastructures. In such networks, availability is crucial and the integration of SIP with a fault-tolerant solution, often based on a replication technique, has become necessary. Because the replicated stateful servers are deployed in distributed networks, state inconsistency may be introduced. Mechanisms have been proposed, which aim at keeping the inconsistency level below a certain threshold by introducing an adaptive delay before the states are committed. The effectiveness of those adaptive mechanisms depends on the accuracy of the inconsistency evaluation during the system operation. In this context, the careful definition of a practically measurable inconsistency metric is necessary in order to benefit from those mechanisms while minimizing their impacting on performance. This paper discusses the relevance of different inconsistency definitions and suggests a common model in which the inconsistency metrics are broken down into a set of measurable and/or analytically derivable contributing factors. We analyze the validity of this evaluation approach with results obtained in a prototype implementation of a 3GPP IMS call control system integrated in a distributed fault-tolerant architecture, so-called RSerPool, for the example of instant message sessions between users.

Keywords: distributed fault-tolerance, state replication, inconsistency, IMS, SIP, RSerPool.

1 Introduction

Third generation mobile networks are offering access to IP-based multimedia services. The Session Initiation Protocol (SIP) [1] has been chosen for establishing multimedia sessions in the IMS part [2,3] of UMTS infrastructures. In such networks, mobile operators put high requirements on their infrastructure, in particular on availability and reliability of call control, and the integration of SIP with a fault-tolerant solution has become necessary. One approach to minimize the impact of server failures in order to offer fault-tolerant service provisioning is to implement redundant servers and to replicate the state between them in a timely manner. In this paper, we study one concept for such a fault-tolerant architecture, namely RSerPool [4,5,6,7,18], in its application to the highly relevant use-case of SIP call control. It is implemented as a distributed set of stateful servers gathered in a so-called pool.

D. Penkler, M. Reitenspiess, and F. Tam (Eds.): ISAS 2006, LNCS 4328, pp. 177–192, 2006.
© Springer-Verlag Berlin Heidelberg 2006

When the replicated stateful servers are implemented in distributed networks, state inconsistency may be introduced. Although there are mechanisms to assure so-called strong consistency [8,9,10], these are not normally viable in the settings of call control in mobile networks since they lead to large overhead and degrading performance (longer call control times), which are not acceptable for the real-time services supported by the IMS. More recently, adaptive mechanisms have been proposed [11,12,17] which aim at keeping the inconsistency level below a certain threshold defined by the operator. Those mechanisms are based on an adaptive timer that delays the state commitment and update, in order to bring the instantaneous inconsistency level below the target value. The effectiveness of the adaptive mechanisms depends on the accuracy of the inconsistency evaluation during the system operation. Therefore, the careful definition of a practically measurable inconsistency metric is necessary.

After presenting the environment in which we consider the state updates and related inconsistency issue, the paper discusses the relevance of a variety of different inconsistency definitions and introduces a common model in which the inconsistency metrics are broken down into a set of measurable and/or analytically derivable contributing factors. This model is not intended to provide fault-tolerant itself, it is used instead to provide numerical inputs for commitment protocols and for architectural considerations. We analyze the validity of this measurement approach, based on results obtained in a prototype implementation of a 3GPP IMS call control system with the distributed fault-tolerant server pooling for the example of instant message sessions between users.

2   The Fault-Tolerant SIP-Based IMS System

In the following, we give a brief introduction to the call control protocol SIP and its fault-tolerant deployment scenario in third generation mobile networks.

2.1   The Session Initiation Protocol (SIP)

SIP was defined by the IETF in RFC3261 [1]. It is an application-layer protocol for creating, modifying, and terminating sessions over IP. A SIP session (also called dialog or call leg) is a series of transactions, initiated and terminated respectively by an INVITE and a BYE transaction. There are also other transactions types, such as REGISTER, CANCEL, OPTIONS, NOTIFY and MESSAGE. A SIP transaction consists of a single request, some potential provisional responses and a final response (usually, the positive 200OK response). A transaction is successfully completed only when the final response is successfully received, processed and forwarded by a proxy server.

SIP is based on the client-server model: typically, SIP requests are originated at a User Agent Client (UAC), pass through one or more SIP servers and arrive at one or more SIP User Agent Servers (UAS), which are in charge of responding to the requests.

2.2 Deployment Scenario in 3rd Generation Mobile Networks: IP-Based Multimedia Subsystems (IMS)

In order to support IP-based multimedia sessions in UMTS, a call control infrastructure that uses SIP was introduced in Release 5 of UMTS standards. In the IMS, the SIP signaling is processed by entities called Call State Control Functionality (CSCF). The basic network architecture consists of three different types of CSCF servers [2] plus an additional supporting database:

- HSS (Home Subscriber Server) is the integrated database that consists of a Location Server, which stores information on the location of users, and a profile database, which stores service profile information for subscribed users.
- P-CSCF (Proxy CSCF) is the server initially contacted by the SIP devices. All SIP requests are sent from the sending device to a P-CSCF.
- I-CSCF (Interrogation CSCF) acts as first contact point for other IMS networks and has the additional task of selecting an appropriate S-CSCF with the help of the HSS.
- S-CSCF (Serving CSCF) is mainly responsible for managing each user's profile and the call states. It performs service control and furthermore provides interfaces to application servers.

Figure 1 shows an example of SIP message paths in the IMS between a UAC and a UAS.

CSCF servers may need to maintain states. In the IMS, most SIP servers are call stateful, meaning that the servers remember the global state for a session from the initiating INVITE transaction to the terminating BYE transaction request. The call state updates occur after completion of each transaction.

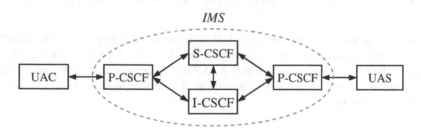

Fig. 1. IMS architecture

2.3 RSerPool: Fault-Tolerant Distributed Architecture

The RSerPool concept [18] relies on redundancy to be deployed anywhere in an IP network, even in different sub-networks. Hosts that implement the same service are called pool elements (PE) and form a so-called pool, which is identified by a unique pool handle (i.e. a pool identifier). The users of a server pool are referred to as pool users (PU). Another entity, called name server (NS), is in charge of monitoring the pool, keeping track of the peer servers' status, and to help the clients know which servers the requests can be sent to. Figure 2 depicts the RSerPool architecture.

The functionality of RSerPool is based on two novel protocols: Endpoint Name Resolution Protocol (ENRP) [5] and Aggregate Server Access Protocol (ASAP) [6]. ASAP provides the name resolution functionality, i.e. the translation of a pool handle, sent by a PU, into a set of PEs' transport addresses (IP addresses and port numbers), and adds a suggestion for a server selection policy. Then, the PU can keep in a cache the information obtained from the name server and uses it for sending future requests. The second RSerPool protocol is ENRP. Name servers use this protocol mainly to disseminate the status of their PEs among their peers to make sure that the information is consistent and up-to-date in every pool since a PE can belong to more than one pool.

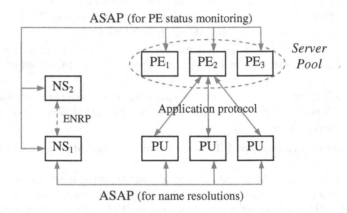

Fig. 2. RSerPool architecture for one pool server. NS1 is the default name server for the server pool; NS2 can be used as a backup NS for this pool and as the default NS for another pool.

Note that the requirements for high availability and scalability defined in RSerPool do not include requirements on state sharing in the pool, i.e. on how the PEs should propagate the session state among them: ASAP itself does not share any state between pool elements. Later, we give the details of the simple state-sharing solution we implemented in our testbed.

3 Inconsistency Definitions and Evaluation Framework

3.1 Inconsistency Definitions

The relevance of an inconsistency definition depends greatly on how accurately it measures to which extent a system's expected behavior is impacted by state-related errors occurring at the servers when committing the state updates and/or when reading the state values. Inconsistent states do not affect all systems and services to the same extent, so the specificities of the system and service(s) are to be considered as well when defining inconsistency in a given scenario.

Most of the time, inconsistency is referred to as state sequence disorder, also called event-ordering problem [14]. With this approach, possible inconsistency definitions are such as the probability that a state update is ordered correctly, or the probability that all the state updates of a session are fully ordered. The latter is especially suited for dependent states, i.e. when state update n is a function of the state value resulting from state update $n-1$, since one disorder occurrence leads to all subsequent state update to be erroneous.

In some cases, a state disorder can be transparent to the service/system: in our SIP call control system, inconsistency can be observed –and, therefore, can have an impact– only when the state is read, e.g. after the communication fails over to the backup server. Not retrieving the correct state value leads to erroneous behavior of the system. Thus, it is more relevant to focus on the correctness of the state when a read operation is done, which is called misread probability. One has to be careful when defining the correctness of the state. With SIP, the state is correct when it has the same value as the one saved at the server of the system that committed the last state update.

For billing purposes, it may be sufficient to read the charging state only once, at the end of the session, in order to deduct the amount of credits spent by the user from his account. In that case, a relevant metric is the distance between the state value read and the actual amount of credits used by the user, which measures the operator's losses. In the prepaid charging scenario, the operator wants to control the access to the network and potentially stop the session when all the user's credits are spent. Then, it is important for the operator to also have access to a consistent charging state during the life-time of a session.

3.2 Evaluation Model

Dynamic, adaptive mechanisms have been proposed [11,12,17] to maintain the inconsistency level below a certain threshold. For systems implementing such solutions, the need for accurate inconsistency evaluation is evident. However, inconsistency occurs in distributed systems, which makes it difficult to be measured in practice (e.g. time stamps are difficult to use because of the clock synchronization issue). Here, we suggest an evaluation framework that uses the characteristics of a system in order to break the computation of the inconsistency level down to influencing factors that can be either measured or approximated from the traffic model and the description of the system. This evaluation approach offers the advantage of not requiring any specific, additional inconsistency evaluation functions to be implemented in the system.

The scenarios (shown in Figure 3) that lead to inconsistency in distributed communication networks are for the example of strict inconsistency, namely, the probability to access an erroneous state at the read operation, i.e. the probability to access a state update that is not the last state update committed in the system. The starting point corresponds to a read operation; the bold lines represent the paths to inconsistency instances, which occur when the last event of a path actually happens (shown in the grey text boxes). This evaluation approach can be generalized to any inconsistency definition that looks at the probability to read, or write, a correct state since it only relies on the probabilities that the events depicted in Figure 3 occur. While some inconsistency evaluation solutions require that the state values follows a known pattern, our approach applies to any type of state values (sequential, non-deterministic, (in)dependent).

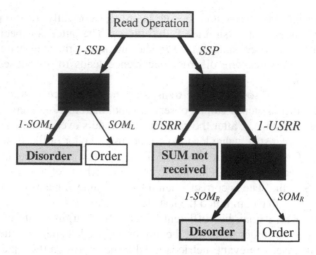

Fig. 3. Representation of all the events sequentially leading to inconsistency, and their respective probabilities

Because of the server selection policy (or load balancing scheme) implemented in a system, a read operation can occur at the server where the last state update was committed, called the local server, or at another server of the system, a remote server. When a read is done at a remote server, the state update message (SUM, see next section) carrying the last state update of the system must be received at this server; nevertheless, this message might never get to the remote server, especially for connectionless communications (e.g. over UDP), and the state would never be updated. Fulfilling only this requirement does not guarantee consistency: also, the latest SUM must be processed at the remote server before the next read operation is executed. The local server has already committed the last state update when a read request arrives and, therefore, cannot be impacted by a SUM loss. However, if a SUM carrying the $n-1^{th}$ state update is received after commitment of local state update n, the correct value might be overwritten and corrupt the correctness of the state before the read operation is processed. Note that the state update policy considered for this paper is such that state update disorder at a local server does not impact the system; the reasons are analyzed later.

This discussion shows that the overall inconsistency depends on three factors:

1. Server Selection Policy (*SSP*): the probability of reading a state in a remote server. This probability depends on three system characteristics:
   - the server selection policy, which chooses the server where the next transaction will be processed (see e.g. [19]);
   - the failure model;
   - the fail-over mechanism, which chooses the server where a retransmitted request should be sent to after a failure was detected (there are many existing policies that determine the destination server for request retransmissions).
2. State Ordering Metric (*SOM*): the probability that the last state update in the system is committed at the server where the read request is received, before this

read request is received. One should be careful when evaluating *SOM* as it is expected to be different for the local server (SOM_L) and a remote server (SOM_R).

3. Unsuccessful State Replication Rate (*USRR*): the probability that the state replication is failed, i.e. that the SUM is not processed at the remote server, either because of packet loss or buffer overflow.

Those factors lead to a new measurement approach for the misread probability, directly derived from the probabilities illustrated in Figure 3:

$$Inconsistency = (1 - SSP)\cdot(1 - SOM_L) + SSP\cdot[USRR + (1 - USRR)\cdot(1 - SOM_R)] \qquad (1)$$

4 Experimental System

We want to investigate inconsistency in the call control part of the IMS, whose experimental logical architecture is shown in Figure 4. More details about this experimental system are given in [15].

The logical entities implement the IMS-like SIP call control servers (CSCFs) standardized by the 3GPP as previously defined. The gray shaded entities represent the RSerPool components. The two redundant S-CSCFs form a server pool of Pool Elements. The choice for the Pool User was motivated by our SIP implementation: the role of the PU could have been taken by the P-CSCF or the I-CSCF. However, since the I-CSCF is only in the SIP path for REGISTER requests and those are not part of the investigated call scenario, the P-CSCF was implemented as PU. Every time a P-CSCF receives an INVITE request, it uses ASAP to request a name resolution from the name server in order to get the list of available servers to forward the requests to. The P-CSCF keeps this list in its cache for the whole duration of the session; the start of a new session triggers a new name resolution request. The other communications during the session are made over UDP.

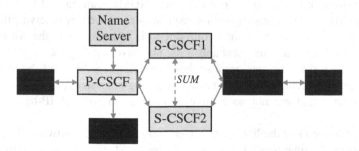

Fig. 4. Testbed logical topology for the IMS/RSerPool system. *SUM* is the message that contains the state information; it is sent from the local server to the remote server after every transaction completion.

CSCF servers usually maintain a large number of session states simultaneously. In our example, the session state is only influenced by the transactions of its own session. Hence, parallel sessions are not required for the evaluation of inconsistency. The UAC follows a simple session/transaction generation pattern. Between the INVITE and BYE transactions, the UAC generates instant message transactions with the MESSAGE request. The inter-transaction time is the time between the moment when a transaction ends (completion or abortion) and the moment when the request for the next transaction is sent. In our testbed, the inter-transaction time is exponentially distributed, with mean value $1/\lambda$ set to one second. The server selection policy is round robin at the scale of the transaction, meaning that each request is sent alternately to either S-CSCF, and the response(s) is sent back via the same S-SCSF (according to the SIP specifications, all messages in a SIP transaction must be processed by the same S-CSCF server). Even though round robin is not desirable to meet high requirements on state consistency, our goal is not to improve the consistency of the SIP call control system; instead, it is to validate our evaluation approach with the experimental system: in our system, there is no inconsistency at the local server, so we need to check the state consistency at the remote server only; as detailed in the next section, the way to check the state consistency is to send the next SIP request to the remote server, which implies that the local and remote server roles are exchanged for every next transaction. For another server selection policy, e.g. persistent backup, our evaluation model still applies; only *SSP* will need to be evaluated accordingly.

Because RSerPool does not specify any state-sharing functionality, we had to implement our own solution in the system. Our state-sharing mechanism is a best effort, message-based solution, over the connectionless transport protocol, UDP. When a transaction is completed at a server, the call state is updated in this server and the state update is replicated to its peer in a file sent with what we call a state update message (SUM), using the direct link between the two servers shown with the dashed line in Figure 4. The simplest models for state commitment and concurrency are used in our system. When the replicated servers receive the SUM, they immediately extract the state update and commit it. In case a server has many SUMs to process (e.g. when several sessions are running in parallel), the SUMs wait in a FIFO queue for processing. Also, when a read operation request is processed by a server, the state is immediately accessed and no delay is introduced in order to insure the correctness of the values read. Again, this mechanism is not favoring high consistency but is adequate for real-time services because they are delay-sensitive and the state should be retrieved immediately when needed. Strong-consistency protocols usually introduce delays that are not acceptable in case of failover of IP-based real-time services.

The characteristics of the link (packet error rate, delay, etc.) between the replicated servers impact the time needed to propagate the SUM; their specific settings in our experimental system are given in a following section.

There was no artificial failure model implemented in the testbed since the focus in this paper is not on the capability of the system to cope with failures of the SIP servers. The prototype SIP implementation that we used was not fully reliable though and failures were observed at all SIP servers. Therefore, the fault-tolerant properties of RSerPool were used for fault recovery. When a failure/error is detected (timeout per SIP request set to 0.5 second), the P-CSCF retransmits the request to the back-up S-CSCF. The transaction is dropped if the timeout also expires when trying with the second server.

5 Inconsistency Evaluation

In this chapter, we explain how we evaluated inconsistency (1) by implementing a solution in the experimental system, called experimental evaluation, and (2) by analyzing the influencing factors introduced previously, called factor evaluation. The goal is to compare the experimental and factor evaluations results in order to verify the validity of the proposed formula (c.f. Equation (1)) and discuss its potential limitations.

5.1 Experimental Evaluation

We implemented an algorithm in the testbed to directly, and experimentally, measure the inconsistency level of the SIP fault-tolerant system. The (distributed) call state element in this example is a charging counter ($CSeq\_server$) in the S-CSCF that keeps track of the cumulative number of successful MESSAGE transactions provided to the user. In this particular example, the approach to directly measure inconsistency is to also implement this counter in the UAC ($CSeq\_msg$) and to communicate the UAC's counter value to the S-CSCF in every SIP message.

When the UAC is aware that the last transaction is completed, i.e. it receives the corresponding final response, $CSeq\_msg$ is incremented before it is put in the next request the UAC sends. At the S-CSCF side, the local CSeq counter, $CSeq\_server$, is saved with the call state. We consider that every request received by an S-CSCF initiates a read operation. Therefore, upon reception of a SIP request at an S-CSCF, we can be sure that the state is consistent at this server, if the CSeq in the message is the next value in the incremental CSeq sequence, compared to the CSeq saved locally at the S-CSCF after the last state update. In other words, there is inconsistency iff:

$$CSeq\_msg - CSeq\_server > 1 \qquad (2)$$

When a State Update Message is disordered (meaning that the SUM arrives at the peer server after the request for the next transaction has been received) or when a SUM is missing, the value is not up-to-date and the read operation increments the inconsistency counter ($InconCount$) at this server.

As described in the previous section, any server of the system can fail. When a transaction is unsuccessful because of a P- or I-CSCF failure, it might happen that the SIP messages are blocked on the SIP path before the state has been updated at an S-CSCF. Then, it would be unfair to the system to check inconsistency with a $CSeq$ value that the system potentially never saved at any of the S-CSCFs. Therefore, a read operation can trigger an inconsistency check only after a successful transaction, i.e. only when we are sure that at least the local S-CSCF is aware of the last $CSeq$ value.

The inconsistency level is measured by dividing the inconsistency instances counter (*InconCount*) by the total number of read operations that requested the inconsistency check (*CheckCount*).

While rather simple to implement in this specific system, this experimental approach proves also to be quite limited. First, it requires dedicated code for inconsistency evaluation purposes, which may not be desirable e.g. for systems with low computational power. It also assumes that the state is monotonic and, therefore, relies on the knowledge of the next state value(s), mandatory in order to assess the correctness of the state. Finally, the UAC is involved in the state evaluation, which seems against the operators' philosophy that suggests giving minimum control to the end users with respect to critical information, especially when dealing with charging-related information.

5.2 Factor Evaluation

In this section, we analyze how to evaluate independently each factor of the evaluation approach described in the evaluation framework Section for the example of strict inconsistency. Many inconsistency definitions/metrics can be broken down into influencing factors equivalent to the ones proposed in this paper; then, those factors can be directly measured or analytically derived from the traffic model and system description.

1. State Ordering Metric (*SOM*): In our system, the state to be retrieved has monotonically increasing values (incremented by one for each new transaction); it should always be bigger than the previous one. Therefore, it does not make sense to update the state with a disordered SUM when its *CSeq_msg* value is smaller than the current *CSeq_server* where it is received. That way, we prevent the propagation of disordered SUMs to several read operations. This would not be the case for non-monotonic state values (e.g. location information), which make it impossible to detect an out-of-date state value in the SUM and, thus, requires that the state is updated every time a SUM is received. Also, with this state update model, inconsistency cannot occur at a local server since an old SUM cannot overwrite the latest state at the local server, which implies that SOM_L is equal to one. Consequently, a disordered state update can only impact a remote server (SOM_R).

   SOM_R is the probability that a read request (i.e. any SIP request in our context) is processed by the remote server after the SUM corresponding to the last state update committed at the local server. To evaluate this factor, we choose the moment when the state is updated at the local server as the reference starting point. Let (1) the Read Operation time (*RO_time*) be the time between the local state update and the next read operation, and (2) the State Update time (*SU_time*) be the time for the remote server to get and commit the SUM from the local server. Then, SOM_R can be expressed as the following probability:

$$SOM_R = \Pr\{RO\_time > SU\_time\} \qquad (3)$$

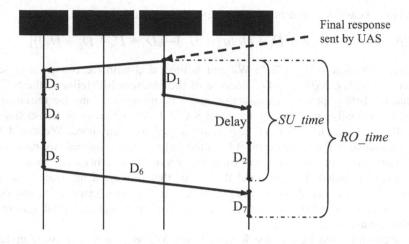

Fig. 5. *RO_time* and *SU_time* delays

Figure 5 shows all the delays that contribute to *RO_time* and *SU_time*: D_1 is the processing time between the final 200OK response leaves the local server and the corresponding SUM is sent to the remote server; *Delay* is the link delay between the two servers (artificially implemented in the function that processes the SUMs at the remote server, here S_2-CSCF); D_2 is the processing time to commit the state update at the remote server after reception of the SUM. D_3 is the processing time at the UAC to complete the transaction after reception of the final 200OK response; D_4 is the inter-transaction time previously defined; D_5 is the processing time between the beginning of the transaction and the moment when the UAC actually sends the request; D_6 is the propagation time of the request from the UAC to the remote server. Note that the two other propagation times, namely between S_1-CSCF and the UAC, and between the two S-CSCFs, are negligible (the bandwidth is 1Mbps); only this propagation time was considered since non-negligible processing times at the P-/I-CSCF are to be considered in the calculation of SOM_R. D_7 is the processing time between reception of the read request and the actual checking of the state values.

Let us break those two times down into their respective delays:

$$\begin{cases} RO\_time = D_3 + D_4 + D_5 + D_6 + D_7 \\ SU\_time = D_1 + Delay + D_2 \end{cases} \tag{4}$$

On one hand, according to the traffic model, D_4 is exponentially distributed, with mean value $1/\lambda$. On the other hand, we can assume that the other delays are deterministic because of the light load in the system. Therefore, in order to evaluate SOM_R, we can isolate D_4 and Equation (3) becomes:

$$SOM_R = \Pr\{D_4 > (D_1 + Delay + D_2) - (D_3 + D_5 + D_6 + D_7)\} \tag{5}$$

And in the case of exponentially distributed D_4, as defined earlier:

$$SOM_R = \exp[-\lambda \cdot ((D_1 + Delay + D_2) - (D_3 + D_5 + D_6 + D_7))] \qquad (6)$$

2. Server Selection Policy (*SSP*): Without failures and with the round robin server selection policy, *SSP* is 100%. Because of the inherent SIP failures, the S-CSCF contacted first to process a transaction might be unavailable and the retransmitted request is finally processed by the local S-CSCF for the previous transaction, i.e. the RO is local; in that case, *SSP* is not equal to 1 anymore. We could have approximated *SSP* at 1, or derive it from the failure model. Instead, we measured it by comparing in the tcpdump files the server that processed transaction n successfully, noted *server(n)*, and the server that processed the read request for transaction $n+1$, noted *server(n+1)*. *SSP* equals the ratio between the number of cases when *server(n)* and *server(n+1)* are different and the total number of comparisons.
3. Unsuccessful State Replication Rate (*USRR*): We assume that no state update is dropped due to buffer overflow since the traffic is very small compared to the memory and CPU capacities of the machines used in the system. Then, the probability that the SUM is not received is directly equal to the Packet Error Rate (*PER*, see beginning of next section) in the link between the two S-CSCFs.

Once the three influencing factors have been evaluated, they can be used in Equation (1) to directly derive the inconsistency level.

6 Results and Analysis

6.1 Results

The previous section showed that inconsistency is a function of the characteristics of the link used for the state replication, namely packet error rate and delay. The latter link characteristics were emulated at the S-CSCFs in the function in charge of receiving the SUMs. To emulate delay in the link, the corresponding thread freezes for the desired time and the received SUMs are randomly dropped according to the chosen *PER*, before they are processed. The bandwidth was fixed to 1Mbps. We ran six tests with different values for those two link parameters, shown in Table 1. For each scenario, the duration of the test in terms of number of sessions established by the UAC is set to 1400 sessions. The number of messages per session is geometrically distributed with a mean value of 10; hence, the overall number of read requests to the session state (at which inconsistency is evaluated) is approximately 14000.

Although the system was lightly loaded, the measurements of the processing delays D_X (D_1, D_2, and D_3, D_5, D_6, D_7) showed that they were not deterministic and were distributed with long tails. For example, D_7 was around 8ms for most of the RO requests but its values ranged from 5-6ms up to 800-900ms. Since the values in the tail of the delay distribution are not relevant for inconsistency, but they influence the mean strongly, we choose to use the most likely delay values of D_X (the modes of the empiric distributions) in the calculation of SOM_R.

Table 1 gives for each test scenario the final inconsistency results for the experimental evaluation (direct measurement of inconsistency) and the factor evaluation (via the right-hand side of Equation (1)), as well as the absolute difference between the two approaches.

Table 1. Comparative results for the experimental and analytical evaluations of inconsistency

Delay (ms)	PER (%)	Experimental evaluation	Factor evaluation	Absolute difference
20	2	2.76%	3.80%	+1.04%
20	2	3.45%	3.92%	+0.47%
0	15	13.77%	13.38%	-0.39%
300	0	19.51%	23.38%	+3.87%
300	15	29.09%	33.77%	+4.68%
300	15	27.45%	33.62%	+6.17%

6.2 Analysis

The results show that the inconsistency level evaluated with the factor approach is slightly higher than the directly measured inconsistency in our experimental system in all scenarios except when there is no delay in the link used for propagating the state update (Row 3 in Table 1). When the delay is much larger, i.e. 300ms, the absolute gaps between experimental and factor results get larger as well: up to 6.17% in the worst case (delay-300ms, PER-15%).

The observation of bigger deviations in settings with higher *Delay* between the two servers can be explained via the empiric distribution of the delays D_X. As stated earlier, the delays that contribute to *RO_time* and *SU_time* are not deterministic and vary (sometimes even reaching large values), even though the load on the SIP/RSerPool system always stayed low. The variations in the D_X values appear to be a consequence of the SIP SW implementation. Both *RO_time* and *SU_time* contain additive delay parts with such variation (the ones that are due to processing time); however, there are more of those in *RO_time*. As a consequence, the deterministic assumption used to compute SOM_R underestimates both *RO_time* and *SU_time*, but *RO_time* more strongly (contains four processing delays as opposed to only two in *SU_time*). Thus, the factor approach overestimates inconsistency due to the variation of the processing delays.

When *Delay* is null (i.e. resulting in smaller *SU_times*), the state is almost always updated at the remote server before the next RO is received, therefore *RO_time* is expected to be longer than *SU_time* and then, even longer *RO_times* do not hide potential inconsistency instances caused by disordering (only remaining cause of inconsistency is packet loss). Hence, much higher accuracy is obtained with the factor evaluation in the scenarios with low or no *Delay* between the two servers.

Note that for the purpose of validation, we picked extreme settings for our tests that lead to very high inconsistency levels; it is rare to reach 15% *PER*, especially in the wired core network between two servers.

6.3 Discussion of Parameter Influence

After discussing how to map the influencing factors to our SIP call control, we concluded that SOM_L is equal to 1. Then, Equation (1) becomes:

$$Inconsistency = SSP \cdot [USRR + (1 - USRR) \cdot (1 - SOM_R)] \tag{7}$$

In Figure 6, we draw the inconsistency level as a function of the delay in the link between the replicated servers, for different given *PER* values; respectively 0%, 2%, 5%, 10%, and 15% from the upper curve to the lower curve. We assume *SSP* to be equal to 1 from the round robin setting, and that *USRR* is the *PER*. As stated earlier, when *Delay* is null, *RO_time* and *SU_time* are almost equal, and SOM_R is equal to 1. Note that in our system, for scenarios with no link delay between the replicated servers, inconsistency has the product of *SSP* and *PER* as lower-bound.

The figure proves to be useful when analyzing the requirements on the system so that the inconsistency level stays below a given threshold. For example, it shows that no more than 10% PER (when no *Delay*) OR no more than 100ms *Delay* (when no *PER*) can be tolerated in our system to keep the inconsistency under 10%. Within those two bounding ranges, all pair values *Delay-PER* allow inconsistency levels under 10%. This analysis highlights the need to consider the tradeoff between *Delay* and *PER*, which can be critical when designing a system. The type of protocol used to propagate the SUMs influences those two link characteristics and, consequently, influences also the inconsistency level. Reliable, TCP-like protocols ensure that fewer SUMs are lost when being propagated (lower *PER*) at the cost of longer delays while

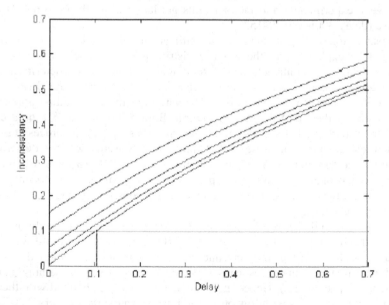

Fig. 6. Influence of *Delay* and *PER* on the inconsistency level. Each curve is the inconsistency level for a given *PER* (from bottom to top: 0%, 2%, 5%, 10%, and 15%).

connectionless, UDP-like protocols offer lower delays but poor reliability to the SUMs. The impact of the protocol used can be analyzed analytically, based on its retransmission and congestion control models applied to the system of interest.

7 Conclusion

In this paper, we introduced an evaluation approach for inconsistency in a replicated call control system. Direct measurements of inconsistency are deployed for model validation but in most cases they are not feasible in practical systems. The introduced new approach is based on an analysis of contributing factors, related to the Server Selection Policy, the packet drop rate between server replicates, and the disordering probability of state update messages. The first two factors are either known from system properties or can be estimated efficiently from the running system. The last factor is derived in this paper from parameters of the traffic model and different delay parameters in the system. The comparison of the evaluation approach via the contributing factors with a dedicated direct inconsistency measurement approach in an experimental prototype of IMS call control shows a close match despite simplifications on assumptions on processing delays. The relation between inconsistency and the contributing factors can also be used for network planning purposes.

Acknowledgements

The authors would like to thank Siemens Mobile Networks, Germany, for supporting this research and our colleague, Marjan Bozinovski, for his valuable support in the testbed implementation. We would also like to thank Robert Seidl, Siemens Munich, for his valuable comments.

References

[1] J. Rosenberg, et al., "SIP: Session Initiation Protocol", *RFC 3261, Internet Engineering Task Force*, June 2002
[2] 3GPP TS 23.228, "IP Multimedia (IM) Subsystem - Stage 2", *Technical Specification*, June 2001
[3] P. Kim and W. Boehm, "Support of Real-Time Applications in Future Mobile Networks: the IMS Approach", *Sixteenth Wireless Personal Multimedia Communications*, October 2003
[4] M. Tuexen, et al., "Architecture for Reliable Server Pooling", *<draft-ietf-rserpool-arch-05.txt>*, February 2003
[5] Q. Xie, R. R. Stewart, "Endpoint Name Resolution Protocol", *<draft-ietf-rserpool-enrp-01.txt>*, November 2001
[6] R. R. Stewart, Q. Xie, "Aggregate Server Access Protocol (ASAP)", *<draft-ietf-rserpool-asap-01.txt>*, November 2001

[7] P. Conrad, A. Jungmaier, C. Ross, W.-C. Sim, M. Tüxen, "Reliable IP Telephony Applications with SIP using RSerPool", *Proceedings of the SCI 2002, Volume X, Mobile/Wireless Computing and Communication Systems II; Orlando, USA, pp. 352-356*, July 2002

[8] M. Rabinovich and E. Lazowska, "An efficient and highly available read-one write-all protocol for replicated data management", *Technical Report 92-07-04, University of Washington Department of Computer Science and Engineering*, July 1992

[9] M.P. Herlihy, "A quorum-consensus replication method", *ACM Trans. on Computer Systems, 4(1): 32-53*, Feb. 1986

[10] A. Kumar, "Hierarchical Quorum Consensus: A New Algorithm for Managing Replicated Data", *IEEE Transactions on Computers*, 1991

[11] H. Yu and A. Vahdat, "Building Replicated Internet Services Using TACT: A Toolkit for Tunable Availability and Consistency Tradeoffs", *Second International Workshop on Advanced Issues of E-Commerce and Web-based Information Systems*, June 2000

[12] H. Yu and A. Vahdat, "Design and Evaluation of a Continuous Consistency Model for Replicated Services", www.cs.duke.edu/ari/issg/TACT/

[13] M. Bozinovski, T. Renier, H.-P. Schwefel and R. Prasad, "Transaction Consistency in Replicated SIP Call Control Systems", *4th International Conference on Information, Communications & Signal Processing and Fourth Pacific-Rim Conference on Multimedia (ICICS-PCM 2003)*, December 2003

[14] L. Lamport, "Time, Clocks, and the Ordering of Events in a Distributed System", *Communications of the ACM, 21(7):558-565*, July 1978

[15] T. Renier, H.-P. Schwefel, M. Bozinovski, K. Larsen, R. Prasad, R. Seidl, "Distributed redundancy or cluster solution? An experimental evaluation of two approaches for dependable mobile Internet services", *1st International Service Availability Symposium (ISAS2004)*, May 2004

[16] M. Bozinovski, L. Gavrilovska, R. Prasad and H.-P. Schwefel, "Evaluation of a Fault-tolerant Call Control System", *Facta Universitatis Series: Electronics and Energetics, vol. 17, no. 1*, April 2004

[17] M. Bozinovski, H.-P. Schwefel and R. Prasad, "Algorithm for Controlling Transaction Consistency in SIP Session Control Systems", IEE *Electronics Letters, Vol.40, no.3*, pp.209-211, February 2004

[18] M. Tuexen, et al., "Architecture for Reliable Server Pooling", <draft-ietf-rserpool-arch-10.txt>, July, 2005.

[19] M. Bozinovski, H.-P. Schwefel and R. Prasad, "Maximum Availability Server Selection Policy for Efficient and Reliable Session Control Systems", to appear in *IEEE Transactions on Networking*.

Measuring the Dependability of Web Services for Use in e-Science Experiments

Peter Li[1,2], Yuhui Chen[3], and Alexander Romanovsky[3]

[1] Manchester Centre for Integrative Systems Biology, Manchester Interdisciplinary Biocentre, 131 Princess Street, Manchester, M1 7ND, UK
[2] Bioanalytical Sciences Group, School of Chemistry, University of Manchester, M60 1QD, UK
Peter.Li@manchester.ac.uk
[3] School of Computing Science, Newcastle University, NE1 7RU, UK
{Yuhui.Chen, Alexander.Romanovsky}@ncl.ac.uk

Abstract. This paper introduces a dependability assessment tool (WSsDAT) for Web Services monitoring and testing. It allows users to evaluate dependability of Web Services from the point of view of their clients by collecting metadata representing a number of dependability metrics. This Java-based tool can be deployed in diverse geographical locations to monitor and test the behavior of a selected set of Web Services within preset time intervals. The graphical user interface of the tool provides real-time statistical data describing dependability of the Web Services under monitoring. The tool makes it possible for the users to identify typical patterns of dependability-specific behavior depending on the time of the day, days of the week or the client locations. In addition, WSsDAT can collect and analyze service dependability measurements during long periods of time, as well as obtaining dependability-related information about current service behavior. The paper reports on a successful series of experiments using this tool for investigating the dependability of two BLAST Web Services which are widely used in the bioinformatics domain. The paper shows how the tool can be employed by e-scientists in making informed choices of the distributed services being used in an *in silico* experiment and thereby improving their overall dependability.

Keywords: Service-oriented architecture, reliability, monitoring, BLAST services.

1 Introduction

Research in dependability has traditionally been focused on closed systems where all components or services belong to the same management domain and are composed statically. This allows the integrators to collect prior information about the availability and reliability of those components and to employ architectural solutions that can provide the required level of dependability [1][2]. This approach is not applicable to the service-oriented architectures where services belong to different organizations and the integrators do not have enough information about their dependability characteristics [3].

D. Penkler, M. Reitenspiess, and F. Tam (Eds.): ISAS 2006, LNCS 4328, pp. 193–205, 2006.

They need special support to make their decisions using valid and up-to-date information collected on-line. Dependability is therefore a major issue in service-oriented environments which are being used for e-Science which is the large scale science that is being undertaken through distributed global collaborations enabled by the Internet and involves the formation of virtual organizations (VO) on an *ad hoc* basis. From a certain point of view, the organizations whose services are invoked within a scientific workflow can be considered to form a VO during its enactment [4]. However, the reliability of the services can be erratic since various types of service faults may be experienced by users and this can lead to failure during the enactment of the workflow. Faults can occur due to an inability to reach the service because of a network problem. The service might also be inoperative because its server is undergoing maintenance or may have become overloaded with requests. Perhaps more critically, the data output generated by a service may be wrong due to incorrect or corrupted requests and this will have serious consequences to the results of scientific workflows.

Issues with the reliability of services are particularly prevalent in the area of bioinformatics. Academic and non-commercial organizations deploy Web Services for public use by scientists in the life sciences community without any prior service level agreements. Such services are used by scientists knowing of their unreliability despite the fact that they may not always be available for the reasons outlined above [5]. These services are orchestrated into workflows which represent '*in silico*' experiments that are analogous to those performed by experimental scientists in laboratories but involve the use of computational resources such as data repositories and analysis programs available on the Internet [4]. Such *in silico* experiments may be long lived due to the large volumes of data being analyzed, whilst there may also be requirements on the timeliness of the workflow enactment. It is therefore essential that such e-Science workflows are executed using the most reliable of services. The possibility of failure can be reduced by selecting those services which are the most reliable based on metadata about the behavioral characteristics of Web Services. Furthermore, the availability of quantitative metadata can provide a means of predicting the reliability of a given service.

In this paper, we describe a tool which was developed to help e-Scientists in improving the dependability of *in silico* experiments that they run over a number of distributed services. We start with a detailed description of the tool architecture and functionality (Section 2). In Section 3, we compare our approach with the existing work in the area of experimental evaluation of Web Services. In the following part of the paper, we demonstrate the applicability and usefulness of the tool by discussing the results of our experimental work in analyzing the dependability of two BLAST services which are used in the bioinformatics domain (Section 4). In Section 5, we discuss how this tool can be used to help the e-scientists and overview our plans for the future work. Section 6 concludes the paper.

2   The WSsDAT Tool

Our work on the tool started with formulating the essential requirements which a general Web Services dependability-monitoring tool needs to meet. The main requirement is that such a tool should be able to monitor a Web Service continuously for a preconfigured period of time and record various types of information in order for the dependability of a service to be measured. Firstly, the tool should provide an interface to accept user's inputs and map these user inputs into internal processing actions. Secondly, the tool has to be able to invoke the Web Service effectively and wait for results; internal and external exceptions should be monitored during this period. When the output of the service invocation is received, the response time for the service should be recorded and analyzed. Ideally, the output of the service needs to be assessed to determine whether the Web Service functioned properly and whether it passed or failed according to the scientists' demands. Moreover, when the test invocation failed then any fault messages generated by the service should also be documented. If available, these messages will provide insights behind the problems causing the service failure. Finally, the tool should be able to produce reports of the test and monitoring procedures.

2.1 Overview

The requirements of a general Web Services dependability-monitoring tool were realized by the development of a Java-based application called Web Services Dependability Assessment Tool (WSsDAT) which is aimed at evaluating the dependability of Web Services. The tool supports various methods of dependability testing by acting as a client invoking the Web Services under investigation. The tool enables users to monitor Web Services by collecting the following reliability characteristics:

– *Availability and Functionality:* Calls are made to a Web Service at defined intervals to check if the Web Service is functioning. The tool is able to test the semantics of the response which are generated by the Web Service being monitored. It is possible to pre-configure the tool using a regular expression which represents the correct response expected by the scientist from a given Web Service and ensure the service is functioning according to that expected by its user. Results returned from a Web Service are recorded for further analysis which can be manually carried out by a user.
– *Performance:* The WSsDAT measures the round-trip response time of calls made to the Web Services. Average response time of successful calls is used as performance metric of a Web Service.
– *Faults and exceptions:* The tool records any faults generated by a failed invocation of a Web Service. Internal and external exceptions, for example, networking timeout exceptions are also recorded for further analysis.

Further to the above metadata recorded by WSsDAT, the tool can also be used to test and monitor the dependability of Web Services at geographically disparate locations through the deployment of the tool on different computers. It is important to understand the behavior of a Web Service from the point of view of the clients, in order to comprehend the networking consequences between the clients and the Web Service.

2.2 General Principles and Architecture

One of the problems with using public scientific Web Services is that their interfaces differ from one resource to another. Therefore, testers would normally have to write a customized invocation script for each service because of the different interfaces and parameters required. The WSsDAT is an off-the-shelf tool offering general solutions for monitoring the dependability of Web Services. This tool is implemented using Apache Axis JAX-RPC style SOAP processing APIs and is based on an extended Model-View-Controller (MVC) pattern. The architecture of WSsDAT is shown in Figure 1. It consists of three main functional components, a graphical user interface (GUI), a Test Engine and a Data Handler. The GUI captures the user's request, and configures the test policy and system settings. These inputs are modeled, mapped and stored in a database for repeated use. The GUI is also a viewport which renders live dependability and performance metrics of the Web Services being monitored. The Test Engine is responsible for generating and executing invocation scripts using the modeled data stored in the Web Services database to invoke Web Services. The Test Engine is able to run a batch of tests and measurements concurrently. The Data Handler processes and models all test and observation measurements data. After statistical analysis, these data are subsequently stored in a MySQL database or as plain text files; relevant information is passed and rendered in the viewport on the GUI.

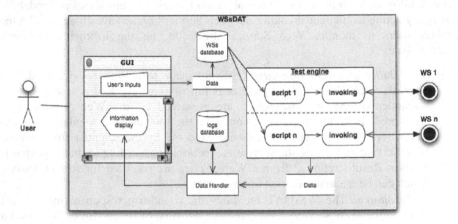

Fig. 1. The architecture of the WSsDAT

2.3 Graphical User Interface (GUI)

We designed and implemented the GUI by which users can interact with the WSsDAT. Users can input information of Web Services on the GUI, set test parameters and configure test policies, as shown in Figure 2. The WSsDAT is capable of testing multiple Web Services simultaneously. Each time the GUI accepts inputs for one Web Service. Once user's inputs are validated, these data are modeled and saved in a database, and the Web Service is entered into a test array. The Web Services in the test array are listed on the GUI and can be selected individually for modification and information display. The viewport on the GUI renders information of Web Services, such as errors, average response time, and graphs of response times. The user can highlight a Web Service in the testing list for display. (See Fig. 3).

Fig. 2. GUI for Web Services information inputs

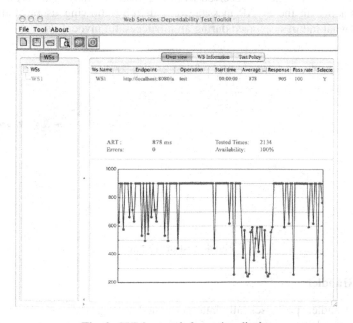

Fig. 3. GUI for test information display

2.4 Test Engine

The Test Engine processes the user's inputs and implements service invocation scripts according to test policies. Tests on each Web Service are established as a single thread and all tests are carried out in parallel. The number of test threads is only restricted by the computer system's capability or restriction. Figure 4 is an UML diagram showing how the Test Engine cooperates with other components in the WSsDAT. The mechanism of a test procedure described briefly as following:

- The Test Engine assembles an invocation script for a Web Service to be monitored according to user's inputs.
- The Test Engine invokes the Web Service with the test script. A timer is started for measuring the response time. The start time of the invocation is logged.
- If a valid result is received from a Web Service, the result is passed to the Data Handler along with other measurements such as start time and end time of the invocation. The test is terminated and will be started again after the preset interval.
- If an exception is detected during the invocation, the exception message is logged along with other dependability and performance metrics. The test is terminated and a new invocation will be initiated after the preset interval.
- If the Web Service does not return any response after a preset timeout period, the timeout exception is logged. The test is terminated and will start again after the preset interval.
- Relevant statistics and analysis are processed and logged after each invocation.

The Test Engine implements the SOAP message processing mechanism. It is able to analyze the SOAP message received from the Web Services by reporting the error message attached in the SOAP message and thereby allowing users of the tool to understand what failures occurred during an unsuccessful invocation.

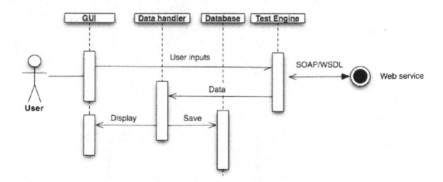

Fig. 4. Test procedure

2.5 Data Handler

The Data Handler processes all data generated during the test. After statistical analysis, these data are stored in a MySQL database, and passed to the GUI if appropriate. If a MySQL database is not installed on the computer, the WSsDAT has an option to save these data in formatted text files. The contents of these files are commented and split clearly and can be easily converted into Microsoft Excel or some other statistics software which can import data from formatted text files such as Profit and SPSS.

3 Related Work

Several solutions for monitoring Web Services dependability and performance are available. Usually these tools are intended to help Web Service providers improve the dependability of the services they develop.

A Web-based monitoring tool has been recently developed by [5] for measuring the performance of Web Services. Web Services developers can use this tool to measure the performance of their Web Services, including ping time and call time to the Web Service and collects information about errors. All tests and measurements are carried out from the dedicated website where the tool is located. In order to use this tool, the users, who must be the owners of Web Services, need to register their Web Services on the Web page of the tool or via its WSDL interface, and provide the URL of the WSDL document of the Web Services. The tool processes the documents with some necessary parameters specified by users to dynamically generate test scripts. The tool is able to log measurements results. The format of log file is compatible with Excel or SPSS. The tool also has a reporting function to show the summary graphs.

The Magpie is a general tool for analyzing the performance of the Microsoft Windows applications [7]. It supports monitoring of the internal components and resources consumed during the processing of incoming requests. It allows system developers to identify the typical behavior of transactions of various types throughout their lifetime. This tool is not specifically intended for monitoring Web Services but it can be very useful in helping system developers to understand the internal behavior of their system.

The Pinpoint approach is a J2EE based debugging tool which implements a runtime tracking mechanism to trace the application requests going through the system [8]. It monitors the behavior of every component of the system processing application requests and applies fault-injection technique to identify the root causes of failures. The tool is not intended for the external users of the Web Services but it can provide valuable insights about internal and external behavior of Web-based applications and helps in detecting faulty components.

There are several Web Services monitoring tools that act as proxies to the Web Services being monitored. For example, the Bionanny system [9], which is actually a Web Service itself, intercepts and monitors all the communication between the clients and the invoked Web Services. Therefore it is capable of monitoring the usage of the Web Services. The Bionanny also provides APIs to log characteristics of the requests and services for further analysis. This tool is developed for Web Services providers. To use the Bionanny, the users need to install Java, Apache Tomcat servlet engine, Apache Axis SOAP toolkit and MySQL database on their system, which in effect means that the users need to build a Web Service environment to deploy the Bionanny. Ideally, the Bionanny tool needs to be installed on the server where the

Web Services to be monitored are located. Tools like Bionanny are intended to help Web Service developers and because they require some changes of the Service under monitoring to be made they can be used by these developers only.

The Keynote System [10] is a commercial solution for monitoring the performance of Web-based applications. It implements real-time methodology and infrastructure for measuring, monitoring and testing Web-based applications including those built using Web Services. This commercial system is deployed over 1,600 measurement computers in about 50 cities worldwide and represents a global infrastructure for performance monitoring and testing Web-based applications across all major Internet backbones. It helps Web-based application developers to understand the behavior of their system from the end-user perspective focusing on the typical general profiles of the requests coming from the wide groups of these users. Although this system focuses on the end-user's perspective, it is not intended for measuring Web Services and the Internet behavior while executing requests coming from a selected client.

eValid™ Web Test and Analysis Suite [11] has been developed for Web page monitoring. It is a test enabled IE-compatible browser tool which has the following functionalities:

- Functional test: it emulates user's behavior to evaluate reliability
- Load test: it measures feedbacks for the emulated payloads for more accurate analysis
- Monitoring: it pings and checks accessibility of a Website
- Performance check: it examines the download times of each element of the server; therefore the users can analyze the bottle-necks.

eValid™ is not a dedicated tool for Web Services monitoring as it does not support Web Services testing or monitoring via invoking their APIs. However it does provide a way to monitor Web Services that has additional Dynamic Webpage accesses.

Paper [12] describes a fault injection tool that allows the dependability of a Web Service to be assessed by injecting various XML messages which have the correct syntax but incorrect values of parameters. This tool is intended for the Web Service developers and works under the assumption that additional software "hooks" can be inserted into the service before the experiment starts.

4   Experiments on Using WSsDAT

4.1 BLAST Services

BLAST is an algorithm which is commonly used in *silico* experiments in bioinformatics to search for gene and protein sequences that are similar to a given input query sequence [13]. BLAST has been deployed on numerous servers around the world but their dependability differs from one service to another. For a computationally-intensive and long running *in silico* experiment, it is important that the most efficient and reliable service is used so that the chances of experiment failure are reduced. To this end, the most reliable BLAST service could be used based on performance characteristics which have been measured by the WSsDAT tool.

4.2 Testing BLAST Web Services

An experiment measuring the performance of two BLAST Web Services was undertaken to test the monitoring capability of the WSsDAT tool. Dependability and performance metrics were measured from a Soaplab BLAST Web Service deployed by the European Bioinformatics Institute, Cambridge, UK [14] and a BLAST service hosted by the DNA Databank in Japan (DDBJ) [15].

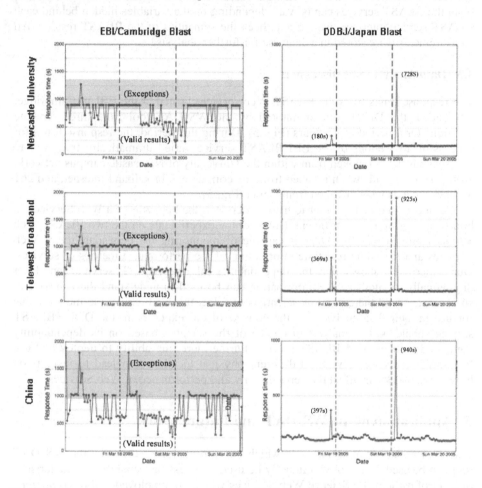

Fig. 5. Performance metrics measured using WSsDAT from BLAST services deployed at EBI and DDBJ when invoked from University of Newcastle campus network, a commercial broadband supplier (UK) and from China. Service failures have been shaded as grey.

We deployed the WSsDAT tool at three different locations and networks to monitor these two BLAST Web Services, simultaneously. Two WSsDAT tools were located in Newcastle upon Tyne, UK; one was deployed from the campus network at University of Newcastle upon Tyne, whilst the other one was hosted on a computer connected with 1MB broadband via a commercial Internet Service Provider, Telewest

Broadband (UK). The remaining WSsDAT was deployed in the China Education and Research Network, an official Internet established by the Chinese government.

In order to observe the variances of dependability and performance metrics at different periods of time in a working day, over the weekend, and during daytime and night time hours, the two BLAST services were monitored from Friday, March 18, 2005 until Sunday, March 20, 2005. The total duration was 72 hours and the interval between successive service invocations was 30 minutes. Since the results returned from the BLAST services can be vary depending on the variables hidden behind each BLAST service interface, we did not check the semantics of the BLAST results. All measurements were stored in a database for further analysis.

4.3 Data Analysis and Discussion

The response times from the BLAST Web services hosted at the EBI in Cambridge, UK and at the DDBJ were monitored by the WSsDAT tool from three separate locations for a period of 72 hours (Fig. 5). During this period, the response times for successful invocations of the EBI BLAST service varied dramatically from 239 to 760 seconds when invoked from within the University of Newcastle campus network, 248 to 1000 seconds when invoked from the commercial broadband Internet, and 261 to 1886 seconds when invoked from China (Fig. 5).

We understand that in order to truly understand the behavior of a Web Service, 72 hours monitoring is not sufficient. However the experiments on the two BLAST Web Services proved that WSsDAT is capable of monitoring the dependability of Web Services and recording real-time information of the performance metrics of services. Our experiment shows that the dependability of one BLAST service can differ dramatically to another. This information can be used to understand the behavior of such services and thereby allow scientists to select those which are the most reliable for use in their data analyses. In the context of our experiment, the DDBJ BLAST service should be the analysis of choice of the scientist based on its dependability compared with the EBI BLAST service. Furthermore, the ability to deploy and use WSsDAT to invoke services in different physical locations can lead to insights on how the network can affect the dependability and performance of Web Services.

5 Application of the WSsDAT and Future Work

There are a number of scenarios in which the information recorded by the WSsDAT tool can be used. The tool will initially be used to assess the reliability characteristics of a set of dedicated e-Science Web Services which are employed within an *in silico* experiment. This information may be collected either before the experiment or during periods when the experiments are usually enacted. The measurements recorded by WSsDAT can be processed in such a fashion which may be used to model the behavior of the service and the models can then be used to predict the reliability of the service. Furthermore, the information could be used to rank conceptually identical services on the basis of reliability.

The information collected and generated by WSsDAT can then be used by the scientist during the construction of the *in silico* workflow experiment. From a list of services which all perform a given analysis, the scientist would select that which was forecasted to be the most dependable. In some situations the scientist can decide against running the experiment if the probability of completing it successfully is not sufficient for his/her point of view. In this case, the experiment can be postponed until a more favorable time. Otherwise the scientist can decide to employ fault tolerance measures which can be implemented in several ways. Firstly, the experimental results can help the scientist to choose correct time-outs for accessing Web Services (this is typically a serious problem as it is usually the case that time-outs are chosen without real grounds). Secondly, the scientist can decide if retries can help in calling specific Web Services and he/she can chose a appropriate number of retries. Thirdly, he/she can decide to run experiment in such a way that after several unsuccessful attempts to call a service, the system switches to using an alternative service which has been ranked with a lower but still sufficient reliability than the first choice service.

Further development of the WSsDAT will focus on better integration with applications in existing e-Science environment. Some specific future work are planned as to allow the following functionalities:

- Interactive APIs for integration with workflows. The WSsDAT is capable to monitor real time dependability of several Web Services simultaneously. However, as an independent application, its users can only predicatively choose Web Services by manually consulting the information provided by the tool. In order to achieve better integration with workflows and bring greater benefits to e-scientists, we planned to implement interactive APIs in the WSsDAT to allow automatic access to metadata recorded in the database of the tool; therefore e-scientists can use those APIs in their workflows to achieve dynamic reconfiguration of using more dependable Web Services.
- Monitoring Web Services workflow. At this stage the WSsDAT can monitor a Web Services in each thread. In future, it will be able to handle interactive communication with the Web Services and monitor workflows automatically.
- Remote control function. Users will be able to deploy several WSsDAT on different computer systems and remotely control the tools and collect data on one computer.
- Roundtrip/time-out tracking. At the moment, the WSsDAT can only track the round trip time of a Web Service operation invocation. If a timeout happened, the tool cannot locate where the timeout exactly happened. In future, the tool will be capable to track the message traveling time in each stage.

6 Conclusions

Developing tools for the experimental evaluation of Web Services dependability is a very active area of research and development. Both service developers and service integrators need to be able to assess the dependability of the individual services. This requires a range of experimental tools that can provide them with the information crucial for making various technical and business decisions.

The aim of our work is to help system integrators who have no access to the service code of the Web Services they use, for example, the Web Services found in the UDDI registry providing their WSDL specifications and descriptions. It will greatly benefit general users especially the workflow developers. The users will be able to flexibly deploy the WSsDAT tool to collect real-time information about the candidate Web Services and to dynamically select the Web Services which will behave more predictably and more dependably. The WSsDAT can also help Web Services developers to improve their Web Services. The platform-independent characteristics of the WSsDAT allows them to conveniently distribute the tool and monitor their Web Services behavior when they are called in different (e.g. from different geographic locations) using various strategies.

The WSsDAT can be freely downloaded at http://www.students.ncl.ac.uk/yuhui.chen/

Acknowledgments

Yuhui Chen is partially supported by the School of Computing Science, University of Newcastle upon Tyne (UK). Peter Li acknowledges support from the Biotechnology and Biological Sciences Research Council (BBSRC). Alexander Romanovsky is supported by IST FP6 RODIN project.

References

1. Tai, A. T., Avizienis, A., Meyer, J. F. (1993) Evaluation of fault-tolerant software: a performability modelling approach. In Dependable Computing for Critical Applications 3. C. E. Landwehr, B. Randell, L. Simoncini (Eds.). Springer. pp.113-134.
2. Randell, B., Romanovsky, A., Rubira, C. M. F., Stroud, R. J., Wu, Z., Xu, J. (1995) From recovery blocks to concurrent atomic actions. In Predictably Dependable Computing Systems. B. Randell, J.-C. Laprie, H. Kopetz, B. Littlewood (Eds.). Springer. pp. 87-101.
3. Ferguson, D.F., Storey, T., Lovering, B., Shewchuk, J. (2003) Secure, Reliable, Transacted Web Services: Architecture and Composition, MS and IBM Technical Report, http://www-106.ibm.com/developerworks/webservices/library/ws-securtrans
4. Oinn, T., Addis, M., Ferris, J., Marvin, D., Greenwood, M., Carver, T., Senger, M., Glover, K., Wipat, A. and Li, P. (2004) Taverna: a tool for the composition and enactment of bioinformatics workflows. Bioinformatics 20: 3045-3054.
5. Stevens, R., Tipney, H. J., Wroe, C., Oinn, T., Senger, M., Lord, P., Goble, C. A., Brass, A., Tassabehji, M. (2004) Exploring Williams-Beuren Syndrome Using myGrid. Bioinformatics 20: i303-i310.
6. Schmietendorf, A., Dumke, R., Stojanov, S. (2005) Performance Aspects in Web Service-based Integration Solutions, 21st UK Performance Engineering Workshop, Computing Science, University of Newcastle upon Tyne. School of Computing Science Technical Report Series, CS-TR-916, July 2005. 137-152. http://www.staff.ncl.ac.uk/nigel.thomas/UKPEW2005/
7. Barham, P., Isaacs, R., Mortier, R., Narayanan, D. (2003) Magpie: online modelling and performance-aware systems, The 9th Workshop on Hot Topics in Operating Systems (HotOS IX) 85—90. Lihue (Kauai), Hawaii, USA, May 2003
8. Chen, M., Kiciman, E., Fratkin, E., Fox, A., Brewer, E. Pinpoint:Problem determination in large, dynamic Internet services. (2002) - Proc. 2002 Intl. Conf. on Dependable Systems and Networks, Bethesda, MD, June 2002

9. Senger M, Niemi, M. (2005) Bionanny - A Web Service monitoring other Web Services, http://bionanny.sourceforge.net/
10. Keynote System Inc, The Keynote Method, 2006, http://www.keynote.com/ keynote_method/ keynote_method_methodology.html
11. eValid, Inc. (2005) eValid™ Web Testing & Analysis Suite. http://www.soft.com/eValid/
12. Townend, P., Xu, J., Yang, E., Bennett, K., Charters, S., Holliman, N., Looker, N., Munro, M. (2005) The e-Demand project: A Summary. The Fourth UK e-Science Programme All Hands Meeting (AHM 2005) Nottingham UK. 19-22 September 2005. http://www.allhands.org.uk/
13. Altschul, S.F., Gish, W., Miller, W., Myers, E. W., Lipman, D. J. (1990) Basic local alignment search tool. J Mol Biol. 215: 403-410.
14. Stevens, R., Robinson, A., Goble, C. A. (2003) myGrid: Personalised Bioinformatics on the Information Grid. Bioinformatics 19 (Suppl 1): i302-i304
15. Miyazaki, S., Sugawara, H. (2000) Development of DDBJ-XML and its application to a database of cDNA. Genome Informatics. Universal Academy Press, Inc (Tokyo), pp. 380-381.

Making Legacy Services Highly Available with OpenAIS: An Experience Report

András Kövi[1], Dánel Varró[1], and Zoltán Németh[2]

[1] Department of Measurements and Information Systems,
Budapest University of Technology and Economics,
H-1117, Magyar tudósok krt. 2, Budapest, Hungary
{kovi, varro}@mit.bme.hu
[2] Nokia Research Center, Nokia Hungary Kft.,
H-1092, Köztelek u. 6, Budapest, Hungary
zoli@cs.bme.hu

Abstract. We report our experiences on application development with the open source OpenAIS framework, which is an implementation of the standard Application Interface Specification (AIS) issued by the Service Availability Forum. Our focus is put on integrating existing (legacy) applications or services into the AIS framework (where the source code of these services is not available) in order to make such services highly available. This is achieved by using Proxy components, which are responsible for managing the High Availability (HA) lifecycle of legacy services (called proxied components). We estimate the availability of legacy services as provided by using redundant proxy and proxied components in the OpenAIS framework on a benchmark service architecture.

Furthermore, as the AIS standard does not contain any recommendation on business-related communication, in the paper, we propose to use communication mediation to forward requests to service provider components and responses back to the service consumers.

Keywords: service availability, AIS, communication mediation.

1   Introduction

Nowadays the range of business functionality is rapidly increasing to better meet customer critical requirements: rapid time-to-market and increased quality of such applications. This can only be achieved if the underlying software architecture overtakes a large proportion of business-independent tasks in order to enhance communication in the overall system. As a consequence, the executing software architecture is typically at least as complex as the business application itself.

In order to enhance communication at the architecture-level, a paradigm shift can be observed in software architectures by placing the service as the basic conceptual element. A service can be provided by many server applications (called service providers, or shortly, services). Moreover a service may use other services, which means that service can take the role of a client as well (called as service

D. Penkler, M. Reitenspiess, and F. Tam (Eds.): ISAS 2006, LNCS 4328, pp. 206–216, 2006.

consumer or shortly, client). The connection and communication between these services is carried out in a standard way (e.g. Web Services, XML-RPC).

However, standardization of service communication does not alone guarantee the required quality of services (QoS). One of the most essential QoS parameter of business services is high availability, which requires the continuity of a service.

1.1 Availability Management by the AIS Standard

In order to obtain highly available services, inexpensive components are made redundant according to some redundancy model. By issuing periodic healthchecks, the Availability Management Framework detects when an active service component fails, and initiates failover, i.e. the service is overtaken by a backup service component, and then the failed component is restarted.

The *Service Availability*^{TM} *Forum (SAF)* aims at providing standardized solutions for making services highly available. The *Application Interface Specification (AIS)* of the Forum standardizes the interface between Service Availability Forum compliant *High Availability (HA)* middleware and service applications. The AIS standard contains specifications for the different functionality groups in HA management. The *Availability Management Framework (AMF)* is a group of functionality which describes the interface needed for the HA management of an application.

1.2 Existing AIS Projects

The importance and the growing popularity of the AIS specification is demonstrated by the increasing number of reference implementations in the telecommunication field as provided by Motorola [3] or Fujitsu-Siemens Computers [4], for instance. In addition, the relevance of an open service availability platform was also highlighted in [5] in an operating systems context by placing the Linux kernel on the top of HA interfaces.

The current work summarizes our experience using the open-source OpenAIS reference framework. It was carried out in cooperation between Nokia Research Center and the Fault-Tolerant Systems Research Group at the Budapest University of Technology and Economics funded by Strategy and Technology, Nokia Networks under the HA2005 project.

OpenAIS is an open-source project to provide a reference implementation of SAF AIS on Linux. At the time of writing, the implementation of AIS services is based on the B.01.01 version and the implementation of AMF is based on the A.01.01 version of AIS, and the latest release version number is 0.69, which is still not a major release. OpenAIS is claimed to have been tested on a variety of Linux platforms [1]. We used Suse Linux operating system Version 9.1 in this project, which was executed under a VMware virtual machine [2].

1.3 Problem Statement

In this paper, we address the very frequent problem of making an existing (legacy) service high available when the source code of the service is not accessible. In other terms, the service provider is assumed to be a "black box", and we have absolutely no assumption on its internal structure.

For this purpose, AMF offers the use of *proxy components*. Proxies are responsible for forwarding messages (e.g. the initiation of healthchecks, restarts or failovers) from AMF to the *proxied (legacy) service components*. As a result, legacy service components can also be made highly available by using AMF without altering the source code of these services.

Since AMF focuses exclusively on HA management, the AIS standard contains no recommendation at all how to carry out core business communication. However, the source code responsible for business communication between the service provider and the service consumer has to be altered to conform to the changes in the execution environment, which requires significant programming efforts many service developers have to face.

1.4   Objectives

In this paper, we first report on the use of proxy components in the OpenAIS framework for standard HA management.

Then we propose two solutions to provide business communication mediation by forwarding business calls between the service provider and consumer using tunnels for connections. We compare if this mediation is carried out by the proxy component itself, or by a separate mediator component also managed by AMF. The main advantage of these solutions is that only the code of the mediator(or the proxy) requires certain adaptation, but no changes are required in the source code of the service provider and consumer (client).

Last, we estimate the availability of a (legacy) service in the presence of multiple proxy and service (proxied) components by using a mathematical model and experimental evaluation on a benchmark application.

2   Towards Highly-Available Legacy Services in OpenAIS

2.1   Benchmark Application

As AIS is designed to be a flexible standard for providing high availability services especially in the telecommunication domain, we used an internal benchmark architecture of the SA-Forum. From the point of view of the current paper, this architecture consists of a client component which aims to access a service (see Figure 1(a)).

In order to make our experiments reproducible, we used a simple web server as the service provider component and a web client as service consumer where a web page is returned by the web server as response to a request coming from the client. In the current paper, we use a simple unified notation as **service** and **client components** so as to better emphasize that both HA management and communication mediation are independent of the target applications or services.

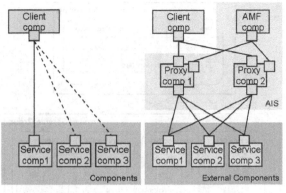

(a) Sample architecture without AIS

(b) Architecture with proxy component

Fig. 1. Main service architectures for legacy services

2.2 Using Proxies

Making an existing service high available in AMF frequently requires the change of the applications that provide the service. However, sometimes this is impossible, e.g. in cases when the service provider is a "black box", what means we do not know anything about the internal structure.

For the latter case AMF offers the use of proxy components. Proxies are responsible for forwarding messages from AMF to the service components. In this context, the black box service components that the proxy is responsible for are called proxied components. In this way, even legacy service components can be made highly available by using AMF.

The system architecture with a proxy component is shown in Figure 1(b).

2.3 Used Redundancy Configuration

In our application we used the following AMF configuration (see Figure 2).

Proxy components: Each Proxy Component was enclosed in a Proxy Service Unit (SU) and SUs were enclosed in a Proxy Service Group. The service group was associated with a 2N redundancy model (i.e. 1 active and 1 standby service unit). Every Proxy Component was registered to mediate for every Service Component when it was associated with the active HA state.

Service components: Service Components in our application were taken as individual SUs. These Service SUs were encapsulated by a service group with N+M redundancy scheme (i.e. N active and M standby), where N=1. Every Service Component may substitute any other Service Component in the Service Group, thus they were enclosed in a Protection Group. Service SUs are registered to be proxied components of proxies since they are implemented by legacy applications that can not be modified to be able to process messages sent by AMF directly.

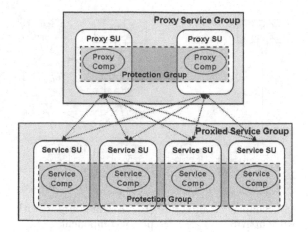

Fig. 2. System architecture with proxy component

2.4   Availability Management of Proxies

AMF inspects the state of the components with continuous healthchecks and takes actions regarding the result of these healthchecks. If once a Proxy or Service component is detected to be down the concerning Proxy or Service component failover process is executed.

Proxy failover. When the active Proxy component is found to be down during the healthcheck the Proxy failover process is initiated. This process is executed in the following steps:

1. The active Proxy SU is taken out of operation.
2. The standby Proxy SU is set up for taking the active state by registering Proxied components, starting certain threads.)
3. The standby Proxy SU is assigned the active HA state.
4. The out of order Proxy is restarted.

Service component failover. When the active Service SU fails a healthcheck the service failover process is initiated. This process stands from the following steps:

1. The active Server SU is taken out of order.
2. A standby Server SU is assigned the active HA state.
3. The faulty Server SU is restarted.

Note that *proxy failover* can be carried out transparently for a client. An example for realizing transparent failover with TCP connections can be found in [6]. However, *service component failover* cannot always be made transparently for a client. In case when the client-service connection is stateless a service failover may only mean the loss of some messages. On the other hand, in case of stateful connections, i.e. when the preceding messages may have an impact on the processing of the current message, service component failover always requires the re-initiation of the connection by the client if the proxy component plays the role of a tunnel.

2.5 Problems with OpenAIS

At the time of writing this report the support for proxy components in OpenAIS is far from product quality. For example, when a proxy component registers its proxied components one-by-one only the lastly registered will be known by AMF. Another problem was that AMF never sent component restart requests as requested by the standard. Because of these defects we had to develop a custom solution for maintaining the availability of proxied components, which can be avoided in the future by using some industrial strength implementation of the standard.

In addition, we found that the OpenAIS does not provide a means to change the system configuration dynamically at run-time. This is unfortunate since the ever-changing user preferences or permanent failures of certain components might require changes in the overall system configuration as well which should be carried out preferably on-line, i.e. during the regular execution of the system.

3 Business Communication Mediation

3.1 Definition of Communication Mediation

As AMF does not prescribe how business related communication should be carried out between the client and the service components, any kind of proprietary solutions would suffice in theory. However, in practice, it requires a significant amount of work to adapt the client to (re-)send its requests to another redundant service component, if the primary service component becomes unavailable.

In the current paper, we propose a general solution for this problem by communication mediation. Our primary solution is to use the Proxy as a mediator for connection between the service and the client units. Furthermore, we also discuss another solution when using separate SA-aware components within AMF for communication mediation.

In both cases, business communication is decoupled between the client and the service units, thus clients will be able to send requests to the same port all the time, while erroneous components are changed transparently in the background.

3.2 Overview of Communication Mediation in Proxies

In this solution, one of the main functionalities of the Proxy is to mediate communication between the client and the service components. This is carried out in the following way (see Figure 3):

– The client connects to the Proxy. The client is unaware of the fact that it is not connected directly to a service.

Fig. 3. Messages of communication mediation

- The Proxy chooses one of the service components that it is responsible for
  e.g. randomly or by applying some load balancing strategy.
- The client sends the request and the Proxy forwards the request to the
  service.
- The service sends back the response to the Proxy.
- The Proxy forwards the response to the client.

With a proxy component in the system there is no change in the behavior
of the service component. The client now should connect to the proxy and not
directly to the service. Naturally, direct connection to the service is still possible,
but the high availability of service cannot be assured in this way.

3.3 Communication Mediation as Separate SA-Aware Components

Another solution for communication mediation is the use of SA-aware mediator
components. The conceptual overview of the system in this case is depicted in
Figure 4.

In this solution, the Client connects to a mediator component and the latter selects the actual service
component for the clients request. Then the mediator
connects to the selected component and starts message
forwarding between the client and the service by tun-
neling. Selection of the service component depends on
many factors. The first and most important is the state
information about the service components which is provided by AMF. The mediator has to know the state
of each service component or at least it has to know
which ones are out of order so as to not to try to connect to a failed service. Some other factors can be, for
example, load balancing, reliability or computational
performance of service components.

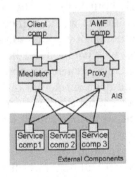

Fig. 4. Mediation with
SA-aware mediator
components

In order to increase the availability, obviously, both
the Proxy and the mediator can also be configured ac-
cording to some redundancy scheme, although it is not depicted explicitly in the
figure.

3.4 Evaluation of Communication Mediation

The main advantage of communication mediation (regardless of the taken approach) is that neither the client nor the service components need to be changed. Additional code is only related to the mediator, which should be developed anyhow to make the proxied components highly available. Note that no business communication is interpreted by the mediator: it only provides a tunnel for forwarding the request to the service components, thus the overhead for the application interactions is negligible.

Furthermore, if the connection of the client and the service components is mediated, load balancing and the pooling of service components becomes possible, which increases the performance of business services. We can use more active service units to upgrade reliability, e.g. with voting or acceptance tests.

A common disadvantage could be that the mediator also has to be made highly available but this is resolved by the use of AMF managed components.

Using separate mediator components provides the following benefits compared to using the Proxy as a mediator:

- Business and AMF related functionality is kept separated since the mediator is responsible for the business communication while the proxy contains the AMF related functionality.
- Due to this separation, higher availability is obtained if only the mediator component fails. (If the proxy functionality fails, then the managed service components are no longer visible for the AMF, thus the mediator cannot access them either.)

On the other hand, using separate mediator components have the following disadvantages:

- There is latency in the state information provided by AMF about the service components (state information is not influenced by failed business methods only by periodic healthchecks).
- Communication overhead is higher since more components are managed by AMF.

4   Experimental Evaluation

4.1   Measurements

In order to access the availability of the system as provided by AMF and our solution for proxies we developed a benchmark example application discovered in Sec 2.1. The client unit makes web requests with given frequency and gathers the statistic information, and the web server (service provider) serves the requests. The proxy component was responsible for maintaining the availability of the service components and it was used as a mediator between the two parties as well. (Communication mediation was introduced Sec 3)

Mathematical model. To have a comparison base on our experimental results we give a mathematic model of the system by a generalized stochastic Petri net shown in Figure 5. The model was created by using the SPNPGui tool [7]. The mathematical basis of our model is introduced in [8].

The parameters of the model are:

- Expected lifetime of components $(1/\lambda)$
- Mean time to restart $(1/\lambda_{restart})$
- Mean time of failover $(1/\lambda_{failover})$
- Number of active server units (Active)
- Number of (hot) standby server units (Standby).

All changes defined by our model assume an exponential distribution with λ (or μ) parameter.

The initial marking is: $M_0=$ {Active: {number of in service (active) service components}, Standby:{number of standby service components}}. Only the mentioned two places have non zero number of tokens.

There are two scenarios according to events. First is when a standby server component fails. In this case, system is still able to serve requests but the failed standby component needs to be restarted. The failure of the component is modeled by the Healthy2Failed transition and the restarting is modeled by the Failed2Healthy transition.

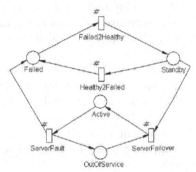

Fig. 5. A Stochastic Petri net model

When an active service component fails the ServerFault transition is fired. It can be seen that in this case we have a failure of service (i.e. our system is down). After this the ServerFailover transition fires, which assigns a healthy standby component the active service state.

The firing rate of transitions. (#(p): number of tokens at place p)

$$Rate(Healthy2Failed) = \lambda * \#(Standby)$$
$$Rate(ServerFault) = \lambda * \#(Active)$$
$$Rate(Failed2Healthy) = \mu_{resrart} * \#(Failed)$$
$$Rate(ServerFailover) = \mu_failover * \#(OutOfService)$$

The firing rate of each transition depends on the number of tokens in given places. For example the firing rate of the Healthy2Failed transition depends on the marking of place Standby, since when there are N standby units the probability of one of them fails is N times greater than in the case when we have only one standby unit. This applies to all other rates as well.

Test parameters. After some tests we came to the conclusion that the following parameters are applicable to our benchmark system: M(lifetime of components)=

	Availability	
#PCUs	Model	Reality
1	87,00%	87,20%
2	98,83%	98,60%
5	99,98%	99,92%

(a) Tabular view

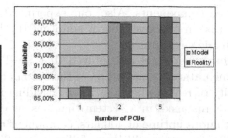

(b) Histogram View

Fig. 6. Computed and measured availability results

10s, M(restart component)= 1.53s, M(failover)= 666μs. Certainly, these values are too pessimistic for real applications but we had to use so small values to be able to get test results in reasonable time. In real applications the typical expected value of lifetime of components can be measured in months but we will show that our model can also be used in such cases.

Measurements. According to the mean values chosen in the previous section the parameters of the model are as follows: = 1/ M(lifetime of components) = 0.1, $\mu_{resrart}$ = M(restart component) = 0.65, $\mu_{failover}$ = M(failover) = 1500. (The lifetime of the service components was simulated by a self killing mechanism.) We made measurements on the real system with 1, 2, and 5 server units. Only one of the server units was active at a time.

We measured the overall availability of the system. In the model this value is indicated by the steady state probability of the Active place (P(#(Active)>0)). In the benchmark application we made a sequence of requests with given frequency and test length for a certain number of server units to compute the availability of the overall service.

First, we computed the availability values with the model. Next, we executed our tests on the benchmark system. We expected that the measured availability values will be very close to the ones that were computed by the model. Results of the tests can be observed in Figure 6.

As we expected, the calculated and measured values are very close to each other although the model slightly over-approximates availability. This is due to the fact that the failover mechanism only provides protection before the data transmission between the client and the server components is started. This means that if the server component fails during communication, the entire request fails, which was not considered in the model. Requests in the real system were generated sequentially and they were much longer (about 10ms) than the failover. As a consequence, a failed request meant longer downtime than a failover, and the overall availability of the real system was worse than the prediction.

Evaluation. The results of our measurements show that a system containing legacy service components can be made highly available with the AIS specification, and OpenAIS, and it does not require the modification of these preexisting service components. Also, our experiments proved that communication mediation is an effective way of adapting the business communication to the high available environment.

Our experiences also proved that the Petri net model which is an intuitive mathematical formalization of the system can be applied for assessing the availability of real applications after providing more precise (realistic) system.

For instance, in a system that has two identical components with expected continuous uptime of 4000hrs, component restart time of 2hrs, and failover time of 20s, the rates will be as follows: λ=0.00025 μ_{rest}= 0.5 $\mu_{failover}$= 200. The model yields the overall availability of 99.999% which is normally acceptable for (non-mission-critical) hot standby clusters of nowadays with these parameters.

5 Conclusions and Future Work

In the current paper, we summarized our experiments in developing highly available applications for legacy services using the OpenAIS framework, which is an open source implementation of the AIS standard of the SA-Forum. As the main conceptual novelty in the AMF framework of the AIS specification, we proposed to use communication mediation for business communication purposes by proxy components or separate mediators, which fits very well to the overall concepts of availability management in AMF.

On the negative side, we experienced that certain features required for the availability management of proxied components in OpenAIS are not yet implemented, thus we had to make a custom implementation in order to assess the availability provided by AMF.

During our experiments, several questions arose when aiming to find an optimal configuration for proxy components that we plan to examine in the future. Our next goal is to examine whether a proxy component should mediate for only a single kind of component in a service unit or it should mediate for the entire service unit.

References

1. Openais, standards based cluster framework. http://developer.osdl.org/dev/openais/.
2. Vmware inc. homepage. http://www.vmware.com.
3. Motorola Company. Netplane software. http://www.motorola.com/content.jsp?globalObjectId=5738.
4. Fujitsu-Siemens Computers. Safe4cs ha 3 including rtp4cs 3 and primecluster 4.1b. http://safe4cs.com.
5. Ibrahim Haddad. Towards carrier grade platforms, linux conference 2004.
6. R. R. Koch, S. Hortikar, L. E. Moser, and P. M. Melliar-Smith. Transparent tcp connection failover. *dsn*, 00:383, 2003.
7. Kishor Trivedi.   Spnp homepage spnp (stochastic petri net package). http://www.ee.duke.edu/~kst/software_packages.html.
8. Dazhi Wang and Kishor S. Trivedi. Modeling user-perceived service availability. In Miroslaw Malek, Edgar Nett, and Neeraj Suri, editors, *ISAS*, volume 3694 of *Lecture Notes in Computer Science*, pages 107–122. Springer, 2005.

Using OpenAIS for Building Highly Available Session Initiation Protocol (SIP) Registrar

Ajay Kamalvanshi[1] and Timo Jokiaho[2]

Nokia Corporation
[1] 313 Fairchild Drive, Mountain View, CA-94043, USA
ajay.kamalvanshi@nokia.com
[2] Linnoitustie 6, 02600 Espoo, Finland
timo.jokiaho@nokia.com

Abstract. Designing for continuous service is a challenge for every telecom application developer. There are various telecom platforms that provide frameworks to address this issue. However, these have proprietary interfaces and are often complex to develop new application. In this paper, we describe our experience with using open source cluster middleware, OpenAIS, for building a telecom application used in IP Multimedia subsystem. The telecom application is a Session Initiation Protocol (SIP) Registrar that keeps user location information In particular, we discuss important design and implementation aspects in making SIP registrar highly available. We also discuss important high availability state transitions, fault handling, application state synchronization. In the end, we share important lessons learned during design, implementation, and deployment.

1 Introduction

The telecom applications are traditionally known for robustness. In fact, numbers of nines are used to describe service availability of telecom equipments. For example, five nines denote 99.999 percent availability with annual downtime of only 5.25 minutes. Such numbers are possible as the telecom applications are built for fault tolerance. Every telecom equipment vendor has developed complex frameworks to meet such requirements. These solutions are very expensive and require a lot of effort to develop new applications.

With convergence of telecom and data communication along with competition to provide low cost solution, the network equipment vendors are exploring the possibility of using solutions based on industry standard, open interfaces and open source implementations.

This paper is based on one of the efforts to build highly available application for IP Multimedia Subsystem (IMS), namely Session Initiation Protocol (SIP) registrar. The SIP registrar is used for registering and querying location of users is made highly available.

This paper starts with a brief overview of IMS stack, the SIP, and SIP registrar to establish the background. We then describe the system design requirements and the

D. Penkler, M. Reitenspiess, and F. Tam (Eds.): ISAS 2006, LNCS 4328, pp. 217–228, 2006.

system design. The system design is followed by the design challenges to make SIP registrar highly available. Later, we describe application implementation including a main routine that handles High Availability (HA) states of the application. After implementation discussion, we cover the software and hardware fault handling from system's perspective. Finally, we conclude the paper illustrating lessons that we learned during our endeavor to make SIP registrar highly available.

2 Overview

An example of layered protocol set for IP multimedia subsystems is illustrated in Fig. 1. At the bottom are traditional physical and data link layer protocols such as Ethernet, ATM, and SONET. Over data link layer, the Internet Protocol (IP) provides functions of a network layer, and TCP/UDP provides the functions of a transport protocol. On top of these protocols, the multi-media protocols are grouped into three categories: Signaling Protocols, Media Transport Protocols, and Quality-of-Service Protocols. The signaling protocols such as SIP establish presence, locate users, and handle sessions. The media transport protocols, such as Real-Time Protocol (RTP), optimize transport mechanism for audio and video packets after a session is established. The Quality-of-Service protocols such as Resource Reservation Protocol (RSVP) and Real Time Control Protocol (RTCP) are designed to meet the negotiated quality contract in terms of performance, throughput, and latency [3].

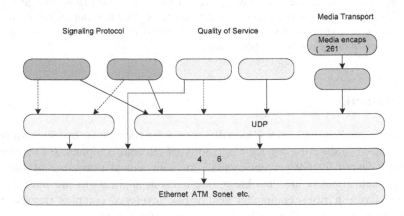

Fig. 1. Protocol set of multi-media communication over IP networks

The focus of this paper is on a network node that implements SIP functionality, so we begin with a brief introduction of SIP. The Session Initiation Protocol (SIP) is developed by the IETF for initiating, modifying, and terminating an interactive user session that involves multimedia elements such as video, voice, instant messaging, and online games. The SIP is also an accepted 3GPP signaling protocol and permanent element of the IMS architecture. It is one of the leading signaling protocols for Voice over IP, along with H.323 [2]. As mentioned in RFC 3261, the primary functionality of SIP includes locating end user system for communication (user location), determining willingness of the called party to engage in communication (user availability), determining media and media parameters for communication (user capability), establishing session parameters and setting up connection equivalent to ringing (session setup), and managing sessions.

An example of message exchange between two users using SIP is shown in Fig. 2. In this example, a user, Bob, uses SIP softphone on his laptop to call another user, Alice. The SIP messages sequence is shown with sequence numbers. After the initial SIP session establishes, a media session is initiated for conversation (step 5). Finally, the session is terminated after completion of the conversation.

The SIP RFC defines a number of network elements based on their functionality to enable the above sequence. The main network elements are: User Agent (UA), proxy server, redirect server, and SIP registrar. The UAs are Internet end points such as softphone, cellular phones, PSTN gateways, PDAs, etc. The proxy server relays call signaling acting both as client and server on behalf of user agents and performs routing during session invitations. The redirect server redirects callers to other servers. The SIP registrar is discussed in rest of the section.

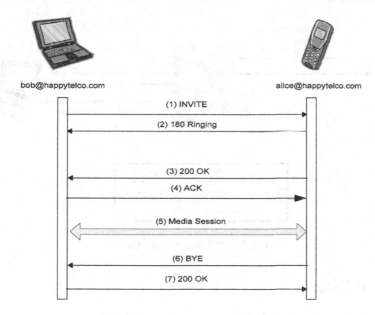

Fig. 2. A session sequence using SIP

The SIP registrar, also referred as just registrar, is a SIP server responsible for keeping track of user's contact location and providing that information to callers. The registrar accepts register message and stores the received information locally in an in-memory database or in a location server as shown in Fig. 3. All multi-media users register their current location with a registrar to allow calls to be made to them using a phone number or alias. Without the registrar, the caller would need to know the correct location attributes such as IP address and port of the telephone, which may be dynamic.

The SIP uses two terms for registering a user: an address-of-record (AOR) and a contact address. The Address-of-record represents identity of a user (generally long term) without any dependency on the end device. It is represented using Universal Resource Identifier (URI) such as <sip:bob@happytelco.com>. The contact-address is also represented as URI, but is associated with a particular device and has device specific form such as <sip:alice@15.121.11.18:1234> or <sip: alice@desktop1. happlytelco.com>.

The two main operations that the SIP registrar performs are:

> Registering user location: The users register their locations using an address-of-record and contact-address pair by sending a REGISTER message. The response message is either an OK message or an error message indicating the result of operation.

> Responding to user location query: A query for the location is made using register request message with and empty contact-address value. The registrar populates the contact-address with the stored location in the response message.

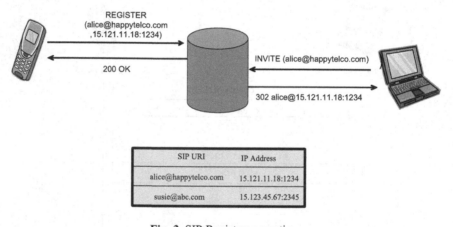

Fig. 3. SIP Registrar operations

3   System Design

With the above overview of SIP registrar, we can infer that SIP registrar is a critical element of the IMS architecture. When the SIP registrar becomes unavailable, the users may lose all the multi-media services of the network and become unreachable. In this section, we explore the system design requirements and system design.

The system design requirements for SIP registrar are to prevent service outage due to hardware as well as software failures. The hardware failure could be result of failed memory, buggy board design, bad disks, or overheating CPUs. The software failure, usually more frequent than hardware failure, could be a result of an operating system crash, application crash, memory exhaustion, unhandled exceptions, deadlock, or application going into an infinite loop. The system must be designed to handle such faults without loosing information of registered users. Furthermore, the clients should not notice that the SIP registry service has failed.

The first solution, a non-clustered approach, is to write a script on a node that periodically monitors the state of SIP registrar. When the process terminates, the script re-spawns a new SIP registrar process. In addition, the client is made aware that the registrar can potentially fail. The SIP RFC defines expiration interval when the UA register their addresses, and the UA contact address is removed when the interval elapses. The RFC defines two ways for setting expiration interval in seconds for contact addresses. The first way is to use expires header field in the register request that applies to all the contact addresses contained in the request. The second way is to use the expires parameter in the contact header. If the SIP registrar is not highly available, the clients may set a small expiration interval (30 seconds to few minutes) and periodically register after expiration of each interval. This will reduce the time during which they are unavailable to others if registrar fails. However, this leads to a lot of unnecessary traffic on the network, and therefore, is not a scalable solution. In addition, this design does not prevent service outage when hardware faults occur.

These issues are addressed by making SIP registrar a cluster application. The basic idea is that when a registrar on a node fails, the registrar on the other healthy node can take up the work load of the failed server.

Our system design, as shown in Fig. 4, is based on a cluster with two nodes connected via Ethernet. We define cluster as a collection of nodes connected together to provide single system image and handle faults at different levels.

The SIP clients send message to the cluster and receive response from a SIP registrar on one of the nodes in the cluster. The SIP registrars provide a Service Access Point (SAP) to the client, such as an IP address and a UDP port number pair, to access registry service.

Each node in the cluster runs Linux operating system, OpenAIS, and SIP registrar. The Linux operating system provides low-level services such as memory management, process management, file I/O, and inter process communication. The OpenAIS is a cluster middleware implementation of interfaces defined in SAF Application Interface Specification (AIS) [8]. In the current OpenAIS distribution (version 0.70), implemented as user-space daemon, the following services are supported:

- Availability Management Framework (AMF) provides a logical view of cluster, redundancy model (such as 2N, N+M), health-check, and failover mechanism.
- Cluster membership service that maintains current view of the cluster members and notifies when change occurs.
- Event service is an interface for publishing and subscribing events in the cluster.
- Checkpoint service enables information synchronization between active and standby components.

The SIP registrar, as shown in Fig. 4, is implemented as a server application in user space.

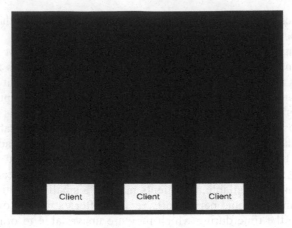

Fig. 4. System Design

4   HA Design Challenges

In this section, we discuss the design challenges to make SIP registrar highly available using OpenAIS cluster middleware. The main challenges with in our design are:

1. Choosing the appropriate scalable redundancy model.
2. Keeping a single service access point when the registrar is hosted on two different nodes.
3. Synchronizing runtime and configuration information between the registrars on two nodes.
4. Handling failovers and switchovers.
5. Handling interval expiry timers.
6. Detecting and handling faults.

The first challenge is to choose the right redundancy model for the SIP registrar. We choose 2N redundancy model, as it is one of the simplest model to implement and address the protection requirements of our application: When a node or application fails due to hardware or software failure, the service is protected by other node. Furthermore, non-revertive redundancy model is used. This means that when the application with standby HA state receives transition to active, it keeps the active HA state even if the failed application on other node is repaired and is available for service. The redundancy model can also be scaled by workload distribution and adding more nodes.

The second challenge is fortunately resolved in the SIP's RFC itself [1]. A well-known multicast address, 224.0.1.75, along with TCP/UDP port, 5060, is defined for SIP. We use this multicast address as the service access point for SIP registry. The registrar joins the multicast group and listens to the SIP request, and the client can send the messages to this address without worrying about actual SIP registrar location. Using multicast address can generate a lot for traffic if there are multiple members of the group. We reduce this traffic by limiting the members of this multicast group to the active registrar serving the request. That is the application on a node that is assigned active HA state joins the multicast group, the application on the other node doesn't join the multicast group.

The third challenge is synchronization of runtime and configuration information. It is an important design decision as it determines the service outage window. The two design choices are synchronizing upon receiving each register request and periodic updates based on timer. Synchronizing every registration request has drawback of excessive communication overhead resulting in reduced performance. The periodic updates open up a window during which the new registrations are lost. We choose the checkpoint mechanism available on the OpenAIS for synchronization and create a checkpoint section for each registry request. The section is deleted when the timer expires or when the UA deregisters its contact addresses.

The fourth challenge of handling failovers is aided by Availability Management Framework (AMF) of OpenAIS, discussed in detail in the following sections . When AMF detects a failure, it notifies the standby application. An application registered callback is called to initiate the switchover.

The timer expiry is handled using checkpoint. Note that timer processing is not done on standby to preserve a master-slave relationship between active and standby applications. The checkpoint records are deleted by component assigned active HA state upon expiry of interval. The checkpoint record also contains start of the timer along with timer interval. When a switchover occurs, the timers are restarted based for start time and expiry interval.

Finally, the detection and handling mechanism is a critical aspect, and is discussed in detail in section 6.

5   SIP Registrar Design and Implementation

Our experimental SIP registrar is implemented as a server application using network programming interfaces (BSD socket APIs). This server application receives the requests on a UDP socket, parses the request, and processes the request based on the request type. To make it highly available, we choose the deployment as depicted in Fig. 4, where the application is deployed on a cluster of two nodes.

The four main steps towards making SIP registrar highly available using SAF APIs are:

➤   Mapping application to SAF system model entities.

➤   Programming changes to integrate application with SAF cluster.

➤   Designing checkpoint mechanism

➤   Application deployment configuration based on entity mapping.

The first two steps are described in further detail in next sections. The application deployment is done based on the OpenAIS configuration file syntax (*groups.conf*).

5.1 Mapping Application to SAF System Model

The application is mapped to SAF entity model as shown in Fig. 5, and is explained from bottom up. At the lowest level, the SIP registrar process maps to the SAF components represented as C1 and C2 on Node 1 and Node 2 respectively. These components are assigned workload using logical entity called component service instance, CSI RegSvcInst. The components, C1 and C2, are contained in service units, SU1 and SU2 respectively. The service units are defined as containers for components providing a service. The AMF assigns the service instance representing a service work load for a service unit, which is represented as RegSvc. In addition, when AMF assigns a service instance, it assigns an HA state (active or standby) indicating whether the service instance performs active or standby role. The HA states of service instance and component service instance are same in a service unit due to containment relationship. Furthermore, a service group, SipRegSvcGrp, contains service units SU1 and SU2, and provides service availability to service instance RegSvc. The attributes of service group include redundancy model, service unit type, and number of service units. As seen in the figure, service group is the highest abstraction in the SAF system model.

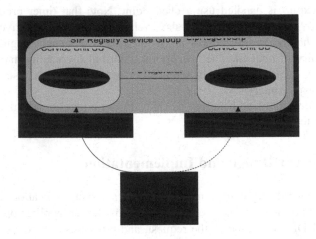

Fig. 5. 2N System Model for SIP Registry Service

5.2 Application Programming Changes

This section captures main programming tasks for our example. We begin with integration of our application with Application Management Framework (AMF) of SAF Application Interface Specification (AIS). These programming changes are:

1. Implementing AMF callback functions to handle the life cycle operations (e.g., health check, termination), work load assignment (e.g., component service instance assignment), tracking changes (e.g., protection group), etc.
2. Initializing and registering callback using safAmfInitialize and safAmfSelectionObjectGet.

3. Using selection object to listen for AMF callback messages and calling dispatching routine, safAmfDispatch, when message is received.
4. Role assignment and processing of application service request when CSISetCallback routine is called.
5. Update checkpoint when a register request is received.
6. Failover or switchover handling in CSI callback.
7. Reporting errors to AMF (saAmfComponentErrorReport).
8. Periodically responding to health-check callback requests.

The pseudo code for an important callback routine, CSISetCallback, is described in Listing 1. In this code, the application state changes with respect to component service instance are described. For example, during cluster startup when SIP registrar on the first node registers with the AMF, it is assigned active HA state and the component can start serving the user registration and lookup requests. When the second node comes up the registrar on that node is assigned standby HA state. Also, note the handling of quiesced state -- a temporary state while transitioning from active to standby state during a switchover. In this state, the application's in-memory runtime state is not purged. The basic idea is to keep the service unit in this state to ensure a standby to active transition is smooth.

```
CSISetCallback(invocation, compName, csiName, csiFlags, haState,
activeCompName, transitionDescriptor)
{
        if (haState is Active){
         join the sip multicast group;
          if (componentHAState is Standby) indicating switchover
then apply the checkpoint data to in memory information;
         set componentHAState to active;
        }
        else if (hastate is Standby){
           set componentHAState to Standby;
           leave the multicast group;
        }
        else if (haState is quiesced) {
           set componentHAState to quisced;
           keep the checkpoints for a possible transition to
active;
           leave the multicast group, i.e., don't accept new
requests;
        }              '
        send response to AMF
}
```

Listing 1. Pseudo code for handling failovers and role assignment

5.3 Designing Checkpoint Mechanism

As discussed in design challenges section, one of the important design aspects is synchronizing information between two components. In our implementation, we use the checkpoint service of OpenAIS distribution that is compliant with SA Forum AIS checkpoint service (AIS B.01.01). The checkpoint is an in-memory database for storing information that needs to be synchronized between components assigned active and standby HA state for a given component service instance. In our example, this information is the records containing address-of-record and its associated contact address. Each record is stored in a checkpoint section and is referred to as checkpoint record. When a register request is received, the in-memory data structures are updated followed by creation a checkpoint record. Similarly, if a request is to remove an association, the checkpoint record is deleted after updating in-memory data structures.

The OpenAIS implementation creates a checkpoint replica, which is a copy of database, on each node the checkpoint is created, so if a node fails a valid replica is available on other node as the components reside on two nodes. When transitioning from standby to active, the component reads the checkpoint records to populate the in-memory data structures.

This concludes our discussion on design and implementation. So far we have covered the mechanism to implement redundancy in our system. However, we have not discussed how faults are detected and eventually handled to provide resiliency. In the next section, we cover these details.

6 Fault Handling

An important design consideration of service availability is fault detection, fault escalation, and fault handling. The faults are classified into hardware and software and the mechanism for detection and handling vary based on the type of failure.

The hardware failures are detected by reading the platform provided mechanism. In our system, a daemon is implemented that periodically monitors the temperature sensors, fans, power supply, and probes hardware components to check for faults. When fault occurs, the faults are logged and the configured actions are taken. The AMF is notified about the fault and if a critical failure occurs the node is shutdown.

In addition to handling hardware faults, software faults are handled to protect services. A software monitoring hierarchy is defined to capture as many faults as possible. Three priority classes are defined: AMF, application, and idle process. The AMF has the highest priority compared to the other classes, so it runs all the time irrespective of application and idle process. The application runs with medium priority and the idle process runs with lowest priority.

Every application registered with AMF responds to periodic health check callbacks. Therefore, when an application fault occurs -- such as unhandled exception like out of memory, NULL pointer exception, and divide-by-zero exception –, the AMF health check fails. The low priority process periodically responds to AMF indicating that every process is receiving fair share of CPU time slice. Furthermore, AMF process periodically resets the watchdog timer. If the AMF process crashes the node will shutdown resulting in failover initiation.

7 Lessons Learned

Our experience with developing highly available SIP registrar on a low cost server with Linux and OpenAIS has been quite positive. However, there are some valuable lessons during development and deployment. Although we have shared some of our experiences in our earlier work [4], we have repeated some to reiterate their importance along with the new lessons. These are:

> Service availability is not replacement for a robust design. In fact, Cluster application must be more robust and carefully designed to take into consideration many race conditions like ownership of checkpoint during switchover.
> Choose a right synchronization scheme, not everything should be synchronized between application with active and standby HA state.
> Design for timers appropriately, a simple replication of code on active and standby results in difficult to debug race conditions and out-of-sync application memory states.
> Include version information and validate version information of checkpoint objects to prevent unnecessary debugging and enable future application upgrade.

8 Conclusions

Building robust application requires a lot of effort, but building for service availability has some unique challenges. In this case study, we have outlined some important aspects of building highly available application using OpenAIS, an open source middleware based on Service Availability Forum's AIS specification. Some of the concepts presented here may apply to many other telecom and data communication applications too. The AIS services that we have used are AMF and checkpoint services.

The service availability of the SIP registrar was then computed by measuring service outage while injecting faults that occur in real world scenario -- like node crash and application faults. The service outage time, about 50-300ms, was found to be sum of network latency, checkpoint synchronization interval, and failover handling time.

This concludes our paper. We hope that the design challenges described in section 4 and design steps in section 5 will be useful to the future HA application developers planning to use SAF specifications. The lessons learned will also prevent future developers to avoid mistakes that we made during our design and development.

References

1. J.Rosenberg, H.Schulzrinne, et. al., SIP: Session Initiation Protocol, RFC 3261 < http://www.ietf.org/rfc/rfc3261.txt>, June 2002.
2. Session Initiation Protocol, Wikipedia, Dec 2005.
3. D.Sisalem and J.Kuthan, SIP tutorial <http://www.iptel.org/sip>, 2000-2002.
4. A.Kamalvanshi and T.Jokiaho, "Building HA Application using SA Forum cluster: A case study of GGSN Application", ISAS 2005.
5. OpenAIS Project <http://developer.osdl.org/dev/openais>

6. T.Jokiaho, F.Herrmann, D.Penkler, L.Moser: "Application Interface Specification of the Service Availability Forum", pp 14-16, Boards and Solutions Magazine, June 2003.
7. T Jokiaho, F Herrmann, D Penkler, M Reitenspiess, L Moser: "The Service Availability™ Forum Specification for High Availability Middleware", October 2003. Presented at Workshop of Dependable Embedded Systems, Florence, Italy.
8. SA Forum Application Interface Specification AIS B.01.01

Searching for Synergy: Java and SAF AIS

Tero Laine[1], József Bíró[2], Jussi Riihelä[1],
Jens Jensen[3], Magnus Karlson[3], and Peter Kristiansson[3]

[1] Nokia Corporation, P.O. Box 785, 33101 Tampere, Finland
{tero.laine, jussi.riihela}@nokia.com
http://www.nokia.com
[2] Nokia Research Center, Köztelek u. 6, 1092 Budapest, Hungary
jozsef.biro@nokia.com
http://research.nokia.com/
[3] Ericsson AB
{jens.jensen, magnus.karlson, peter.kristiansson}@ericsson.com
http://www.ericsson.com

Abstract. Service Availability Forum [TM] (SAF) has specified interfaces
for highly available software and has since 2001 published the Application Interface Specification (AIS), and the Hardware Platform Interface
(HPI). All specifications have been written using the C language calling
conventions and the assumption was that all usages would be through
native executables rather than through a more compound environment
like a Java Virtual Machine (JVM). This paper concentrates only on the
AIS interfaces and its possible mappings to the Java world. We have
studied AIS and high availability software from a Java perspective to
see the implications of using AIS in the Java world and to ensure that
we do not violate the way Java programming is usually done. During
these studies we have shown which specifications and how these could be
implemented in Java, as well as specified and implemented a Java adaptation for selected SAF AIS services. We believe that a Java adaptation
is an important addition for the standardization of high availability interfaces because it enables the creation of highly available applications
also for the software domains where Java is dominating, including mixed
environments where some parts are written in Java and some in other
languages, which will most probably be the prevalent environment for
some years in the telecom world.

Keywords: Java, high availability, Service Availability Forum, Application Interface Specification.

1 Introduction

Service Availability Forum [SAF] is a consortium of companies working together
to develop and publish interface specifications for highly available software. One
of its specifications is the Application Interface Specification [AIS] that defines
the interface between the applications and the middleware providing service
availability within a cluster to enable a system with no single point of failure.

D. Penkler, M. Reitenspiess, and F. Tam (Eds.): ISAS 2006, LNCS 4328, pp. 229–252, 2006.
© Springer-Verlag Berlin Heidelberg 2006

AIS captures commonly used high availability (HA) patterns and provides a variety of services for carrier grade applications.

AIS has been defined using the C programming language calling conventions and thus it currently does not support the usage of Java in a high enough degree. Java has become a mature technology over the years, with one of the largest developer base worldwide and it brings numerous benefits to software systems including improved productivity, modularity, robustness and portability. However, despite its obvious potentials, Java has not been used extensively in the inner parts of carrier grade telecom systems so far.

Considering the aforementioned general benefits and also its extended use mainly in the service layer of telecom networks, both Nokia and Ericsson have been contemplating the application of Java in highly available systems and have been carrying out projects to investigate the problems Java faces in this new domain. The potential synergy between SAF AIS and Java has been a natural target of these studies from the beginning and both companies saw it as worth while to work on adoptions of AIS to Java. This paper presents the results of the related work carried out by the two companies.

Ericsson and Nokia have partly worked together but investigated two different approaches for integrating Java technologies into the HA framework defined by AIS. They will be described in more detail in their respective sections but in essence the two approaches are A) to investigate which existing Java solution there is already, the need for communication between Java and C to see what could be the minimal subset of the SAF API that has to be mapped, and how one would connect SAF implementations to existing Java solutions (Sect. 3 and 4) and B) to create a Java API representing a semantically identical mapping of the native AIS API with minor object oriented modifications (Sect. 5). It should also be noted that the companies have used different presumptions concerning potential changes to AIS: approach A assumed that the architectural model for SAF could be extended and modifications could be done to the existing specifications, whereas approach B considered only the existing specification without potential modifications.

These two approaches do complement each other and presenting them in a joint paper gives a broader picture of the possible and desirable ways for SAF to move forward into the Java domain. Indeed, both companies assumed from the beginning that this type of work should really be driven within the appropriate standardization bodies. The main motivation of this paper is to trigger such activities within SAF and the Java Community Process (JCP).

2   Background

In some software application domains, such as the telecom domain, carrier grade high availability and fault tolerance, as well as fault recovery, have been standard requirements for a long time already. Such a system must be continuously available and "always on". In practice, availability can be expressed as $A = MTBF/(MTTR+MTBF)$ where A is the degree of availability expressed as a percentage, MTBF is the mean time between failures, and MTTR is the mean time to repair or resolve a particular problem (See [BP]). Availability is often specified as a number of "nines", e.g. five nines availability (99.999%, the level required for carrier grade systems), matches to a maximum of five minutes downtime per year, including planned maintenance, software upgrades, hardware maintenance etc.

Proprietary high availability solutions have been used in such software systems for years and implementations have relied on low-level programming languages like C or C++, or even proprietary programming languages and special hardware. Some availability or fault tolerance related design patterns have been published (e.g. [BP] and [BCT]), but individual patterns can be applied only to very limited problems. System level high availability is always a concatenation of large number of attributes that need to fit together.

Migrating from proprietary systems towards standardized solutions has been the main goal of SAF. The "need for standard interfaces in the telecom domain is driven by requirements of rapidly evolving and converging network services. These factors – which include new technologies, rapid deployment and cost constraints – point to a modular, building-block equipment architecture for carrier-grade systems" [SWP]. SAF has been defining HA interfaces since 2001, the latest releases were published at the beginning of 2006. The SAF specifications have now for the first time truly reached such a maturity that they could be used to build contents and control servers in the telecom domain which has been the initial goal for SAF.

A SAF compliant HA middleware contains the following major elements, as mandated by AIS version B.02.01:

- Availability Management Framework (AMF, see [AMF2]) is the software entity that provides service availability by coordinating redundant resources within a cluster to deliver a system with no single point of failure.
- Cluster Membership Service [CLM2] maintains membership information about the nodes.
- Checkpoint Service [CKPT2] provides a facility for processes to record checkpoint data incrementally, which can be used to protect an application against failures.
- Event Service [EVT2] is a publish-subscribe multipoint-to-multipoint communication mechanism that is based on the concept of event channels: one or more publishers communicate asynchronously with one or more subscribers via events over a cluster-wide entity, named event channel.
- Message Service [MSG2] provides a communication mechanism for processes on the same or on different nodes. Messages are written to and read from message queues.
- Lock Service [LCK2] is a distributed lock service, intended for use in a cluster, where processes in different nodes might compete with each other for access to a shared resource.
- Information Model Management Service [IMM2] manages the SA Forum information model (IM): the different entities of an AIS cluster, such as components provided by AMF, checkpoints provided by the Checkpoint Service, or

message queues provided by the Message Service are represented by various objects of the SA Forum information model. The objects in the Information Model are provided with their attributes and administrative operations.

- Log Service [LOG2] provides high level cluster-significant, function-based information suited primarily for network or system administrators, or automated tools to assist troubleshooting issues such as mis-configurations, network disconnects and unavailable resources.
- Notification Service [NTF2] is provided for system management purposes and is used by a service-user to report an event to a peer service-user.

The SAF Application Programming Interfaces (API) have been defined using C calling conventions to ensure that they will have an as broad as possible usability. This is a very wise choice in an industry that has to maintain a huge amount of legacy code, traditionally written in C or other similar languages, and that uses a wide variety of software platforms (operating systems, in-house middleware, etc.) for most of which the C language is an ideal lowest common denominator. However the emergence of Java as a widely spread technology to address differences between very different platforms and to enable rapid creation and integration of different software modules (often created by 3rd parties) raises the need to introduce Java support to SAF interfaces.

When Java was first launched in 1995, it had an immediate commercial success with support for dynamic content in web browsers. Although this breakthrough made Java synonymous with applet technology for the general public, Java was from the beginning intended as a general-purpose language designed for reliability, modularity, portability, concurrency, networking and security. This made it especially suitable for server systems. Soon Java was used to extend web servers with Java servlets, and with the introduction of Enterprise JavaBeans technology in 1997 Java was used to implement full-featured application servers.

One of the important goals of Java is reliability. This reliability is achieved on a first level by the language constructs and by the runtime environment with features such as clear syntax, strong typing, extensive exception handling, automatic memory handling and controlled execution in a JVM (Java Virtual Machine). In server systems reliability is also achieved on a second level by executing components in a container, which among other tasks has the responsibility of fault isolation and fault recovery.

Although the Java specifications do not require application servers to provide features such as high availability, session retainability and multi-server scalability, the specifications have intentionally designed the container-component contract with the APIs that are necessary for such systems. As server side environments often specify availability requirements, some effort has been put into creating Java platforms supporting such requirements. Leading application server vendors IBM WebSphere [WS], BEA WebLogic [WL] and open source middleware initiatives [JBHA] support these requirements. These efforts should be taken into account when we consider integrating Java with the HA middleware specified by AIS. Sections 3 and 4 provide an overview of the elements of these efforts (along with definitions of Java SE/EE and an overview of their current state) that could potentially be useful for AIS.

Sun has chosen to implement an open mechanism to introduce new Java standards. The mechanism is called Java Community Process [JCP]. Hundreds of standards (called JSRs: Java Specification Request), have been created using JCP. It is foreseeable therefore that the creation of Java APIs supporting the HA middleware defined by SAF will have to be controlled by a cooperation between SAF and JCP.

3   Java Domains

In the Java world there exist two different editions for server applications, the Java Standard Edition (SE, see [JSE]) and the Java Enterprise Edition (EE, see [JEE]). The standard edition contains the base functionality for desktop and server applications. It is also the foundation for the enterprise edition and lightweight containers. The enterprise edition adds a lot of functionality to the standard edition to give more support for server applications. The enterprise edition is a collection of specifications and there exist implementations from many different vendors. As a reaction to the heavyweight complexity of the enterprise edition the open source community has developed alternatives called lightweight containers. When the SAF concepts are to be introduced in Java all three alternatives should be taken into account to ensure full usability in the Java environment.

3.1   Java SE

The Java SE environment provides support for developing server applications. It lacks protection for unhandled exceptions and is designed to have one application per JVM. As the JVM has a too large footprint to make this acceptable additional failure handling is needed. The standard edition also lacks support for deployment of smaller components.

3.2   Java EE

Java EE defines a standard for developing enterprise applications. Java EE bundles a lot of services that are needed for these types of applications i.e. communication support, database access etc. The container handles failures and can persist application data automatically. Java EE contains complete standardized specifications and compliance tests that make it possible to write applications that are portable between different implementations. The problem with Java EE is the complexity and that it is heavyweight. Currently the Java EE community is working on improvements that will make it easier to use and more lightweight; EJB 3.0 (Enterprise Java Beans, see [JSR220]) is a step in that direction. But even with this the Java EE environment is much more complex and heavyweight than many of the open source lightweight containers. When SAF is introduced in the Java EE concept it is possible to hide much of the functionality in the container and in this way make the impact on the applications smaller. Many of the services already provided with Java EE overlaps with the services specified in specifications from Service Availability Forum. This has to be taken into account when deciding which SAF services are necessary and reasonable to introduce in Java.

3.3 Lightweight Containers

As a reaction to the heavyweight complexity of the enterprise edition, the open source community has developed alternatives called lightweight containers. The most popular ones are Spring Framework [SPRF] and PicoContainer [PICO]. The lightweight containers strive to provide services for the simplest component possible. The objects that are deployed into the lightweight containers are POJOs, plain old Java objects. The objects themselves do not depend on the container and can be run outside of the container for better testability. The containers also provide mechanisms for rapid extensions by third parties which make it possible to use services defined in the Java EE standard or new SAF services defined for Java. The containers have a short start-up time and a small footprint. Even when they are more lightweight than traditional Java EE containers they still give the same support for failure handling by the containers and they can bundle the services needed. The problem with the lightweight containers is that they are not standardized today.

4   Integration Between Java and C

4.1   Java Support Levels

When introducing Java in the SAF community it can be done with different support levels. The first level is a C-like Java API that is a direct mapping of the current C APIs in SAF. This would make the mapping simple but are so far from what the Java community is used to, that it would not be accepted by them. But it can serve as an intermediate solution for cases when a SAF application has parts written in Java and the complete standardization work has not been completed.

The next level of Java support is to use the concepts from the SAF standardization and create a Java representation for it. This would give the Java programmer an object oriented API that is designed using the conventions and the patterns common in Java APIs. It is more work and this would have to be done in co-operation with the Java community, in a JSR.

The third level of Java support could be to reuse some of the existing Java standard APIs and declare them as part of AIS. In some cases these standards need to be enhanced. This work should also be done in a JSR.

4.2   Multiple Components in Java

Another aspect of the integration is to make it possible to have multiple components in a single JVM. Two factors have to be considered in this respect.

First, in AIS the current specification only allows one operating system (OS) process to be mapped to one AIS component. This implies that the JVM itself will become a component and that it can not contain multiple components. This needs to be solved within the SAF standardization and some work in this direction is currently ongoing: one possible solution would be to allow multiple components in one "container" (a JVM in this case), an interface created to allow sub/proxy- Application Management Framework entities that could control and supervise these multiple components in one container.

The second factor is how to achieve an adequate isolation between components executing in the same JVM. One approach to this problem is to require the JVM to provide this isolation. Current JVMs do not provide this support, but the emerging Isolation API (JSR 121, see [JSR121]) may change this and eventually produce JVMs that have support for multiple isolated applications within a single JVM instance.

An alternative approach, which is currently widely used, is to implement a container-component architecture. With this approach, components are deployed into and executed within a container, which provides a controlled environment for the components. The container is itself a Java program executing in the JVM and utilizing the JVM features in order to provide fault isolation between the components and fault recovery. In this way it can be guaranteed that a fault in one component cannot corrupt the state of another component. However, there are a few rare faults (such as lack of memory) that will lead to the termination and the restart of the JVM, the container and all of the components. It is appropriate to view the JVM and the container as an extension of the OS. Like the OS provides isolation between processes, the JVM and the container provide isolation between more fine-grained components.

4.3   Integration Methods

There are different ways to integrate Java and C implementations depending on whether they need to interact and where the best implementation currently is.

If a service implementation is present in C (see Fig. 1), a Java API can be provided with a JNI interface. The Java interface can provide object oriented interface and does not necessarily need to be a direct mapping of the C API. It is not necessary that the Java interface is implemented with JNI. It can also be a pure Java API that communicates with the C parts using some other protocol like a socket based protocol.

If there exists a solution in both the Java and C space and if applications in the different spaces need to share data, a bridge solution is preferred (see Fig. 2). In this solution it is not necessary that the two implementations are based on the same set of APIs it can be the case that they solve the same problem in different ways. This could be a good solution if a Java solution already exists

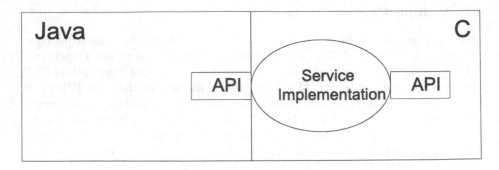

Fig. 1. Service implementation in C

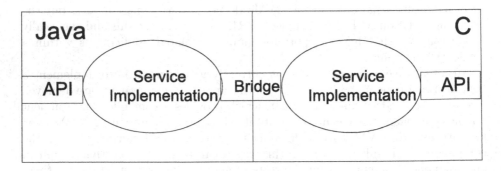

Fig. 2. Bridging service implementations in Java and C

for one of the areas where SAF have a specification. The bridge would solve the interaction between the C and Java application.

For the cases where the applications in Java and C do not need to interact and there already exists a solution in Java, the C and Java implementations can be used without linking them (see Fig. 3).

In the future it is possible that some backend solutions written in Java could be used from C (see Fig. 4). This could be the case when there already exists a feature rich high availability service in Java, even when a SAF service has yet to be specified or has a less feature rich interface. However, this is not a likely scenario in the near future due to that a SAF HA implementation would not use a JVM but requiring it, and that would not be acceptable for small foot-print (memory) system solutions.

4.4   Dependencies Between SAF Services

When investigating which SAF services are candidates for Java standardization it is important to know the dependency between the different services. If one service is dependent on another this has to be taken into account when and

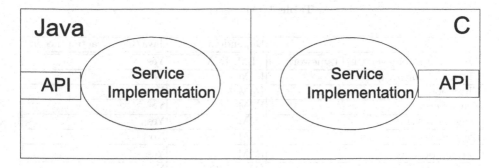

Fig. 3. Service implementations in Java and C without bridging

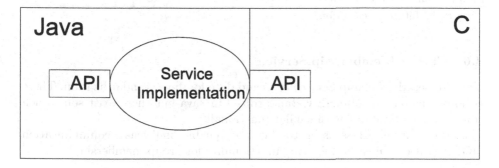

Fig. 4. Service implementation in Java

if the service is standardized in Java. It is also expected that Java for SAF services, when available, will spread gradually and mixed-language application will be dominant for a long time. This means that it is important to know if the Java and C parts need to interact for a specific service.

4.5   Availability Management Framework

One of the very fundamental rules applicable for reliable systems is that having more than one entity that tries or believe that it is in control of the system is a difficult problem to solve. Therefore, if we are to enable Java and C applications in the same cluster it is advantageous that both are controlled by one (main) instance of the AMF. The most plausible solution is that AMF is implemented in C, as there already exist a number of implementations, and the AMF APIs are provided for Java applications. The Java APIs should be object oriented and based on the concepts specified in the AMF specification. The standardization of the Java APIs should be done within the Java community in a JSR. Today there is no service like AMF for Java.

Table 1. AIS services

SAF Service	Dependent on	Java/C interaction needed
Availability Management Framework	CLM, IMM	Yes
Cluster Membership Service	IMM	Yes
Checkpoint Service	IMM	No
Event Service	IMM	Yes
Message Service	IMM	Yes
Lock Service	IMM	No
Naming Service[1]	IMM	Yes
Log Service	IMM, MSG	Yes
Timer Service[1]	IMM	No
Notification Service	IMM, LOG, MSG	Yes
Information Model Management Service	–	Yes

[1] potential future specifications

4.6   Cluster Membership Service

The Cluster Membership Service is a candidate for Java standardization. There is no overlapping functionality standardized in Java but there exist some open source implementations with similar functionality.

JGroups from JBoss is a toolkit for reliable multicast communication [JGRPS]. It contains the following functionality for group membership:

– Knowledge about which group the members are in.
– Notifications when a member joins, leaves or crashes.

This could be used as an alternative to the Cluster Membership Service but it is not standardized.

4.7   Checkpoint Service

The Java community has standardized alternatives to the Checkpoint Service and there are alternative solutions in the open source community.

One of the alternatives is the Java Persistence API, part of JSR 220. The Java Persistence API is lightweight framework for persisting Java object. It is considered the way forward for both Java EE and SE applications. Even if it is mainly designed to use a database for storing the data it can be extended to protect the data in other ways, i.e. in memory replication. The Persistence API combines the best ideas from other popular persistence frameworks as Hibernate [HIBR], Java Data Objects [JDO], TopLink [TL] and others. There does not exist any commercial implementation of the Persistence API today.

JBoss Cache [JBC] is an open source implementation that is not standardized but it solves the same problem as the SAF Checkpoint Service. It works as a distributed cache for Java objects with in memory replication. It has three different caching modes:

- Local Cache without replication.
- Replicated Cache using non-blocking asynchronous replication.
- Replicated Cache using blocking synchronous replication.

It also has transactional support and pluggable policies for database integration.

As there are solutions within the Java community, including solutions with a higher support level than the current SAF specification, it is not reasonable to try to standardize the SAF solution. Also, since it is hard to imagine a Java and C applications that will share the same checkpoint data, any integration between the Checkpoint Service and the solutions in the Java community seems unnecessary.

4.8 Event Service

In the same way as for the Checkpoint Service there are alternative solutions to the Event Service in the Java community. JMS (Java Message Service, see [JMS]) has more or less the same functionality as the Event Service from SAF.

JMS provides two types of messaging models, publish-subscribe and point-to-point queuing. In publish-subscribe one producer can send a message to many consumers through a channel. Subscribers can choose to subscribe to a specific topic and any message addressed to that topic is sent to all the consumers that has subscribed to it. The publisher is not dependent on the consumer that receives the message. JMS publish-subscribe is very similar to the SAF Event Service and it would be hard to introduce something new in the Java community that does not provide any new functionality. To conclude, the Event Service is probably not a candidate for Java standardization but as Java applications and C applications in a cluster must be able to communicate a bridged solution is necessary.

4.9 Message Service

JMS also contains one model that has overlapping functionality with the SAF Message Service.

JMS point-to-point messaging model allows JMS clients to send and receive messages asynchronously via queues. A given queue may have multiple receivers but only one receiver may consume each message. JMS takes care of distributing the messages within a group of receivers and guarantees that the message is delivered once and only once.

It is not necessary to standardize SAF Message service, but as interaction between C and Java applications is needed, a solution should allow this. This means that a bridged implementation is probably the best solution.

4.10 Log Service

Java has a logging API so a new logging API based on SAF logging should probably not be defined. The log handling though needs to be integrated. All logs produced by applications in a cluster should be handled in the same way, and probably it would also be beneficial if an application that is implemented in both Java and C can actually write into the same log file, although it would still be acceptable without this possibility.

4.11   Information Model Management Service

In some parts of JMX (Java Management Extension, see [JMX]) and Java Preferences (supporting configuration storage, see [JSR10]) has overlapping functionality with IMM.

JMX provides a standard way to manage Java based applications. An application or another resource is instrumented by an MBean (Managed Bean), which represents the management interface of the resource. This interface exposes the attributes that can be accessed, the operations that can be invoked and the notifications that can be emitted. Besides the instrumentation level, JMX defines an agent level, which makes use of the instrumentation level in order to enable the management of the resources. It consists of an MBean server and a set of services for handling MBeans. The JMX agent provides a generic management API, which can be used by connectors and protocol adapters in order to expose a management view of the JMX agent and its MBeans and to enable the control of them. Protocol adapters adapt this interface to specific protocols, such as SNMP or HTTP.

The JMX agent has a similar role as the IMM service. However, there are also considerable differences and there are some complex features in the IMM service that are lacking in JMX.

A Java standardization of this service should be handled as an enhancement of the JMX specification to support the lacking features. It is especially important that this is defined on the instrumentation level (the MBeans) that is the management interface of the applications, even though it may be optional for JMX agents to support all of the new features.

An implementation can be based either on a C implementation with the Java MBean API or on a bridged solution (which currently will have a limited functionality).

4.12   Notification Service

The functionality in the SAF Notification Service is partly covered by JMX in Java. JMX defines an API for notifications. JMX defines the common content for all notifications and the extended content for a few specialized notifications, such as attribute change notifications and monitor notifications. JMX also defines APIs for notification filters, notification listeners and notification emitters.

Even though JMX permits customized extensions of a basic notification, JMX ought to be enhanced in order to standardize the event types and the attributes defined by the SAF Notification Service. An implementation can be based either on a C implementation with the Java MBean API or on a bridged solution.

4.13   Naming Services

The Java Community has standardized a naming service that is widely used, JNDI (Java Naming and Directory Interface, see [JNDI]). JNDI is an API that provides naming and directory functionality. Applications can store and retrieve named Java objects of any type. It also provides directory operations such as searching for object using their attributes. JNDI is independent of any specific naming or directory service implementation. Different implementations can be plugged in seamlessly behind a common API. This could be a way to integrate the emerging AIS Naming service and JNDI. Integration is needed as Java and C applications in the same cluster needs interaction for a naming service.

4.14   Timer Service

Timers are normally local events to a component and not shared among several components, considering that Java already have reasonable support for timers it is not likely that there will be a need to map any future timer specification from SAF into the Java world.

5   Experimental Java AIS API Implementation

Sections 3 and 4 have provided a high level view of relevant state-of-the-art Java technologies and a broad investigation of several architectural aspects of the potential integration of these technologies and SAF AIS. This investigation has produced a variety of integration concepts. The following section describes the experimental work that has been carried out to prove the feasibility of some of these high-level concepts. An adaptation of native AIS APIs to Java has been carried out, including the specification of draft Java AIS APIs, a prototype implementation of a Java framework supporting these APIs and finally the creation of an example application that utilizes the specified Java APIs. Below we explain some problems and solutions related to the specification and implementation of the API.

The specified APIs represent a semantically identical mapping of the native AIS services, although some effort has been made to make the API conforming to object oriented principles and Java conventions. Still, the resulting experimental API could be classified as the first level support mentioned in Sect. 4.

The prototyping work has been based on the assumption that Java AIS API, when available, will spread gradually and mixed-language application will be dominant for a long time. Thus, the prototype has been built upon native SAF AIS implementation and the Java adaptation layer mostly propagates calls between the native AIS implementation and the Java applications. This is the approach referred to as "Service implementation in C" in Sect. 4 (see also Fig. 1). Although Sect. 4 mentions that the approach does not necessarily mandate the usage of JNI, it is the most obvious implementation candidate and the prototype was indeed implemented using JNI.

During the experimental work we have not considered any potential changes to AIS or future trends of Java technology either; instead we wanted to create and investigate solutions that are possible today. The work is based exclusively on B.01.01 of AIS (published on 22 November 2004, see ([AISO1], [AMF1], [CLM1], [CKPT1], [EVT1], [MSG1] and [LCK1]).

5.1   AIS Clarifications

Below we clarify some essential definitions in SAF AIS that are relevant for the subsequent architectural considerations.

A process is an "entity that a system provides to manage executing software" (see 3.1 of [AISO1]). A process is executable as a unit, has its own memory area and dedicated resources, such as files and finally it has its own thread (or threads) of execution. Although this definition is taken from AIS, a process is in fact the well known entity managed by the operating system.

A component (see 3.1.2 of [AMF1]) is "the smallest logical entity on which Application Management Framework (AMF) performs error detection and isolation, recovery and repair". On the one hand, a component must be "small enough" so that its failure "has as little impact as possible"; on the other hand, it "should include all functions that cannot be clearly separated for error containment or isolation purposes".

AIS specification (AMF in particular) defines that a component may include one or more processes. However, we think that the "one component - one process"

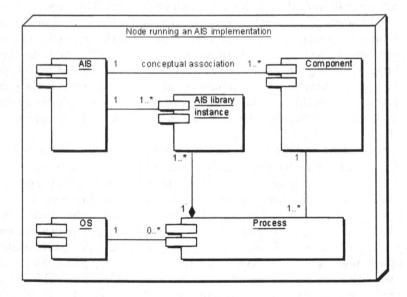

Fig. 5. Relationship of AIS middleware and operating system, process, component and AIS library instance

mapping is the ideal match, because the isolation required by the component (for error containment) is automatically provided by the process. A component containing more processes produces components bigger than ideal and we think this match is supported by AIS mainly for legacy reasons or for special design constraints.

We use the term library instance as a dynamic association between the process(es) of a component and AIS. A library instance contains a handle, identifying the instance when the component calls AIS, a set of callbacks implemented by the component called by AIS and a "selection object" to enable the polling of pending callbacks. A process may establish multiple library instances for an AIS service; allowing multithreading of API calls and dispatching of callbacks.

On conceptual level the AIS middleware sees the application as a set of components. In practice (see Fig. 5), the AIS communicates with the processes of the components using library instances.

5.2   Mapping the Java Virtual Machine to AIS Components

One of the key problems is to find a sound mapping between AIS and Java entities so that the isolation requirements are met. The virtual machines (VMs) available on the market today (see Fig. 6) are dominantly targeted for a single computer, run in a single operating system process and support a single Java application, provided that "application" means the same isolation as in operating system processes.

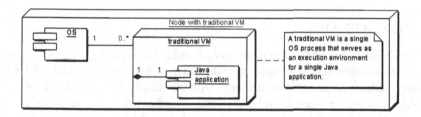

Fig. 6. Relationship of operating system, VM and Java application

Such VMs are naturally mapped to AIS components; Figure 7 presents the overall view of this architectural mapping, also showing how the concept of library instance can be utilized:

From the reliability point of view, this mapping seems optimal because the applied VM technology is mature and can be assumed to be as reliable as the operating system. Furthermore, the effect of VM faults is limited to one component. However, a drawback of the mapping is that the native AMF implementation cannot tell the difference between VM and component faults.

From the performance point of view, component lifecycle events are slowed down because VM startup/shutdown is involved, this influences recovery as well.

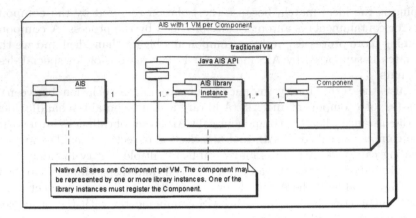

Fig. 7. Architectural mapping between VM and component

However, an important positive effect of the mapping is the limited influence on other components due to separate VMs.

A significant constraint of the mapping is that no multiple processes per component are allowed. This could be overcome by using the alternative mapping of one process per one VM. Architecturally there is no major difference between using a process or a component within a single VM, so this is just a variation of the first mapping. The drawbacks are increased footprint and slower speed (e.g. component startup/shutdown involves startup/shutdown of multiple VMs.)

5.3   Java AIS API

Design View. Java APIs are generally organized into packages, so our first step must be to define the packages into which the Java classes of the API will be placed. A single package is usually sufficient for simple APIs, while a hierarchy of packages is used for more complex APIs, especially if the API supports independent functionalities. The latter criterion applies to AIS, so we will distribute the API into several subpackages. The root package is `org.saforum.ais`: it serves as storage for global AIS constants and types. Each AIS service will have its own subpackage, like `org.saforum.ais.amf`, for the Application Management Framework, `org.saforum.ais.ckpt` for the Checkpoint Service API, and so on.

AIS services are defined as a set of C functions. Since Java does not allow standalone functions, we need to introduce classes that host the methods defined by the API. Below we present an approach, that – while still copying the native API very closely – is more suited to the object oriented paradigm of Java. The enclosed diagram (see Fig. 8) presents Checkpoint Service classes but other Services are designed along the same principles.

The core class of each service is the one representing the library instance, `<Area>LibraryHandle`. This class encapsulates library lifecycle and support for AIS-component interactions: it associates Java callbacks with the library

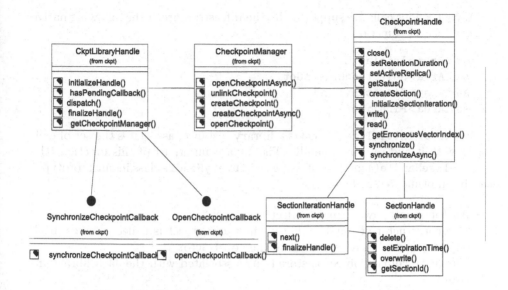

Fig. 8. Key Java classes of the Java Checkpoint Service API

instance and finally it is a gateway to other classes representing the API calls of the particular AIS service.

For example, the API calls for Checkpoint Service have been organized into four classes (see Fig. 8: readers familiar with the native AIS Checkpoint Service API will find that the operations of these classes are more or less direct mappings of the native API functions). `CheckpointManager` can be used to create a new checkpoint, open or unlink an existing one. The newly created checkpoints are represented by `CheckpointHandle` objects that enable the application to read or write the content of the checkpoint, change some checkpoint attributes and manipulate sections belonging to the checkpoint. Newly created checkpoint sections are represented by `SectionHandle` objects, while a `SectionIterationHandle` object can be used to retrieve descriptors of a selected set of sections. The detailed design contains miscellaneous other classes as well but they have been omitted here for the sake of simplicity.

Process View. The native AIS framework supports both synchronous and asynchronous communication programming interfaces. Mapping these interfaces between the Java API layer and the native API layer is explained below.

Synchronous calls, either with or without time-out, can be implemented in a straightforward way. The only serious issue is related to the blocking nature of the calls. If the virtual machine uses native threads, this is not a problem, but if it uses green threads, this is a major concern, because then a blocking native call will block the whole VM, i.e. all other Java code. Fortunately, most VMs for the standard and enterprise edition use native threads.

Asynchronous calls are supported by the infrastructure of the following native library lifecycle functions:

- sa<Area>Initialize(),
- sa<Area>SelectionObjectGet(),
- sa<Area>Dispatch() and
- sa<Area>Finalize().

Sa<Area>Initialize() creates a library instance, associates the set of callbacks with it and returns a handle. The Java counterpart of this function (the initializeHandle() method of <Area>LibraryHandle class in our prototype) can be implemented as follows:

- An (optional) Java callback object is created.
- The constructor of the Java library instance object is called. The callback object is passed as a parameter to the constructor.
- The Java callback object is stored and associated with the Java library instance.
- The native side is entered, where the native library initialization is performed by calling sa<Area>Initialize(). The native callback (part of the Java API implementation) is passed as a parameter.
- The native handle (returned by sa<Area>Initialize()) is stored and associated with the Java library instance.

Figure 9 presents the above steps as a UML sequence diagram.

Sa<Area>Dispatch(), in native AIS, calls pending callbacks in the context (i.e. thread) of this function. The Java counterpart of this function can be implemented as follows (see also Fig. 10):

- Save the current thread into the library instance
- Call the native sa<Area>Dispatch() function. The native AIS implementation will invoke the registered native callback of the Java AIS API in the context of the thread of the sa<Area>Dispatch() function. The native callback will execute as follows:
  - Get a reference to the current thread
  - Search the table of library instances for the one referring to the current thread
  - Get the callback object of the library instance and
  - Call the appropriate Java callback.
- Delete the current thread reference.

Sa<Area>SelectionObjectGet(): The native AIS call returns a "selection object" that can be used to poll for pending callbacks. The principles of the Java implementation are as follows:

- Save the native selection object into the Java library instance object (upon the first usage or - optionally – during the initialization of the library handle).

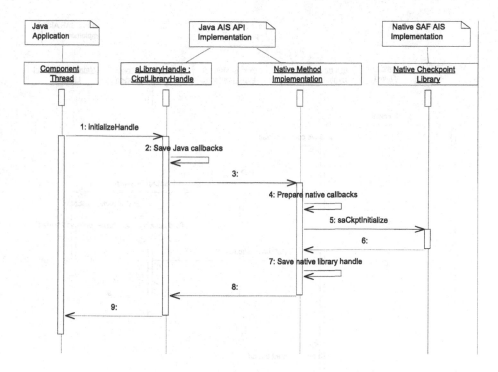

Fig. 9. Library instance initialization

- Provide a high level interface in Java: currently we support a method named
  isCallbackPending(), returning a Boolean value indicating a pending callback. More advanced schemes are also possible: future work is planned on
  more sophisticated versions of isCallbackPending() and dispatch(), supporting blocking versions and timeout. We also intend to elaborate a rich
  Java interface to support event-based dispatching, similar to the POSIX
  select() call.

Figure 11 presents the implementation of the isCallbackPending() method.
The native sa<Area>Finalize() function call in AIS closes a library instance that has been created earlier by sa<Area>Initialize(). Since this
is a fully synchronous operation, the Java counterpart of this function (the
finalizeHandle() method of <Area>LibraryHandle class in our prototype)
is simply mapped directly to its native equivalent.

Status of Prototyping Work. We have created a prototype Java AIS API
implementation based on the design presented above. So far two services, the
Cluster Membership Service and the Checkpoint Service have been finished. Currently work is being done on the implementation of the Availability Management
Framework. Further AIS services will be implemented later, if the concept proves
to be viable. We expect to use this prototype to create demonstration applications and experiment with the platform in various ways.

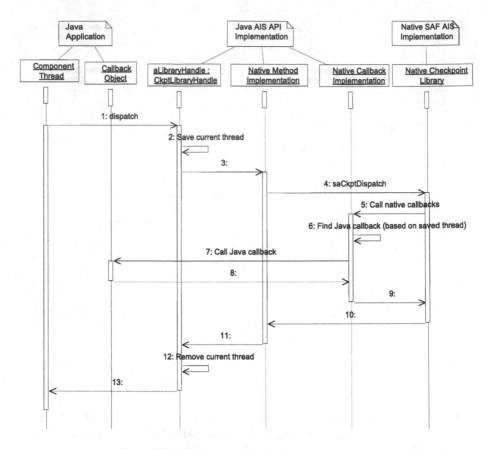

Fig. 10. Java callback dispatching

The main criteria for selecting the two services already implemented were that they provide the essential support for the demonstration application (to be described in the next subsection) and that while not extremely complicated, they exhibit every key constructs of the native AIS APIs that need special attention during the adaptation work.

Assuming that the presented APIs are embraced by SAF, there can be several ways of utilizing them. One is to use them directly by Java applications. This can be a valid approach for those services that do not have existing Java counterparts even in the long term. AMF and Cluster Membership Service are obvious examples, but for Java SE applications most other services fall into this category, including the Message, Event and Checkpoint Services.

However, we also think that for certain services there are already existing Java APIs (especially in Java EE and in lightweight containers: many examples are given in Sect. 4), so another way of using the presented API implementation is to use it as a low-level implementation layer and create another Java layer on top of it to support the existing higher-level Java API.

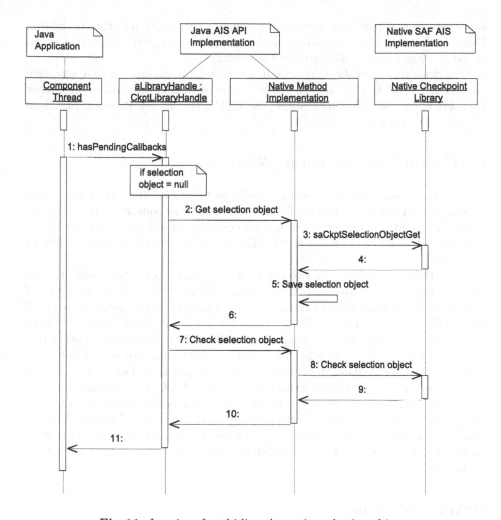

Fig. 11. Java interface hiding the native selection object

Verification. The operation and feasibility of the prototype Java AIS API was verified by constructing an example failover enabled Java application. The application uses the callback functionality of the Cluster Membership Service to trigger failover actions and the Checkpoint Service to store, retrieve, and replicate the state of the application. The purpose of the example is to show that the AIS APIs can be used from a Java application.

The implementation of the example application consists of multiple threads. One thread is dedicated to only query and execute callback methods from the Cluster Membership Service. This design allows simple and clean implementation of the actions triggered by the cluster change. The callbacks are executed in their own thread separated from the threads that serve clients. The essential state of the application can be represented as an object tree. When the state is saved, the object tree is serialized into a byte array, which is then written to the checkpoint. During this operation it has to be considered that the size of the byte array might be larger than the size allocated for the checkpoint.

Functionality of our Java adaptation layer and our example Java application against SAF AIS B.01.01 was successfully demonstrated on a two-node cluster by using native AIS implementation (see [RTP]) and Java 2 Platform Standard Edition 1.5 on Linux server.

6   Conclusions and Future Work

During the studies we have shown which specifications and how these could be implemented in Java. Four different integration methods were identified between Java and C. One approach was successfully experimented by specifying and implementing Java interfaces for AIS Cluster Membership and Checkpoint Services.

From the work done we can conclude that it makes sense to modify the architecture picture created by SAF to enable "contained in"/container type of relations to components to enable execution of multiple components in a "thread-safe" JVM including potentially a way to have a proxy AMF in the JVMs to do functions like start of Java components and the heart-beating and other reasonable AMF functions. Another area that has been found to need much more studies is the management side, affecting SAF specifications like NTF and IMM with respect to the existing Java solutions such as JMX and MBeans.

Both companies have already from the beginning been working with the assumption that this type of work should really be driven by SAF and JCP, rather than as company internal initiatives to ensure any form of adoption. Our main motivation has been to try to establish a working foundation for future work within SAF and JCP.

Acknowledgments

Nokia wishes to thank Fujitsu Siemens Computers for contributing a SAF enabled platform to enable test implementations.

References

[AIS]   Application Interface Specification,
           http://www.saforum.org/specification/AIS_Information/, Ref. February, 2006.
[AISO1]   Application Interface Specification (B.01.01) Volume 1: Overview and Models.
[AMF1]   Application Interface Specification (B.01.01) Volume 2: Availability Management Framework.
[AMF2]   Application Interface Specification (B.02.01): Availability Management Framework.

[BCT]   J. C. Laprie. Dependability: Basic Concepts and Terminology. In Dependable Computing and Fault Tolerant Systems, Vol 5. Springer Verlag. 1992.

[BP]   E. Marcus, H. Stern: Blueprints for High Availability, 2nd Edition. Wiley, 2003.

[CKPT1]   Application Interface Specification (B.01.01) Volume 4: Checkpoint Service.

[CKPT2]   Application Interface Specification (B.02.01): Checkpoint Service.

[CLM1]   Application Interface Specification (B.01.01) Volume 3: Cluster Membership Service.

[CLM2]   Application Interface Specification (B.02.01): Cluster Membership Service.

[EVT1]   Application Interface Specification (B.01.01) Volume 5: Event Service.

[EVT2]   Application Interface Specification (B.02.01): Event Service.

[HIBR]   Hibernate,
          http://www.hibernate.org/, Ref. February, 2006.

[IMM2]   Application Interface Specification (A.01.01): Information Model Management Service.

[JBC]   JBoss Cache,
          http://www.jboss.org/products/jbosscache, Ref. February, 2006.

[JBHA]   JBoss High Availability,
          http://wiki.jboss.org/wiki/Wiki.jsp?page=JBossHA,   Ref.   February, 2006.

[JCP]   Java Community Process,
          http://www.jcp.org/, Ref. February, 2006.

[JDO]   Java Data Objects,
          http://java.sun.com/products/jdo/, Ref. February, 2006.

[JEE]   Java 2 Enterprise Edition,
          http://java.sun.com/j2ee/, Ref. February, 2006.

[JGRPS]   JGroups,
          http://www.javagroups.com/javagroupsnew/docs/index.html,
          Ref. February, 2006.

[JMS]   Java Message Service (JMS),
          http://java.sun.com/products/jms/, Ref. February, 2006.

[JMX]   Java Management eXtensions,
          http://java.sun.com/products/JavaManagement/, Ref. February, 2006.

[JNDI]   Java Naming and Directory Interface,
          http://java.sun.com/products/jndi/, Ref. February, 2006.

[JSE]   Java 2 Standard Edition,
          http://java.sun.com/j2se/, Ref. February, 2006.

[JSR10]   JSR 10: Preferences API Specification,
          http://www.jcp.org/en/jsr/detail?id=10, Ref. February, 2006.

[JSR121] JSR 121: Application Isolation API Specification Isolation API,
          http://www.jcp.org/en/jsr/detail?id=121, Ref. February, 2006.

[JSR220] JSR 220: Enterprise JavaBeans ^{TM} 3.0,
          http://www.jcp.org/en/jsr/detail?id=220, Ref. February, 2006.

[LCK1]   Application Interface Specification (B.01.01) Volume 7: Lock Service.

[LCK2]   Application Interface Specification (B.02.01): Lock Service.

[LOG2]   Application Interface Specification (A.01.01): Log Service.

[MSG1]   Application Interface Specification (B.01.01) Volume 6: Message Service.

[MSG2]   Application Interface Specification (B.02.01): Message Service.

[NTF2]   Application Interface Specification (A.01.01): Notification Service.

[PICO]   PicoContainer,
          http://www.picocontainer.org/, Ref. February, 2006.

[RTP]   RTP4 Continuous Services,
          http://www.safe4cs.com, Ref. February, 2006.
[SAF]   Service Availability Forum,
          http://www.saforum.org, Ref. February, 2006.
[SPRF]   Spring Framework,
          http://www.springframework.org/, Ref. February, 2006.
[SWP]   Standards for a Service Availability ^{TM} Solution,
          http://www.saforum.org/about/solution_backgrounder.pdf, Ref. February, 2006.
[TL]   TopLink,
          http://www.oracle.com/technology/products/ias/toplink/index.,
          html Ref. February, 2006.
[WL]   BEA WebLogic,
          http://www.beasys.com, Ref. February, 2006.
[WS]   IBM WebSphere,
          http://www-306.ibm.com/software/websphere/, Ref. February, 2006.

The Emerging SAF Software Management Framework

Maria Toeroe[1], Peter Frejek[2], Francis Tam[3], Shyam Penubolu[4], and Kannan Kasturi[5]

[1] Ericsson Canada Inc., 8400 Decarie Blvd., Town of Mount Royal, QC, H4P 2N2, Canada
maria.toeroe@ericsson.com
[2] Fujitsu Siemens Computers GmbH, Otto-Hahn-Ring 6, D-81739 Muenchen, Germany
peter.frejek@fujitsu-siemens.com
[3] Nokia Research Center, P.O. Box 407, 00045 Nokia Group, Finland
francis.tam@nokia.com
[4] Motorola Inc., 2900 S. Diabolo Way, Tempe, AZ, 85282, USA
shyam.penubolu@motorola.com
[5] OpenClovis Inc., 1310 Redwood Way Suite B, Petaluma, CA, 94954, USA
kannank@openclovis.com

Abstract. This paper describes the emerging Software Management Framework of the Service Availability Forum (SAF). It defines the steps required for a software upgrade in a high availability system. Although the orchestration of the upgrade is an important task of the Framework, it is not the only one. It is essential that the software to be upgraded is made available to a target node and that there is some bookkeeping about which versions of software are available, on which nodes they are installed and which entities are configured to deploy them. This necessitates the definition of an information model for software management.

The Software Management Framework takes on the software upgrade issue from the perspective of SAF: SAF has defined the Availability Management Framework (AMF) and therefore the Software Management Framework assumes only AMF entities as highly available and uses AMF to handle the high availability issues of their upgrade. At the same time it is also suitable for controlling the upgrade of software which does not make use of AMF, however with no availability guarantees for them.

Keywords: Cluster, open standards, service availability, software upgrade concepts, availability managed upgrade.

1 Introduction

Software upgrade is a key issue in high availability environments. Such environments are characterized by applications that implement business critical services, e.g. call services running on systems of telecommunications providers. Since service outage results in loss of revenue for service providers and/or service users, business critical services are required to run with minimal interruption over a long period of time. In other words, the availability of these services must be 99.999% and above. This poses the requirement of no single point of failure, and therefore such high availability systems are usually implemented by clusters. The cluster infrastructures may range from

D. Penkler, M. Reitenspiess, and F. Tam (Eds.): ISAS 2006, LNCS 4328, pp. 253–270, 2006.

a two-node local cluster to a large cluster with hundreds or thousands of nodes that may be distributed over long distances. These are the infrastructures that are considered for software upgrades by the Service Availability Forum (SAF), and accordingly by this paper as well.

During the life of such systems, many software upgrades will be necessary to fix problems in existing software, to add new applications, to migrate to new or to remove obsolete versions. Each of these upgrades is a critical intervention in the service infrastructure as it modifies certain application and/or system components. Some or all of these components may need to be taken out of service at least temporarily for the time of the upgrade. Thus, the system becomes more vulnerable to service outages. A software upgrade must therefore be carefully prepared, particularly as its execution is usually restricted to a given window of time. If the upgrade fails or it must be cancelled due to any problem, it is a *must* to re-establish the status of the system before the upgrade.

1.1 Requirements and Challenges

The primary requirement in a high availability system is that the software upgrade should be achieved with no or minimal service interruption. To be able to satisfy this requirement a number of issues need to be addressed and resolved as discussed below.

Software Image Management. Software is delivered in the form of software packages. The distributed nature of clusters creates the need for a centralized software repository where all available packages are stored for a system. Then the lifecycle of a software package from an operator's viewpoint starts by putting it into the software repository. When the package needs to be deployed, it is fetched from this repository, distributed to a selected number of target locations where it is installed. A target location can be a node or a common area used by multiple nodes like NFS. After a while the software may become obsolete when it is removed from the nodes to free up resources, and eventually it is removed from the repository as well.

Thus, there is a need of *software image management*. The image management is responsible for importing a package into the repository, for distributing it onto the target nodes and for installing it on these nodes. It is also responsible for uninstalling and removing packages from the nodes and the repository as necessary. Today some of these tasks are accomplished by package handlers others are not handled at all. Issues like package versioning, compatibility with existing packages and dependencies on required packages are also covered by most package handlers, however only within the scope of a given installation location.

Component Level Version Management. The image management must keep an inventory of installed packages, together with the information about package versions, compatibility and dependencies. However high availability upgrades often require a finer granularity of upgrade control in a cluster. The different software components contained in a package can have individual compatibility conditions and dependency rules concerning other components in the cluster, and these relations can be essential for an upgrade with highest availability. For example, multiple versions of components must coexist and collaborate in such systems simultaneously. Therefore it is not sufficient to have such information only at the package level. Component-level information has to be provided to and needs to be processed by a *software version management*.

Upgrade Specification. To deploy a package on a set of target nodes, it is necessary to establish a sequence of steps to be performed by a *software upgrade management*. Such an upgrade management must provide a way to select between different (basic) upgrade schemes, e.g. rolling upgrade or split-mode upgrade, and it must permit user-defined controls to refine the upgrade execution. High availability applications may also require customization at the application level.

The sequence of steps is dictated by the selected scheme and by the user-defined controls, but it must conform to the contents of the version management database. For example, the user might define that a split-cluster upgrade has to take place over two groups of nodes, but the version management database might imply restrictions on how the cluster can be split for upgrade purposes.

Upgrade Prerequisites. It is also necessary to define the conditions under which an upgrade may take place, e.g. an acceptable service outage, the different resources that are necessary for the upgrade like free memory, free disk capacity, free processing capacity, etc. The upgrade management needs to be able to assist in the evaluation of the system whether such requirements are met by the current system status.

Upgrade Control and Monitoring. Once the upgrade has been instrumented, it can be launched. The upgrade management must allow a highly automated upgrade mode as well as manual intervention and the execution of lower-level upgrade steps by administrative control.

Applications need an interface to the upgrade management so that they can track the progress of the upgrade in order to perform application-specific actions like backup/restore, preparation of switch-over etc.

Recovery from Errors During Upgrade. A key requirement is that it must always be possible to return to the state before the upgrade, even if a critical error occurs, or any of the compulsory conditions for the upgrade are not met. For a high availability upgrade, the requirements against the error recovery procedure are the same as in the case of the forward path: During its execution, the services must remain available. If this is impossible, the downtime must be minimal. For these reasons, a multi-staged repair concept is desirable.

Traceability. In addition, all activities of the upgrade management need to be logged in a way which facilitates the analysis of the course of events, mainly in the case of errors.

1.2 Related Work

The topic of software upgrade is not new and has been addressed even by standardization.

The Free Standards Group in the Linux Standard Base (LSB) specifies the RPM packaging format [1] as the common denominator for upgrades. It requires from Linux distributions to provide mechanisms to install applications distributed in this format. Among others, RPM defines the exact format in which the information necessary to resolve compatibility and dependency issues must be provided. It is up to the implementer how this information is used during the installation. The standard does not address any of the procedural aspects of upgrades.

The Open Group's Distributed Software Administration (XDSA) [2], which is based on the IEEE 1387.2 standard goes beyond the issues tackled by LSB. The XDSA specification defines the package layout as well as it addresses the software administration requirements of distributed systems and applications. The specification defines a set of administration utilities that enable management applications to control the packaging, distribution, installation, update and removal of software across multiple nodes of a cluster. XDSA still does not address the service availability in any way.

Online upgrade has been a subject of investigation by both academics and practitioners for a period of time [3], [4]. Recently, the Object Management Group has published the Online Upgrades specification [5], which addresses the upgrade of a CORBA object implementation. Let us take a closer look to what extent it deals with service availability.

First of all, it defines the interfaces provided by the *upgrade manager* to prepare an object for upgrading, to perform the upgrades of one or more objects, to rollback upgrades of objects, and to revert an object from its new implementation to its old implementation.

The first step of an upgrade is to put both the old and new implementations into an object group, followed by the query to the old implementation to determine whether it is safe to perform the upgrade. A vendor specific implementation of the *upgrade mechanisms* is expected to stop new messages being delivered to the old implementation, instead, it queues them for delivery to the new implementation. When the old implementation responds positively to the upgrade request, the current state of the old implementation is transferred to the new one. The queued messages are then applied to the new implementation, and all future messages for this object group are directed to the new implementation. The old implementation is then removed from the object group before the upgrade is committed. Multiple objects can also be upgraded together by setting a parameter in the upgrade request method. If some part of the upgrade fails, rollback and reverting an upgrade could be used to recover. However, how these measures are facilitated is considered to be implementation specific and they are not defined.

Some important features appear to be missing from the current specification, for example, implementations are not versioned; concurrent operation of the old and new implementations is not supported; when an upgrade is available and when it should be applied to an object cannot be determined; to name just a few. The current specification does not really support a true online upgrade, in the sense that services provided by the object to be upgraded are not available although the incoming messages for that object are preserved. To overcome this it is recommended to enhance the Fault Tolerant CORBA [6] specification with Online Upgrade to exploit the inherited redundancy for having minimum, or even no loss of service during an upgrade. However, the standards currently do not contain any suggestion how to integrate them seamlessly considering the somewhat conflicting features such as Fault Tolerance that relies on redundant object implementations while Online Upgrade that does not support versioning and simultaneous operations of the old and new implementations.

1.3 The SAF Proposal

This paper describes a framework for software management that defines the steps required for a software upgrade in a high availability system. Although the orchestration of the upgrade is an important task of the framework, as we have seen, it is not the only one. It is essential that the software to be upgraded is made available to a target node and that there is some bookkeeping about which versions of software are available and on which nodes they are installed and deployed.

The Software Management Framework (SwMF) takes on the software upgrade issue from the perspective of the Service Availability Forum's (SAF) work of availability management. SAF has defined the model and the application programming interfaces (API) of an Availability Management Framework (AMF) [7]. AMF ensures the availability of services that follow this model and use its API. Therefore the Software Management Framework relies on AMF to handle high availability and complements it with handling the remaining issues of an upgrade. It can also handle upgrades of software that does not make use of AMF albeit with no availability guarantees.

In the rest of the paper first in section 2, an overview of the SAF Software Management Framework is given, followed by the software management information model used by SwMF in section 3. Section 4 discusses the phases of software upgrades and through that defines the main upgrade concepts. It also demonstrates the use of the information model in this process. Subsequently an example is given in section 5. Finally section 6 draws the conclusions and projects the future directions of this work.

The paper assumes some familiarity with the SAF specifications, particularly with the Availability Management Framework.

The presented work is still work-in-progress within SAF, and therefore there are no guarantees that the future specification of the Software Management Framework will specify the behavior and data structures exactly as described here.

2 Overview of the SAF Software Management Framework

In a SAF cluster the Software Management Framework is the software entity that orchestrates the software upgrade process. It accomplishes this task within the SAF ecosystem in tight collaboration with other SAF services as shown in Fig. 1. To facilitate the discussion of its functionality, it is described here as a composition of three functional modules that are referred as: the Image Manager, the Version Manager and the Upgrade Manager.

Since a SAF cluster may be a heterogeneous system that deploys multiple file systems and different package formats (e.g. RPM [1]), an Image Manager is defined that acts as a broker between the different native package handlers (e.g. XDSA-like [2]) and the rest of the SAF system including the Version Manager and the Upgrade Manager.

The Image Manager allows the delivery, verification, and installation of software packages of different formats in a normalized way. Furthermore, it is capable of extracting from the software packages some descriptor files that contain SAF specific information and delivering them to the Version Manager.

The package descriptor files provide information necessary for the information model used by the Software Management Framework. This information model – as described in section 3 – is maintained by the Version Manager using the Information Model Management Service (IMM) [8]. It describes, among others, the software available for the system and the locations it is installed in the cluster.

The Upgrade Manager drives the actual deployment of the new software. If entities managed by AMF are upgraded, then the Upgrade Manager acts as a management client of the Availability Management Framework in order to provide availability during the upgrade.

As part of the upgrade procedure, the Upgrade Manager may use other SAF services such as Logging, or Security. It also interacts with the Hardware Platform Interface (HPI) [9]. This is necessary when the subject of an upgrade procedure is a firmware of an HPI resource, or when a software upgrade requires HPI-level action such as node reboot. The Upgrade Manager interacts with the HPI entities using the HPI API and its proposed extension for firmware upgrade.

AMF entities and other software entities running in the system may coordinate their actions during an upgrade through the Upgrade API provided by the Software Management Framework. After registering their interest with SwMF, entities will receive callbacks whenever a relevant upgrade operation is initiated and as it progresses through its different stages so they can synchronize their application level actions with the ongoing upgrade. These software entities are referred as *upgrade aware entities*.

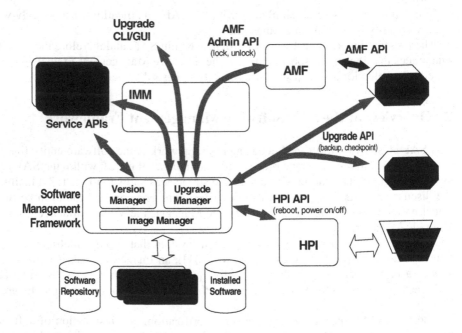

Fig. 1. The Software Management Framework in the SAF ecosystem

3 Software Management Information Model

It is essential for the Software Management Framework to have up-to-date information about the software available for the cluster, installed within the cluster, and the entities derived from it. It also needs to be able to determine package and component level dependencies as necessary. These dependencies need to be satisfied not only by the software repository, but also at each installation location and by the deployed software. To facilitate these tasks the software management basic information model is introduced (Fig. 2.).

3.1 Basic Information Model

To store and manage the information model the Software Management Framework's Version Manager uses the Information Model Management Service [8]. The basic information model may be refined to meet the requirements of the different parts of a SAF system such as the Availability Management Framework as discussed in 3.2.

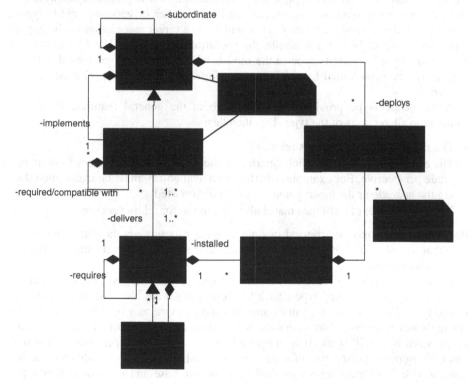

Fig. 2. Software management basic information model

Configured Software Entity. The Software Management Framework refers to any running instance of an executable piece of software in the cluster or a logical entity that is associated with such pieces of software as a *software entity*. Examples of software entities are a firmware instance, an operating system instance, or a process; logical entities can be AMF entities such as service units, components or component service instances.

The model contains all the configured software entities irrespective of whether they are instantiated at a given moment or not.

Software Entity Type. The generalization of similar software entities is called software entity type. Any software entity that is present in a SAF system and managed by the Software Management Framework belongs to a certain type. In the model, bi-directional links are maintained between the software entity type and its configured software entities.

The software management information model distinguishes two related classes of the software entity type: the *base entity type* and the *versioned entity type*.

Base Entity Type. Base entity types are not directly associated with executable pieces software. Instead they represent the functionality these pieces of software deliver. A base entity type may be specialized by a number of versioned entity types; then each of these versioned entity types will have a direct association to the appropriate set of executables. For example, the operating system (Red Hat Linux) may be represented by a base entity type in the model, while each of its versions that is deployed may be represented by a different *versioned entity type (e.g. Fedora Core 3, Fedora Core 4)*.

A base entity type provides information about the general features, which are common to all versions of the type. This includes:

- The name that all its versions refer to.
- The entity type category, which determines the handling of the entities from an upgrade perspective. For example, whether high availability must be maintained during the upgrade or the hosting node needs to be restarted.
- It may have a set of attributes that shall be common for all its versions.

Base entity types may be arranged in a hierarchical structure via the subordinate relation that specifies a containment relation for those types. More details on this are given in section 3.2.

Base entity types may have no versions on their own if they are implemented via versions of other base entity types. Such base entity types are like aspects of those versioned types. For example, the same communication service may be provided by different applications. In case of the operating system this can be the communication capability provided by its IP stack. It is inseparable from the software perspective, but it is separable from the perspective of a service user as other software may also provide the same service. The operating system will have its own base and versioned entity types accordingly representing the software aspects; but the common communication service aspect that is important for a user may be represented as a non-versioned base entity type from which its own different service instances are derived and configured in the cluster according to the assigned IP addresses and other parameters.

Versioned Entity Type. As discussed, a base entity type can be implemented by multiple versions of software and accordingly each such version is associated with a versioned entity type. A versioned entity type expands the base entity type with versioning and version-specific information. It contains the list of compatible and required versions of its own and other versioned entity types. It also defines all the attributes together with their default values and/or value ranges that are inherent for the software entities derived from it.

Package and File-Set. A package object of the information model describes a software package that has been delivered to the system's repository. A package may specify dependencies on other packages.

A software package may deliver different versioned entity types, but typically it will not deliver multiple versions of the same type. The package object refers to all the versioned entity types that the associated software package delivered. On the other hand, some versioned entity types may be delivered by a set of packages.

A package may consist of multiple file-sets in which case each of them is described by a file-set object, which is a specialization of the package object.

Installation Location. Software delivered to the repository in the form of a package cannot be executed right away. First it needs to be installed. A package may be installed in a number of locations. The list of locations where a package is installed is maintained as an array of installation location objects in the model.

At least one of the locations must be accessible from each place the relevant versioned software entity types need to be deployed. There could be a number of entities instantiating each given type at those places. Moreover their number may vary over the system lifecycle. Therefore the information model contains the configured software entities as well.

Only entities derived from versioned software entities may have reference to an installation location.

3.2 AMF Entity Types

AMF defines a hierarchical model for its entities [7]. The Software Management Framework reflects this by a hierarchy of entity types from which AMF entities are derived. This hierarchy of base entity types is shown in Fig. 3.

The base application type, base service group type, base service unit type and base component type are always specialized as versioned entity types and respectively referred as application type, service group type, service unit type and component type. The other two are not specialized as they reflect the service aspects of the first group and accordingly they are implemented through versions of those. Namely, a service type is referenced by the versions of a service group type and its service unit types that can provide that service type, while a component service type is referenced by versions of component types capable of supporting it.

Note however that the model does not require the completeness of this type hierarchy. Some versioned AMF entity types may exist in a partial tree. Each of the AMF entity types can be a topmost (or root) element if it is intended to be reused by multiple composite AMF entity types of higher level. In this case these composite entity types reference the appropriate root entity type rather than redefining it. Application, service group and service unit types are composite AMF entity types, i.e. each of these types is the root of a partial tree of subordinate entity types. Examples of such cases are: a service unit type that supports any redundancy model and therefore used by different service group types defining different redundancy models; or a generic proxy component type that can be used with a range of proxied component types.

AMF entities derived from a given AMF entity type inherit the attributes of the type. The set of attributes for each AMF entity type is going to be standardized by SAF together with the appropriate XML schema to be used for the SAF specific descriptor files. (Note that the data types of these attributes must be in accordance with the data types already specified by the UML system model [10] of the AMF entities.)

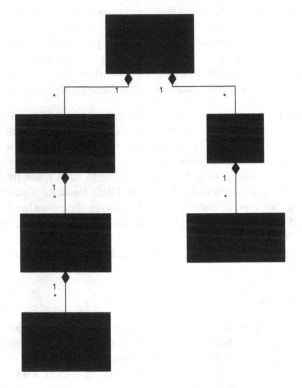

Fig. 3. UML diagram of base AMF entity types

AMF Version Map. The software management information model includes an inventory of AMF entity types as described above, and the AMF information model comprises an inventory of AMF entities configured in the system (i.e. the software entities of the basic information model configured for AMF). The AMF Version Map can be viewed as the set of linkages between the AMF information model and the software management information model. A pictorial representation of the AMF Version Map is shown in Fig. 4.

The links between the AMF information model and the SwMF information model are set by the Upgrade Manager during an upgrade. The links are bi-directional as the

Version Map is used to fetch all the AMF entities, which are derived from a certain base AMF entity type for which a new version was delivered and therefore potentially could be upgraded by it. All these compose the default *upgrade target*. On the other hand, it should also be possible to determine the entity type from which a certain AMF entity is derived to verify, for example, requested configuration changes.

Fig. 4. Relationship between the AMF and software management information models

Note that the basic software management information model calls for similar maps for all configured software entities.

4 Phases of Software Management

Now that we have defined the Software Management Framework and its information model we are ready to take a closer look at the process of software management. It has two clearly distinguishable phases:

- The delivery of software packages; and
- The deployment of the new software i.e. the *upgrade campaign*.

These two phases can be executed separately in time. However, the deployment phase usually requires the successful accomplishment of the software package delivery phase.

4.1 Software Package Delivery Phase

In the delivery phase packages are made available to the cluster. A software package may be copied to the software repository from a remote file server, a CD or some other media. This action is initiated by an administrator and executed by the Image Manager.

First, the Image Manager verifies that the package is from an authentic source and has been delivered untampered. The Image Manager needs to support standard means for verifying authenticity and integrity of the package. In the future the SAF Security Service may also be involved in this checking. Next, the Image Manager checks if all the required packages are available in the repository and if all these checks succeed, it extracts the SAF specific files from the package and delivers them to the Version Manager. This means that the following information is retrieved:

- Package descriptor – this information can be delivered as a file or it may be included in the package header depending on the package type. This, among others, provides a listing of one or more files (binaries, configuration, etc.) included in the package and package dependency information. This information is not SAF specific, but it is used to build the package object of the information model.
- Entity types file – this file describes the content of the package in terms of software entity types. This includes all their attributes as specified by the XML schema supplemented with dependency and compatibility information as necessary. All packages that deliver SAF entity types are expected to contain entity types files.

If the new software can be installed in advance, i.e. while the old software is still running, software installation may be part of the delivery process. Otherwise it is done within the upgrade campaign. In either case the new software is installed on various locations so that it can be accessed from all the nodes on which entities need to be upgraded. For each of the locations an installation location object is created in the model.

The Version Manager using the information of the package descriptor and the entity types file reflects all the changes introduced by the package to the software management informational model. In particular, it introduces the new software entity types, package, file-set and installation locations objects, and the links between them. It also determines the default upgrade target using the version map. That is, all software entities that are derived from base entity types that were updated with a new version, are potentially upgradeable by these new versions. Additional constraints and configuration may be used to adjust this default set to define the actual upgrade target, for example, if new software entities are configured they expand this set, or if there are two instances of an application running in the system and only one of them shall be upgraded the other is removed from the default set.

4.2 Software Deployment

The delivered software is deployed in the system by an *upgrade campaign* which is executed by the Upgrade Manager. Fig. 5 presents the major activities comprising an upgrade campaign. The goal of the upgrade campaign is to upgrade all entities identified as the upgrade target. To do so, the upgrade campaign is specified as an ordered set of *upgrade procedures* each of which upgrades a subset of the upgrade target (e.g. a service group) using the most appropriate for that subset upgrade method (such as a rolling upgrade).

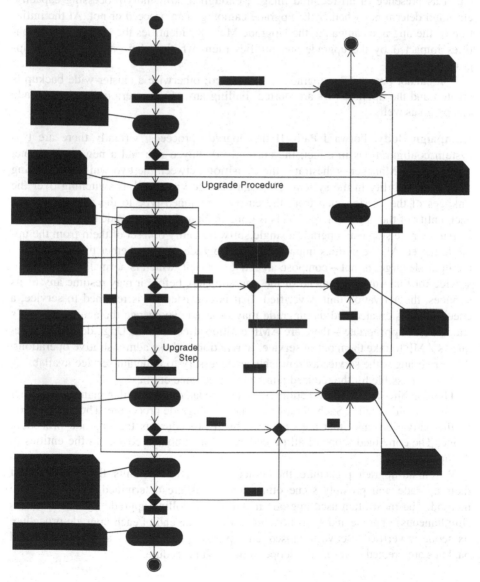

Fig. 5. Software upgrade activity diagram

Campaign Initialization. An upgrade campaign is handled in the manner of transactions and accordingly an 'initiate upgrade' and a 'commit upgrade' or 'terminate upgrade' determine the transaction boundaries.

During the upgrade campaign, the Upgrade Manager interacts with the upgrade aware entities (i.e. those implementing the Upgrade API) and this interaction also influences the course and the outcome of the upgrade.

SwMF introduces the concept of acceptable service outage as one of the prerequisites for a campaign to start. The Upgrade Manager also checks other prerequisites (such as presence of all required images, enough disk/memory/processing capacity, etc.) and determines whether the upgrade campaign can proceed or not. At the initiation of the upgrade campaign, the Upgrade Manager identifies the upgrade-aware entities impacted by the upgrade and notifies them whether their state permit an upgrade.

If it cannot proceed the upgrade is terminated; otherwise a cluster-wide backup is created and the upgrade logs are started. Failing any of these terminates the upgrade campaign as well.

Campaign Body. Forward Path. If the upgrade proceeds, virtually there are two system configurations in effect: the currently deployed one and a new desired one. The Upgrade Manager orchestrates the transition between the two while maintaining service availability in the system. This can also be visualized as switching over the linkages of the version map from the current versioned type to the desired one for each entity of the upgrade target. This is done in a number of upgrade steps.

An upgrade step may upgrade a single software entity or a set of them from the upgrade target. All the entities impacted by an upgrade step – whether they are part of the upgrade target or not – compose an activation unit, which is normally taken out of service for this time. At the end of the upgrade step, before it may resume any of its services, the activation unit is verified. If it is consistent, it is returned to service, a check point is created and the upgrade may proceed. To change the activation unit's state, if it is appropriate – there are AMF entities affected – the Upgrade Manager requests AMF to take them out of service. In reaction to these administrative operations, AMF rearranges the service assignments as necessary to maintain service availability as high as possible for the reduced number of in-service entities.

The combination of these actions may be repeated in a similar manner for other similar activation units. Such iteration defines an upgrade procedure. The composition of the activation units that are upgraded by a procedure is the upgrade procedure scope. The combined scope of all procedures of a campaign covers all the entities in the upgrade target.

Within an upgrade procedure, the choice of the activation units, the sequencing of their upgrade and possibly some other constraints are determined by the upgrade method. The most often used upgrade methods are: rolling upgrade, synchronous (or simultaneous) upgrade and split-mode upgrade. At the end of each upgrade procedure its scope is verified. Between subsequent upgrade procedures of a campaign partial backups are created covering the scope of the next procedure.

Campaign Body. Reverse Path. *Recovery from errors.* The combinations of upgrade checkpoints, cluster-wide and partial backups and the systematically performed verification allow for different recovery strategies to be deployed depending on when the failure is detected.

If an upgrade step or its verification fails and the step can be retried, the last checkpoint is restored in a single-step rollback and the step is reapplied. If retry is not allowed, the procedure within which the step failed needs to be rolled back all the way to its beginning provided that all checkpoints within the procedure were kept.

If the rollback is not possible for any reason (no checkpoints, no time, an irreversible change has been applied), or in case of a failure during rollback, the Upgrade Manager immediately triggers a 'fallback' to a backed up state. That is, rather than backtracking the executed procedure, one of the states stored in a backup is restored in a single step during which no service can be provided by the impacted entities. This can be a scope fallback, in which case the latest partial backup is applied; or a system fallback, when the cluster-wide backup is restored, depending on the severity of the error.

Note that during the upgrade the system provides services that may change the system state. Since restoring the backed up state, discards also all the permanent changes made in the system during the upgrade that were not part of the upgrade, these are recovered in a 'rollforward' after the fallback using the upgrade logs that have been started at the creation of the backup.

Note also that after restoring a partial backup, the system is in a state which is different from the initial system state, but the upgrade campaign is not completed. As discussed below different options are available.

Campaign Wrap-up. Once all the upgrade procedures are completed or the campaign is terminated due to a failure the entire system is checked for consistency. This consistency check may involve application level verification possibly over some time period. It may also require a human decision.

If the final verification is passed and it is determined that the system is in a consistent operational state, the upgrade campaign is committed leaving only one system configuration in effect. During the wrap-up phase all the protective measures (e.g. checkpoints, logging) are terminated in an orderly manner, the upgrade status is reported and saved. Upgrade aware applications may do the same for their application specific information.

Failure of the final verification results in a system fallback or in a complete rollback depending on the circumstances. In some cases, the corrective action can be another upgrade campaign that restores partially or fully the system configuration in effect before the failed campaign by downgrading the required entities. Downgrade is favorable compared to a fallback as it is less intrusive action and the system is capable of providing services.

All the presented upgrade concepts together allow for a rather flexible specification and handling of software upgrades and their recovery procedures that can maintain services at the highest possible level. For better understanding, the next section demonstrates some of these concepts with an example.

5 Example

Let assume that in a SAF system an application type is deployed that has a service group type built from service unit type A. There were two versions delivered of this SU type so far: 1.0.0 and 1.1.0. There are two instances of the application type in the system *app1* and *app2*. One (*app1*) deploys SU type A in a 2+1 redundancy model, while the other one (*app2*) according to the 2N model. Accordingly the first application has three service units of type A: *app1:A1*, *app1:A2* and *app1:A3*. They all run version 1.0.0. The other application runs version 1.1.0 in two service units: *app2:A1* and *app2:A2*.

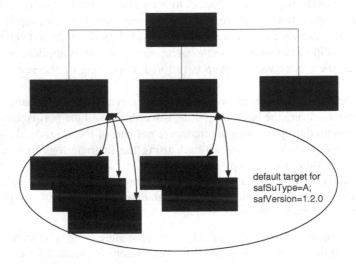

Fig. 6. Example configuration

A new software package contains a new version for service unit type A, version 1.2.0. This can be used to upgrade both application instances in the system and therefore the default upgrade target can be defined as: *app1:A1*, *app1:A2*, *app1:A3*, *app2:A1* and *app2:A2* as shown in Fig. 6. However, it may be desired or some dependencies may define that only the SUs of the second application instances (*app2*) can be upgraded, i.e. the upgrade target is reduced to *app2:A1* and *app2:A2*. It is further assumed that we want to deploy a new application instance *app3* with one service group using a N-way redundancy model, the upgrade target would then be expanded to include *app3:A1*, *app3:A2* and *app3:A3*. Fig. 7 gives the desired configuration after the upgrade.

When selecting the upgrade method one needs to consider the impact of the upgrade on the services. Since the services of *app2* are already provided, its service units must be upgraded while these services are maintained. As its service units are in a 2N redundancy, either rolling or split-mode upgrade method is appropriate. On the other hand, since *app3* is new and does not provide any service yet, the fastest and simplest upgrade method is a synchronous upgrade, when the required code is installed and deployed in all of the nodes simultaneously and once the upgrade is verified the new application is put into service. Provided that none of these actions

impact any other service, we can define our upgrade campaign to contain two procedures: one that upgrades *app2*'s service units in a rolling fashion, and a second that
installs and deploys *app3* with all its service units synchronously. The first procedure
has two activation units *app2:A1* and *app2:A2*. The second procedure has only one
activation unit that contains the all the SUs of application *app3*.

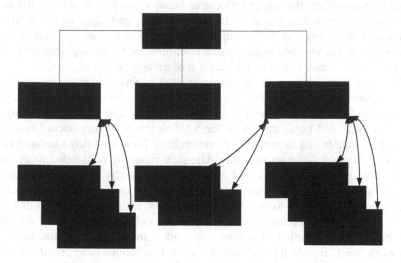

Fig. 7. Example configuration after the upgrade

If the installation or the upgrade impacts other entities, the availability of the service provided by those need to be considered when selecting the upgrade method and
defining the procedures. For example, if a reboot of the hosting node is necessary to
deploy a service unit of SU type A version 1.2.0 that changes all the considerations.
Since with the upgrade of a single SU the entire node is affected, the activation unit
must be at least a node. In this case our campaign may have a single procedure that
upgrades all the nodes on which there is a service unit to be upgraded one by one in a
rolling fashion.

After performing a successful upgrade the system configuration shall change as
shown in Fig. 7.

6 Conclusions

This paper provides an overview of the emerging Software Management Framework
of the Service Availability Forum. Due to complexity of the subject we presented
only some highlights of the Framework such as the different functionalities provided
by SwMF and how they are used in the different phases of software management. It is
also a work in progress and as such it will change and evolve before it is published as
a complete specification.

We also introduced the software management information model that maintains an
up-to-date inventory of software available in the cluster. It is expressed in terms of
packages, but also in terms of software entity types, from which the actual software

entities configured in the cluster are derived. By linking these two, the types and the derived entities, the model facilitates the upgrade itself. From this perspective an upgrade can be defined as setting the links between the entities and their types as each of the entities is upgraded to that type.

There are a number of ways an upgrade can be done. To facilitate the specification of different upgrades, this paper introduces some concepts to identify the different sets of entities targeted (e.g. upgrade target, activation unit, upgrade procedure scope) by different procedural units (e.g. upgrade campaign, upgrade procedure, upgrade step). By doing so, we hope to establish a common understanding between the different parties when it comes to the specification of an upgrade.

The issues not addressed in this paper are the different upgrade methods, coping with compatibility issues during upgrades, the methodology of upgrade campaign planning, the SwMF Upgrade API and its utilization by applications and many others. Not all of these will be addressed by the SAF Software Management Framework as its goal is to enable and to provide a common base for availability managed upgrades and not necessarily solve all its issues. Upgrade planning or the design of smoothly upgradeable applications each could be a research topic by itself and the intention is to leave those as fields of competition for the different vendors and providers.

Accordingly, the main focus of the future work within SAF is to refine the presented ideas to the level that implementers, vendors and providers can use them for specification and execution of software upgrades and in the implementation of the framework itself. Beside the mentioned issues, this requires the specification of the administrative and user upgrade APIs, and the upgrade notifications. This work is continuously synchronized with other SAF standardization efforts such as AMF and system management.

References

1. Free Standards Group, Linux Standard Base Core Specification, Package Format and Installation, http://refspecs.freestandards.org/lsb.shtml
2. The Open Group, Systems Management: Distributed Software Administration (XDSA), CAE Specification, document number C701, 1998
3. Software Engineering Institute, Workshop on the State of the Practice in Dependably Upgrading Critical Systems, Special Report, CMU/SEI-97-SR-014, August 1997.
4. Dependable On-line Upgrading of Distributed Systems, Workshop held in conjunction with COMPSAC'02, United Kingdom, August, 2002. http://homepages.cs.ncl.ac.uk/alexander.romanovsky/home.formal/doluds.html
5. Object Management Group, Online Upgrades Specification, SMSC review copy, smsc/05-10-02, November 2005.
6. Object Management Group, Fault Tolerant CORBA, in Common Object Request Broker Architecture: Core Specification, chapter 23, Version 3.0.3, formal/04-03-12, March 2004.
7. Service Availability Forum, Application Interface Specification, Volume 2: Availability Management Framework, SAI-AIS-AMF-B.02.01.
8. Service Availability Forum, Application Interface Specification, Volume 8: Information Model Management Service, SAI-AIS-IMM-A.01.01.
9. Service Availability Forum, Hardware Platform Interface Specification, SAI-HPI-B.02.01.
10. Service Availability Forum, Overview, SAI-Overview-B.02.01.

The Service Availability Forum Security Service (SEC): Status and Future Directions

P. Badovinatz[1], S. Balakrishnan[2], M. Pourzandi[3], M. Reitenspiess[4], and C. Tindel[5]

[1] IBM Corporation, STG Telecommunications, Linux Standards, Beaverton, OR, USA
[2] Intel, 15400 NW Greenbrer Pkwy, Beaverton, OR 97006, USA
[3] Ericsson, Open Systems Lab, 8400 Decarie Blvd, Ville Mont-Royal, QC H4P 2N2, Canada
[4] Fujitsu Siemens Computers, Domagkstr. 28, D-80807, Muenchen, Germany
[5] Hewlett-Packard Company Bldg. 5L, ms 43 Fort Collins, CO 80528, USA
wombat@us.ibm.com, Santosh.Balakrishnan@intel.com,
Makan.Pourzandi@ericsson.com,
Manfred.Reitenspiess@fujitsu-siemens.com, Chad.Tindel@hp.com

Abstract. The Service Availability Forum is specifying high availability interfaces for carrier grade applications. Along with the direct support for applications an implementation of these interfaces implies that it can itself be highly available. To ensure this availability an implementation must be secure, but these security mechanisms must themselves not reduce the availability of the overall system [1,2]. The security of high availability interfaces (and their middleware implementations) therefore requires a careful design to address potential cross influences.

In this paper, we first discuss the general security scope for SA Forum systems, do a threat analysis and list a number of assumption of the execution environment. Then, we present a strawman architecture for the SA Forum Security service (SEC). Rather than presenting a detailed design, with this architecture we attempt to provide guidance, expose issues to be addressed and offer solution ideas for those issues.

Keywords: Service Availability Forum, SA Forum system security, Carrier Class systems, Clusters, Middleware security.

1 Introduction

The Service Availability Forum (SA Forum) is a consortium of computer and communications companies working together to develop open standards for supporting hardware, application high availability, and local and remote systems management for such systems [3]. The SA Forum develops and publishes interface specifications, and promotes and facilitates the adoption and use of the specifications that it develops [4]. The specifications are directed at three domains: the Hardware Platform Interface (HPI) [5] which abstracts hardware-level details; the Application Interface Specification (AIS) [6] which abstracts services of the clustering middleware software (like cluster membership information or cluster-wide checkpoint data); and Systems Management specifications that define facilities for managing clusters supporting all of the services in these specifications [7] [8]. These specifications provide a unified software architecture which is needed by a rapidly growing market of telecom services [9].

D. Penkler, M. Reitenspiess, and F. Tam (Eds.): ISAS 2006, LNCS 4328, pp. 271–287, 2006.

With the increasing number of security threats, efficient and flexible security has now become an essential requirement for these systems. The term "security" can be confusing when discussed in the context of APIs which abstract High Availability (HA) middleware. In an HA environment, nodes must not only defend themselves against potential threats but must also grant privileges and act cooperatively with other cluster nodes. The current SA Forum specifications consider security only to the extent that it should be handled by the middleware implementation out-of-band. In this paper, we present a high-level design for a new SA Forum Security Service (SEC). The SEC abstracts security at the middleware level, and provides an API that can be used by the various SA Forum services.

In the early sections, we discuss the general security scope for SA Forum based systems (section §2) and provide a high level security analysis of SA Forum environments (section §3). We continue with a review of different security requirements for SA Forum services (section §4). We then propose a security model for SA Forum systems, and discuss a strawman design of the SA Forum Security service (SEC) before exploring the relationship between the SEC and other SA Forum services (section §5).

2 Scope

Security is not a new topic for the SA Forum but it had not been addressed directly before; until now the specifications have assumed that security would be taken care of "out of band" by the middleware implementation itself. After the stabilization of the initial specifications, the SA Forum sees the need for a Security specification, and has issued a work item for the following areas:

- **Local Security for the AIS Interfaces:** Allows AIS services to authorize particular activities for certain processes within the cluster. This is necessary to protect the HA infrastructure from misuse. In addition, this avoids the unauthorized access to the SAF application, its managed data and preserves its integrity. This paper will focus on this specific issue.
- **Security for HPI:** Restricts HPI information to authorized users, and creates a specification for the delivery and receipt of security alarms which the domain manager can forward to the SA Forum Notification service.
- **Broad Security for an SA Forum Implementation:** Involves areas of cluster security which are peripheral to the middleware implementation such as communication security.

The SEC is not an attempt to define the actual methods or techniques that will be used to implement security, and it is assumed that standard security algorithms and techniques will be used to protect the systems as appropriate. Instead, the SEC provides interfaces that allow security controls to be applied in uses of the SA Forum AIS interfaces. The SEC is standards agnostic with respect to the various telecommunications and security standards available; any of them should be able to work within the SEC (see Figure 1). Therefore, the SEC implementor can base its implementation on various existing security mechanisms, from the network protocols like IPSec and SSL/TLS,to use distributed

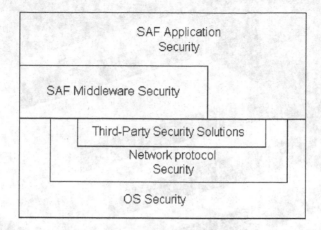

Fig. 1. The SA Forum Security service uses different OS level and third party software security mechanisms to provide the needed functionality to the SA Forum applications

authentication and authorization mechanisms like Kerberos, or use secure middleware services like Corba Security Service, Web Service Security and so on.

Administrators will be able to configure different security policies for the various SA Forum services. For example, some users might be allowed to initialize and use only the LCK interface, while others are allowed to use all SA Forum interfaces. However, it is the business of each SA Forum Service working group to define the security-sensitive areas and level of granularity for their service.

The SEC is concerned with access and use of the SA Forum services, it is not concerned with providing mechanisms such as encryption for the data that passes through those services, such as in checkpoints or message queues. However, the users of those services may certainly apply such mechanisms if desired.

To further constrain this discussion, we first recognize that by concentrating on only the AIS interfaces we do not provide a complete security picture for an SA Forum cluster. While the following are items that need to be addressed in such an implementation, we recognize that many techniques may be applied to these, and we do not further cover them in this paper.

– The security of interactions with the systems management services
– Actions of processes other than their use of the AIS interfaces
– Testing of security features and their functionality
– Secure installation of an SA Forum system

3 High Level Security Analysis of SA Forum Based Application Environments

Before discussing security requirements and security services of SA Forum interfaces, we need to develop a threat model to understand the potential threats to an implementation of the interfaces. This is a subset of the overall security analysis for the full system.

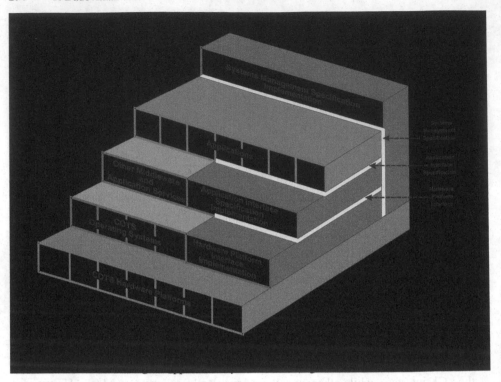

Figure 2 is used as a representation of an application system using SA Forum middleware.

The security assumptions and a threat analysis presented in this section will form the basis for the SEC security requirements.

3.1 Threat Model

On a very generic level (see Figure 2), the AIS interfaces can be interpreted as an extension to the underlying operating system that executes on a number of compute nodes. Application programs use the available interfaces to achieve carrier-grade availability.

What are the security threats to a system as described above?

- The correct operation of applications as well of the HA middleware itself is crucially dependent upon the **integrity** of the managed data. Change access to data under control of the HA middleware needs to be verified and secured.
- The same holds for the **availability** of the data as well as of the SA Forum implementation itself. Access to critical resources needs to be available under all circumstances (denial of service attacks, resource exhaustion).
- We view **confidentiality** for the HA middleware to restricting access to important repositories of information items related to application or system status. Examples are checkpoints, events, locks, etc.

– **Accountability** is an important aspect in the operation of a highly available system as actions and traces must be clearly associated with the responsible system entity (e.g. in events).
– Last, but not least, **legal liability** is typically an issue on application level, for example in proving the correctness of a billing information.

We do not cover masquerading attacks, theft of identity and other related authentication attacks as we expect that these will be addressed by the overall broad security plan for each installation.

3.2 Security Assumptions

A number of assumptions are made in the design of the SA Forum Security Services.

1. An encompassing threat analysis has been done for the surrounding system (application system) leading to adequate protection against vulnerabilities and threats. In some cases, the classification of the application system according to Common Criteria may be required resulting in application specific security profiles. Firewalls or virus analysis tools are typically installed as the application system is always assumed to be connected to the Internet in one way or the other.
2. A sufficiently detailed user model and role model is implemented in the application system to assure accountability for any activity on the system, at least for those activities which affect the operation of the HA middleware and the security of the application system. Sufficiently strong user authentication should be used. Administrators, in particular security administrators or administrators for HA components including the SA Forum implementation, must be trusted to not engage in malicious behavior.
3. The software and hardware components of the application system have been designed and developed based on proven techniques and using proven tools. This includes the development of the HA middleware itself.
4. The physical protection of the application system and the hardware it is running on is an important aspect to be taken into account (e.g. service personnel may have to replace faulty hardware and needs access to the system).

4 Security Requirements for SA Forum Based Implementations

As can be seen from the threat analysis of SA Forum based application environments, the integrity and availability of data as well as accountability of actions need to be supported by the SA Forum Services and in particular the SEC. Subsequently in this paper, this very generic requirement will be broken down into a number of individual requirements based on the following requirements categories:

– SA Forum Security Service
– Support for user application processes
– Security policy implementation

- Management of security
- Enforcement of security

The SA Forum Security Service is not stand-alone, but is embedded in the overall system and is assumed to take advantage of existing security mechanisms of the operating environment the service is running in (see §3.2). The SEC has to support user application processes to be compliant with the overall security policy. The SEC also has to support the security policy of the application environment. If required this may also mean the support for a "no security" policy. The security management and the enforcement of the defined security policy also result in requirements on the SEC, but also on the SA Forum services in general. Note that in the following, we only consider the requirements which have been approved at the time of writing. These requirements are to be extended in the future.

4.1 SA Forum Security Service

In regards to the security service itself, two requirements are specified:

- SA Forum security service shall be self-secure.
- SA Forum Security service shall be agnostic to underlying crypto algorithms and libraries if any. These shall be used in a transparent way (as much as possible) by the SA Forum Security service (or other SA Forum services when necessary) to provide adequate security to user application processes.

These requirements enforce the adherence of SEC to the defined security policy. Because the SEC cannot take advantage of the security services it implements, additional precaution is required in its implementation. The service has to protect itself against attacks. At the same time, the service implementation must be flexible enough to accommodate different security policies depending upon the application environment. As security mechanisms are available in most operating environments or can be defined by the application set-up (e.g. biometrics based authentication), the SEC must be able to take advantage of the available services.

4.2 Support for User Application Processes

User processes are clients of SEC. The SEC therefore has to help user processes maintain their security state:

- SA Forum Security service shall manage the security contexts of different user application processes.
- SA Forum Security service shall provide the credentials and the associated privileges of user application processes to the different SA Forum services.

We assume that user processes do not control their security contexts, i.e. their security environment, themselves. Instead, the SA Forum security model assumes that the security contexts of application processes are managed by the SA Forum layer. This model has a number of advantages:

- the security context is under the control of SEC and therefore not vulnerable to attacks on the user processes.
- the security context will reflect the requirements of the security policy. Changes to the policy are under control of SEC and propagation of policy changes can easily be managed.
- all user processes are known to the SEC. Otherwise they would not be able to participate in an SA Forum environment due to unavailable credentials.

Processes must have valid credentials for their participation with the SA Forum services and the overall application environment. The central handling of their credentials (including their privileges) will considerably reduce the vulnerabilities to bad application processes. At the same time, the use of credentials and the interpretation of privileges will be flexible to support a number of security policies.

4.3   Security Policy Requirements

The security of SA Forum based environments needs to be flexible to accommodate the use of SA Forum services in application areas with differing security policies. For example, the integration of SA Forum applications in a corporate data center must support their adaptability to the corporate security policy. The support of the concept of security policies is therefore a key requirement of SEC.

In regards to the security policy, SEC needs to fulfill the following requirements:

- It shall be defined what are the security aspects of the SA Forum system which are covered by the security policy. Possible aspects of a security policy configuration might include different Quality of Protection for SA Forum AIS services, access rules for different user application processes, auditing settings for different SA Forum services, etc.
- SA Forum security service shall include a management API to allow for predefinition and modification of security policy at runtime.
- SA Forum Security service shall propagate the modifications in the security policy to concerned SA Forum services.
- "No-Security" policy shall be supported. This does not mean that the overall system will not have any security mechanisms, but that these will be provided out-of-band of the SA Forum Services and the SA Forum Security service.

The definition of supported security aspects of the SEC security policy is necessary to allow its integration with the security environment of the applications being supported. For the same reason, an administrative interface (management API) is required, which can be used to integrate the SEC security policy into the overall management environment.

In particular, the run-time adaptation of the security policy is important from an availability perspective. Let us assume that the rules for the access to administrative functions changes because the service operator has changed the authorization structure. SA Forum based applications usually cannot be brought down (neither due to faults nor due to maintenance). The change of the authorization structure must therefore be handled on-line with the application services running.

4.4 Security Enforcement Requirements

Implementing a security policy also requires the enforcement of the policy. The following requirements have been established to this extent:

- The SA Forum services shall enforce the security policy within the SA Forum system.
- Each SA Forum service shall respond to changes in the security policy.
- For all SA Forum services, and according to the security policy, only user application processes with the proper credentials shall be able to perform life cycle operations.
- The changes in the security policy for SA Forum services shall not decrease the availability of the service for the authorized users.
- The error return-codes shall be standardized.

The enforcement of the imposed security policy is delegated to the SA Forum services within a SA Forum system. It is important to note that the requirements do not expect SA Forum security to go beyond the SA Forum boundaries and that the policy enforcement is not dependent upon application services. However, SA Forum services must be prepared to adapt to changes in the security policy and thereby support the overall security management of an application system which includes SA Forum services.

4.5 Security Event Handling

The handling of security events requires a close cooperation between the application processes, other SA Forum services and the SEC. This is reflected in the following requirements:

- SA Forum Security service should listen in to receive all security alarms for further actions. Some examples of possible security alarms are failed authentications, or denied access to SA Forum services.
- The list of all security alarms triggered by each SA Forum service shall be defined. This can be extended in the future to other alarms not directly related to the security. For example, alarms on checkpoint data might indicate a security failure even though the application creating checkpoint data might have successfully passed service authentication.
- All security sensitive operations and information shall be logged. The format and type of these log messages shall be formalized.

It is obvious that the SEC needs to track security relevant alarms and notifications ("events") to invoke adequate responses. But this can only be achieved if these security events are defined by the SA Forum services. The SEC is responsible for consuming all such alarms and interfacing with the systems management infrastructure for resolution of the security situation. This may range from simply logging the event through dispatching an incident response team."

5 Future Directions

In the following sections we propose a security model for SA Forum based systems and then discuss different security issues and the solutions to them. We end this section by proposing a strawman architecture for the SEC. The goal of this architecture is to provide guidance and expose the difficulties ahead instead of presenting a detailed design.

5.1 Security Model

The basic entity used for authentication, authorization and accounting is the user application process. We do not consider covering all processes running in the SA Forum system but those only using SA Forum service interfaces. Thus, unless otherwise specified, all use of process in the remainder of this text refers to processes using, or requesting to use, the SA Forum AIS interfaces.

Authentication. The processes are authenticated at the operating system (OS) level. The authentication information is then used by the SEC when the process accesses any SA Forum services resources. The SEC does not specify any specific means for OS-level authentication as it is out of scope of the SEC This is then completely implementation dependent.

For the SEC to use the OS level authentication for access control, it maps the OS level authentication into SA Forum security rules defined in the security policy (see section 5.3).

Authorization. The authorization in the SA Forum context concerns granting or denying access to different SA Forum service resources for different user application processes. This authorization is based on the rules defined in the SA Forum security policy. These rules map permissions to the identity of different processes. These identities are acquired during the authentication.

In the current approved requirements, the authorization is only performed when a process accesses each SA Forum service for the first time and upon termination, i.e. the permissions of a process are only verified upon the initialization and termination of SA Forum services. In the future, this will be extended to a more fine grained access control (the process' permissions are verified when executing the different SA Forum Service operations[1]).

The different SA Forum services use the SEC API upon a request by a process to initialize the use of each service. The SEC encapsulates the processing necessary to make the access control decision, and returns to the requesting SA Forum service an indication of whether it should grant or refuse the request. This centralized approach makes managing and upgrading the security mechanisms themselves easier and more powerful and frees the various SA Forum services from having to understand these mechanisms.

---

[1] Note that the list of the different operations which need security verifications is to be established as part of future releases of the SA Forum Security service specifications.

Auditing. The SEC auditing consists of examining the different logs of activities to test for the compliance with the security policy, and the detection of possible security breaches. For example, the analysis and correlation of logs from different SA Forum services to detect possible breaches in the system.

All security incidents like failed authentication or refused accesses are reported by the SA Forum services to the SEC through the SA Forum logging service. The SEC is in charge of analyzing the logs of different SA Forum services and correlate them with security events. This functionality is then internally implemented in the SEC and is not exposed to the user process applications. This analysis provides its output as security alarms or warnings toward the system management using SA Forum Notification service.

Communications Security. This issue is a general problem to many systems and we are not going to provide any particular solution for that as it can be handled securely at the operating system and network protocol point of view. There are already several projects providing efficient secure communications [10]. Therefore, we recommend the use of standard network protocols to establish secure communications between different processes in an SA Forum environment. The way these protocols are used and how they map into different processes is out of scope of the SA Forum Security service.

Basic Example. To illustrate the security model in the SA Forum eco-system, we consider the simple case when the user login is used for authentication. In this case, the security policy defines the different permissions for the user logins to different SA Forum services. Upon process initialization, the user login of the process is used for authenticating the process. From then on, the user login is used to identify the SA Forum user processes and to define the process permissions to the different SA Forum services. The authorization is based on the mapping of the process user login to the security rules in the security policy. The same process user login is used for logging the security sensitive operations or to identify the origin of security alarms. At the end, the user login information is used to establish security attributes for the communications between different processes. Note that this example is informative and not meant to give any direction for future implementations.

5.2 SA Forum Security Service and High Availability

To support failover with continual access to data, all active and standby processes sharing resources should have the same permissions in order to avoid access rights problems when the newly activated process accesses the resources of the failed process (these resources can be checkpoints, or log streams previously created by the failed process). In practice, both processes should have the same SEC-ID, see 5.3 for more details. [2]

Another aspect is to consider the modifications of the security policy at run-time and how these changes are going to be enforced at run-time. Of particular interest is the modifications of the credentials of a user application process at run-time.

---

[2] Note, that the AMF can issue a warning when the SEC-IDs are different for active and standby processes in a SA Forum system. The SEC provides an API to get the SEC-ID of a process based on its OS-ID.

5.3 Security Policy

The security policy describes the general behavior of the entities from a security point of view. It comprises how the entities are authenticated, what are the access rules for them, the security attributes for communications between different entities and their accountability, etc.

The security policy is defined by the system management. It is then interpreted by the SA Forum Security service and propagated to different SA Forum Services which enforce the security rules defined in the security policy (see Figure 3). For the time being, we do not consider standardizing the security policy syntax. For the future iterations, we consider using a standardized language like SAML or XACML [13,14].

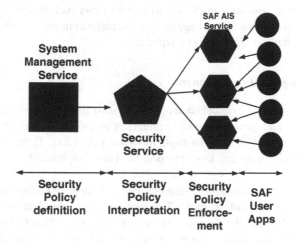

Fig. 3. Security policy definition, maintenance and distribution in SA Forum systems

Security Policy Scope. The SA Forum security policy only covers the SA Forum related security aspects of the SA Forum eco-system. The security policy comprises two aspects in the SA Forum system:

- SA Forum user application permissions: These are the security rules defining the permissions for different SA Forum user applications in regards with the SA Forum service resources. The current security requirements are only concerned with the accessibility of the SA Forum services by the user applications.
- SA Forum services security attributes: These are the security attributes for the SA Forum services including the SEC. These attributes define the security behavior of different SA Forum services. For example, the security attribute auditing level can be defined to express the necessary level of internal auditing for each SA Forum service. This attribute can be set by the SA Forum system management to enabled or disabled.

SEC-ID. Using the basic security entity, i.e. the user application process to express security rules in the security policy makes the task of elaborating and maintaining the security policy for a complex (possibly distributed) system cumbersome and error-prone. To provide the security management with a higher degree of abstraction, we introduce the concept of SEC-ID. All processes with the same SEC-ID have the same permissions. The SEC-ID does not identify an individual process but a group of processes. We then assimilate SEC-ID to what group IDs represent for Unix systems.

The security permissions in the SA Forum eco-system are then defined according to the SEC-ID. The security policy is a set of the tuplets $< SEC - ID, SAF - Service, Permissions >$[3]. The tuplets define access rules to different SA Forum services for SEC-IDs. For example, $< SEC - ID1, saEventService, Granted >$ means that processes authenticated as SEC-ID1 can use SA Forum Event service.

The authorization assertions in the security policy can include run-time conditions such as time limitations (validity, usage time, time interval in the day for usage, etc) or load factor limits that the SEC needs to evaluate.

5.4   Decision Logic and Enforcement

The access control is based on decisions made against the security rules expressed in the security policy and general security context. Therefore, there is need to interpret the security rules and implement the logic to make a decision. There are several possible strategies about where and how interpret the rules, implement decision logic, and enforce those decisions.

In our approach, we separate the interpretation, and the decision making logic mechanisms from the security enforcement. The interpretation and decision logic are implemented in the SEC and the decisions are enforced in the different SA Forum based systems. Note that from a practical point of view, the SA Forum services do not need to know about the details of the rules or how to interpret them. They are mainly concerned about the decision to grant or deny the service to the SA Forum user applications.

Therefore, the SEC API abstracts the decision-making logic from the SA Forum services. We define the "saSasAuthorize" call in the SEC API to allow the SA Forum services to decide to grant or deny the use of the SA Forum service. Upon this call, the SEC evaluates the operation against the security policy and the security context and returns the decision to the caller.

The "saSECAuthorize" passes the "SAF-Operation" as an argument to the SEC. The "SAF-Operation" is the SA Forum logical operation which the SA Forum service needs to grant or deny access. The SAF-Operations are defined for each SA Forum service (for example a SEC-Operation can be initialization of CLM service: "SEC_CLM_INIT"). These operations should be standardized for each SA Forum service. For time being, there are few SAF-Operations as the current approved requirements are limited to the access control upon initializing and closing different SA Forum services. Hence, only the initialize and terminate SA Forum service necessitate SAF-Operations. Beyond initialization, subsequent releases of the SEC would become more granular. By this we

---

[3] The tuplet is then a logical concept as we do not consider any particular syntax to represent them.

mean that the operations specific to each SA Forum service could become sensitive to security operations. Examples would be read and/or write access to specific check-points, message queues, event channels and lock resources. More extreme examples would be controls on individual messages and events, lock modes, and other fine grain controls. At this time we do not envision using the SEC to mediate to this finest level.

The SAF system management (SMS) can modify the mapping of process OS-ID and SEC-ID. This automatically implies new privileges for the process. Though, these changes should be transparent to the user process applications, and different SA Forum Services in charge of enforcing the security should be informed. In order to be able to support run-time changes in the credentials of different processes, the SEC API provides the saSasTrackChanges() to the SA Forum services to track the changes in the credentials for specific SEC-IDs or all SEC-IDs. Upon changes in the credentials for the user application processes, the SEC uses the callback provided by each SA Forum service when calling saSasTrackChanges() to inform the SA Forum service about the changes. The responsibility of updating the access rights for different SA Forum user processes is upon the SA Forum service by re-calling saSasAuthorize() for the concerned SEC-IDs.

Regardless of the targets, this approach makes the security policy interpretation, decision-making logic, and the handling of run-time changes in the security policy completely transparent to the SA Forum services. It would then become a SEC implementation issue (see section 5.3 for details). In addition, by concentrating these mechanisms in the SEC, we ease the evolution of these mechanisms over-time. This is particularly of interest for our target highly available environment when the security and related mechanisms should evolve without interruption through software updates at run-time.

5.5   Security Management

We consider that the SEC should be managed through the changes to the SA Forum security policy object in the Information Model Management Service (IMM). We do not exclude the creation of an admin API later on if there is need for a secondary or ad-hoc uses. However, we prefer the security management to be done through the IMM OM-API rather than an admin API.

The SA Forum system management (SMS) is in charge of managing and updating the security policy. This approach assumes direct dependency between the SMS and the SEC but eliminates the direct dependency between the SMS and different SA Forum services.

The SMS should use IMM OM-API to update or modify the security policy object in the Information Model (IM). The SA Forum system management can use any SNMP/MIB or DMTF/CIM agents [15,?] to access the OM-API of IMM. Upon the changes in the security policy object, the SEC is called by the IMM as the Object Implementer (OI) for that object (see Figure 6). The SEC can then interpret those changes and reflect them on the SA Forum system. The way that the SA Forum service modifies its run-time behavior is implementation dependent.

The security policy can be modified at run-time. Different SA Forum services (and perhaps later SA Forum application processes) should be informed about the changes at run-time in security policy and modify their behavior accordingly. The SA Forum services should reflect the changes in the security policy independently of the SA Forum user application processes, i.e. the SA Forum service should not rely on the user application to enforce those changes.

5.6 High Level Design

In this section, we give a high level architecture of the SEC (see Figure 6). As mentioned before, our purpose is not to present a detailed solution but rather represent the main components of the SEC.

We do not discuss the secure communications. The secure communications should be used whenever needed for the communications inside and outside of the SA Forum system.

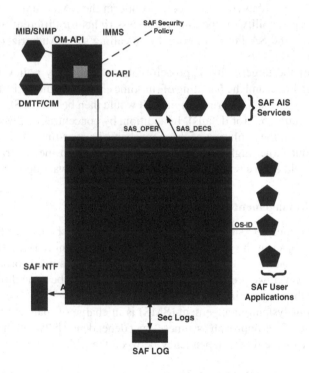

Fig. 4. The high-level overview of the SEC

The main components of the SEC are defined as:

– The management interface: This component is in charge of interacting with the SA Forum system management. It receives the management commands and information from the SA Forum system management and sends the security related information and changes to the SA Forum system management. It interacts with the SA Forum system management through the changes to the SA Forum security policy object in the IMM. This component receives the callbacks from the IMM for the changes in the SA Forum Security policy object. It reflects the changes in the SEC to the SA Forum security policy object in the IMM. The management interface forward the relevant information received from the system management to internal components.

- Rules: These are the current valid security rules in a SA Forum system. They are updated at run-time by the SAF system management through the SEC management interface.
- Security contexts: These are the current security contexts for different user application processes, resources... in a SA Forum system. They are the combination of the SA Forum security policy and the OS level security information. An example is the mapping between the SEC-IDs and the OS-IDs.
- The decision logic engine: This component implements the logic for decision making. Based on security rules, security contexts for the service and the SEC-ID of the requester, it makes a decision to grants or deny access to the resources. This component sends the service denials to the auditing component for further actions.
- The authenticator: This component authenticates a user application process according to its OS-ID. It maps this OS-ID into a SEC-ID which is sent to the decision logic engine. This component sends the failed authentication or unknown users to the auditing for further actions.
- The auditing: The auditing component is in charge of auditing the SA Forum system (for example analyzing the logs) and based on those results and the events received from internal components trigger security alarms using the SA Forum Notification service. Upon reception of security alarms, or the detection of security breaches, the auditing component will inform the decision making component (not represented in Figure 6). The auditing component also logs all changes in the security status for SA Forum systems using the SA Forum Logging service.

5.7   Relationship Between SEC and Other SA Forum Services

SA Forum Services Using the SA Forum Security Service. All SA Forum services use the SA Forum Security service to enforce security. Therefore, all SA Forum services depend on the SA Forum security service. While this leads to complex issues, it is not a new concern in the implementation of these interfaces, as there are already a number of complex interdependencies [6]. In addition, this paper will view this issue summarily and consider full explication beyond its scope.

The SEC should run prior to the initialization of other SA Forum services. In the case where an error occurs accessing the SA Forum Security service, the behavior of the different SA Forum services is defined as a parameter in the security policy. In turn, this parameter is defined by the SA Forum system management. The valid options for this behavior are to be defined as part of future SA Forum Security service specifications releases. These options can vary from denial of access to resources for all new requests to simply ignoring the error and grant access to all requests.

SA Forum Security Service Using Different SA Forum Services. The SEC service uses the SA Forum Log system to read the logs in order to analyze them [11]. In addition, the SEC service uses the SA Forum Notification service to trigger security alarms [12]. Even though, this is not part of the current requirements, the SA Forum log system and the SA Forum Notification service implementations should be enhanced to guarantee a secure transport and delivery of information. The SA Forum log system should guarantee the integrity of security logs during the transport and the storage. The SA Forum Notification service should guarantee the integrity of the security log messages during the transport.

SA Forum Services and Non SA Forum Software. We envision the future SEC as a system being able to exchange security related information with the system management or other third party security software like log analysis tools etc. These exchanges will be through security alarms sent and received by the SA Forum Notification service to and from the SA Forum system management or other third party software.

6 Conclusions

This paper has first presented the general security issues related to SA Forum based systems and detailed the current security requirements for them. We then proposed a security model for SA Forum environments and discussed different security issues related to its application to SA Forum middleware. We concentrated our efforts on the issues specific to the highly available middleware. Based on that discussion we developed a high-level design for the SA Forum Security service. Although our design does not cover all possible issues, we believe that it exposes the main issues ahead and give possible solutions to them.

Therefore, we expect this paper to be useful to the future implementers of the SA Forum Security service by providing them a general view of the SA Forum specific security issues, and some insight into the difficulties and their possible solutions. In addition, we hope that this paper would spark new ideas and feedback from security experts on on-going work for securing SA Forum based systems.

As future work, we plan to investigate more into details of the design and the interactions between SA Forum services and the SA Forum Security service. For example, it should be clarified what to do when a security breach has occurred in one or several applications running on a SA Forum system. Should we stop those applications or continue to provide the service in order to avoid any service interruption? What is the most important asset here, the security of the system or its high availability? At the end, perhaps it is the SA Forum system administrator who should set the default behavior in such cases through the SA Forum security policy.

References

1. M. Reitenspiess: "Availability in Industry and Science - A Business Perspective - ". In: Dependable Computing - EDCC 2005: 5th European Dependable Computing Conference, Budapest, Hungary, April 20-22, 2005. ISBN: 3-540-25723-3, p. 226. http://www.springerlink.com/index/10.1007/11408901_17.

2. R. Dierstein: "Sicherheit in der Informations technik - der Begriff IT-Sicherheit". Informatik Spektrum Bd. 24, Heft 4, August 2004, p. 343-353.
3. Service Availability Forum (SA Forum), http://www.saforum.org/home.
4. Shahane, Moser: Open standards for high availability and system management, 2005. http://www.embedded-control-europe.com/pdf/basapr05p31.pdf
5. HPI-B.01.01 Service Availability Forum Hardware Platform Interface, version B.01.01. http://www.saforum.org/specification/HPI_Specification
6. Service Availability Forum, Service Availability Interface, Overview document, SAI-Overview-B.01.04, Candidate B.02.01.
7. Service Availability Forum, Distributed Systems Management, Distributed Systems Management for AIS-SNMP SAI-SMS-AIS-SNMP-A-01-01.
8. Service Availability Forum, Distributed Systems Management, Distributed Systems Management for HPI-SNMP SAI-SMS-HPI-SNMP-B-01-01.
9. Kamalvanshi, Jokiaho: Build the next generation of telecom systems with open interfaces, Part 2, 2005. http://www.commsdesign.com/design_corner/showArticle. jhtml;jsessionid=OB3CJKWTFE3QQQSNDBCCKHSCJUMEKJVN?articleID= 163700304
10. Carrier Grade Linux, http://www.osdl.org/lab_activities/ carrier_grade_linux.
11. Service Availability Forum, System Management Specification, Volume 10: Log Service, SAI-AIS-LOG-A.01-01.
12. Service Availability Forum, Application Interface Specification, Volume 9: Notification Service, SAI-AIS-NTF-A.01.01.
13. Security Assertion Markup Language (SAML), http://www.oasis-open.org/ committees/tc_home.php?wg_abbrev=security
14. eXtensible Access Control Markup Language (XACML), http://www.oasis-open. org/specs/index.php#xacmlv2.0
15. SNMP, SNMPv2, SNMPv3, and RMON 1 and 2. William Stallings. 1999. Addison Wesley.
16. CIM Specification 2.3 . Distributed Management Task Force, http://www.dmtf.org/ standards/cim/.
17. Service Availability Forum, Application Interface Specification, Volume 2: Availability Management Framework, SAI-AIS-AMF-B.02.01.

Author Index

Lecture Notes in Computer Science

For information about Vols. 1–4252

please contact your bookseller or Springer